BUDDHA.
THE CEO

EXORCISING THE GHOSTS
OF EXCELLENCE

JAGDISH CHANDRA

INDIA • SINGAPORE • MALAYSIA

Notion Press

No.8, 3rd Cross Street
CIT Colony, Mylapore
Chennai, Tamil Nadu – 600004

First Published by Notion Press 2021
Copyright © Jagdish Chandra 2021
All Rights Reserved.

ISBN 978-1-63633-711-1

Contents

SECTION 3

Preface

There is a reason why I started this book.

A scalping, dry April noon some six years ago had led me to a bunch of mid-segment entrepreneurs who appeared more trapped than learning something valuable in a seminar they were attending on leadership and enterprise. And with hardly any interest in the details, I could sense the focus was on business and spirituality.

The name of the workshop was '**Buddha CEO**' and the organization was Pyramid Valley International. The idea appeared powerful! But the transaction I witnessed was insipid!

The reason for this wonderment-disillusion couple was my own background. I romanced with humanities and entered into a formal study of it after graduating to be a teacher of science from a well-known teacher training college. The teacher training college had obviously taught us the futility of memorizing huge chunks of interesting data and rehearsing procedures; the romance, the institute had taught, comes from an ardent inquiry into the framework of the syllabus. And this dictum was faithfully violated by all of us students as exigencies of exam scores and other blunt realities created a dead-end—an inescapable trap! And during my post-graduation in humanities, this would become even starker—students would practice a text, say **Pride and Prejudice,** prescribed for the syllabus, and would regurgitate in the exam. This is not uncommon still.

That appeared plain stupid; if not stupid, at least, amusing. Each text provided a sample for a far wider exploration that can include a metonymic understanding of social structures and radical shifts in a zeitgeist. An exploration that could have been philosophically inter-disciplinary in nature was reduced to a mere preparation for exams; that was absolutely unimaginative, unromantic and was un-aspirational.

Coming back to the point of what I saw in **Buddha CEO** workshop, it was reminiscent of my university days—uninspiring and textual. A very big name had gone unused and the target audience was hardly addressed. A well-conceived name by itself, I felt, wasn't enough to get into the intricacies of human performance.

This is what led to my rumination on how Buddha would act had he been the CEO of modern corporations. That rumination led me to work on curating a programme on 'organizational excellence' to begin implementing in Pyramid Valley itself where I worked during that time. Those thoughts have led to this book.

Just as the workshop was insipid, the organization that conducted it found itself stranded without realising its own dream of breakthrough performance. So, as the book explores why organizations fail, sometimes, so miserably, I had an opportunity to peep into Pyramid Valley International and say why it would never work and generalize it broadly enough for any organization.

The key question for me was this—why was Pyramid Valley dysfunctional despite a wondrous infra, the power of 'Pyramid Meditation' and a track record of transformations? Even miserable failures are great learning opportunities. Pyramid Valley is an extraordinary ambition and, within it, provided an opportunity for me. These thoughts emanated from there. Two things collided in bringing it to shape—my loose journaling and the enigmatic ambiguity of the lockdown!

Acknowledgements

My experience into organizational transformation has been minimal. Nevertheless, the truth is that more than the experience, the keen observations I have had the opportunity for and a holistic, earnest involvement in the transformational process should be sufficient right now. I will be taking a spiritual organization Pyramid Valley International, on the outskirts of Bangalore as a constant running undercurrent throughout the process of this narration.

As obvious, any organization by itself has a design to it. Pyramid Valley also has one such. I am very thankful for my experiences there that have helped me carve out this writing. At the same time, my analysis may appear critical of some practices there. Our analyses sometimes are largely limited to our perspective like the proverbial blind men exploring different aspects of an elephant. What may look like, in my description, a dysfunctional entity is entirely my viewpoint based on my intense personal analysis. Secondly, the intention itself is not to reflect on the 'dysfunctional' but to resolve issues that humanity in general and organizations in particular face. It should in no way show up as a critique of the people who run it. They have been by far some of the most dedicated and most sophisticated individuals who have performed extraordinarily well in their own fields.

I have immensely benefitted from Pyramid Valley International where I came across the term 'BUDDHA CEO' in a programme that was, nevertheless, not satisfying. Pyramid Valley has an extraordinary ambience and an energy field that's unmissable. I acknowledge my major source of inspiration from it.

Sri Sri Ravishankar whom we all affectionately call Guruji has been a source of inspiration. His commentary on Patanjali and Ashtavakra have generated silence within me which otherwise would have been a long drawn process for me. Guruji has truncated an effective part of my struggle to the bare minimum, leading into extremely satisfying quantum leaps in my understanding of texts.

My experience in running an experimental school in Madhya Pradesh, Central India, has been an 'awfully' beautiful experience. It was awful in the numerous demands from parents and the blunt questions about life—like examination and syllabus coverage and the beautiful things included the rich environment and generous freedom I experienced.

Kaushik Daga, the School Chairman, went on to forge a relationship that is far beyond the confines of the school. I owe whatever intensity the relationship has entirely to his gregarious nature. He is profoundly simple, disarmingly loving at that. I somehow acknowledge him as a strong element in forging my consciousness in terms of both the respect and freedom he generously offered me and also in terms of the exposures he sponsored me into. Kaushik is unbelievably shrewd, gentle and humane—all put together. I deeply and, even more, warmly acknowledge him for his generous contribution to my life.

My conversations with a fiercely independent and irritatingly ethical spouse—Ashwini. She doesn't read as much as I do; that's her advantage. When she says things, it's crystal clear. Numerous conversations with her have generated extraordinary insights for me. Her nuances and an ability to grasp have added tremendous value to my conceptualization.

In the same line as above, I should mention Ravishankar! My younger brother's talkative friend who's much closer to me than my own brother with whom he has had an eternal quarrel. His alertness for what is worthwhile reading and his critical intensity in reading has been very useful to me. His pace of reading and the ability to process information amazes me.

Numerous readings from books have been an extraordinary source of propulsion. Some of them are awe-inspiring and their scope far beyond the scope of the present work. Given space and the limited mandate, I have just been able to summarize them to the basic minimum requirements. I recommend earnest and deeper engagement with each one of them. I am thankful to all these works—whether I have just mentioned them or quoted to some extent!

These and much more have resulted in this work. At the risk of making a 'blanket statement', just wish to express my immense gratitude at this juncture. Gratitude has no direction; it's a scalar quantity. I am grateful!

Introduction

The book you are about to read is ostensibly a book about business, institutional imperatives, leadership and organizational excellence. However, as we are about to see throughout the book, just as there is a limit to what we can hear or see or feel, there is an alleged limit to our cognition as a whole, through which narratives that make up organizations are pigeonholed into time and space-boxed constraints that hinder the paradigm shift essential for auto-renewal. In addressing this, the book is essentially an exploration into the process of auto-renewal at its core. The central question that keeps morphing into various expressions in the book is this—can we answer the call of organizational excellence through the known paraphernalia of our times?

An organization is a complex narrative. Its origins, history, existence, the paths it has traversed through success, failure, mediocrity, sustenance, times of prosperity and despondency, market pressures, respect from its peers, etc. are all parts of a grand narrative. Grand narratives are only alive through confabulations within an ecosystem in which they flourish. For an organization to thrive wholesomely, the narrative must be healthy, free to grow and it must encompass not only desirable but also undesirable elements of its constituent components, as well as its shadows.

Charting the course of an organization's journey, delving into its structural components, its ordering, its growth, obstacles in its path, the way it overcomes to achieve excellence and the journey it takes to renew and reinvent itself to remain relevant is not short of any Hollywood thriller blockbuster script! However, a careful and meticulous analysis into the depths of each of these aspects of an organization's existence is easier said than done. Juxtaposing this analysis with the actual confabulations of the complex grand narrative of the organization throws up a curious fact. And that fact is—as the grand narrative deviates from its origins, it keeps its central tenets ever more firmly rooted while its confabulations morph into temporal and spatial relevance into whatever is required to sustain itself and grow.

A palpable shift has occurred in the make-up of the ecosystem of organizations and institutions in the last two decades across the world. Whether this shift is only a story of the prevalent market forces, business imperatives, technological advancements and industry behaviours, or whether there are other not-so-obvious realities at play for this shift to emerge, concerns a major thematic investigation in this book. At a macrocosmic level, the acknowledgement of the ecosystem's truths meant knowing the story, its growth and the forces of its sustenance. The story of IBM (a business organization) or that of the Red Cross (a humanitarian institution) follows this script of genesis, growth, overcoming circumstantial obstacles, getting imprinted on the collective consciousness of generation upon generation of the population (even unrelated or untouched in many cases) as having some tangible value and emotional weight and finally, consistently renewing their relevance to the world through design and providential intervention. Now, irrespective of the causal seismic activity that triggered the aforementioned shift, the present age is not the one that has the luxury of confabulations.

Examining the aforementioned shift closely, it is apparent that the modern mechanistic science may have obviated the ecosystem in the narrative process. Just as a modern doctor may not want to inquire into the 'ecosystem' of a patient's symptom, the supremacy of modern mechanistic science, with its penchant for conclusions, may have obviated the need for an ecosystem in the narrative process. Handling a symptom doesn't need understanding but rehearsed action. Rehearsed action is enough for survival but doesn't provide scope for a shift in the paradigm. Ever-evolving stories have a way of retaining their pristine glory and organically stretching into what is relevant. This transformation of things that are ordered and predictable naturally lent itself into a set of standardized processes of which outsourcing and the impersonalized efficiency of assembly-line manufacturing are prominent. This meant that the 'ecosystem' of the organic narrative had to be done away with. Ashlee Vance aptly summarizes this strand of decontextualization when she evokes Jonathan Huebner's analysis of 'declining trend in worldwide innovation' in her book ELON MUSK. The best engineers, she quotes a Facebook engineer, are thinking of how to make people click the digital advertisements. The digital age is such. It cannot deal with whole information but in pieces, convenient clips and footages that can be telecast repeatedly.

The motivation for this book comes from the author's insight into the possibility of this state of affairs as a problematic proposition. It is quite easy to see that in any given context that the spontaneity of oral narration is quite unlike any rehearsed action. Rehearsed action although promises infinite efficiency is, in fact, a quick recipe for the mediocrity of intent and execution that hastens the arrival of a standstill. To write a story is to play with the real danger—the danger of establishing pathways out of the standstill. The story that keeps re-writing is the only story that lives. No need here to extrapolate this to the grand narrative of organizations and institutions.

Confabulation as the Life Force of Relevance and Perpetration

This is where we are right now, right here. In a state in which we can expand the narrative and accommodate our experiences, travails and our imaginary lands.

Let us look at the Mahabharata, which is one of the finest examples in the traditions of confabulations. (This is dealt with to appropriate length at a relevant section within the book. Hence, suffice here to expand just what would be relevant within the confines of an introduction.)

The Mahabharata is not a monolithic text. To ascribe to the Mahabharata, the simplification of a quarrel between two groups of cousins that grew into a war is to miss a whole bunch of points. And as was said in the beginning, this largely conservative view of portraying a 'strand' as a whole is an easy 'winning formula' for duplication and multiplication. This marketplace of 'summary' narratives narrows down the variety that's possible.

One of the finest meta-stories is how the Mahabharata was written into existence. The origin of the Mahabharata is generally traced to Parikshita's passionate need to know life itself, a quest that eventually became perpetually relevant as generations upon generations piled on the narrative into a grand narrative of infinite confabulations. Parikshita's quest to 'know' stemmed from this severe urgency and his authentic "ignorance" was very accommodative. It had to include everything. The Mahabharata takes its form in Parikshita's questioning - he wanted to understand it all - the smallest things, the minutest phenomena, the grandest universal truths. Parikshita gets so intrigued that his questions included even as mundane as 'what had his great-grand-uncle carried to the pilgrimage?' Mahabharata became an infinitely flexible web of accommodation. It included everything. No question remained marginalized.

Yet, the confabulations are seen as extra-baggage today by us. We either ignore them completely or employ them for their quality to evoke something exotic as a differentiating aspect that represents our affordability to stand apart—something akin to our personal engagement with spirituality; something readily dispensable. But why do we ignore these narratives in the first place? How does an obviously interesting story with all its innumerable tentacles get marginalized? Since narratives are built around the questions of the listener as it happened in Parikshita's case, stories morph themselves in size, form and purport to suit the age. That probably explains the proliferation of disjointed, single strand stories of the present times.

This disengagement with the narratives, confabulations and the natural outgrowth of the collective, connected wisdom is symptomatic of our age. For our convenience, I would like to classify them into three interrelated symptoms:

1. **The primacy of cognition:** *We live in a world where grandmother's tales have all but disappeared. Even more seriously, the value of fiction and imagination is fast eroding both in a child's school life and also as a way of building the adult's consciousness. It is a world in which 'whatever is read or listened to should make* **rational** *sense'—everything else is actively marginalized. Even schools marginalize what cannot be rationalized into 'extracurricular' activities; to have these marginalized activities at the harmless peripheries of value-based action is never a problem. Cognition rules.*

Even the little 'extracurricular' reading that really happens is reduced to the competitively priced information. This 'information', gleaned out of such reading through an involuntary process of evaluation, is placed above everything else, and what doesn't appear to lead to a linear and predicted result is devalued and relegated. Leisure and free time are filled with passive, consumption-led entertainment. Formatted content that is pre-masticated for easy ingestion on the present-day social media apps, cable TV and FM radio channels stand testimony to this fact.[1]

Though industry, modern pedagogy and psychology speak about out-of-the-box thinking and creativity, it's not personalized but just part of a coffee-table conversation. Not surprising that the Mahabharata is accommodated within what's understandable—cognition is primary—only have something that can be easily remembered and propagated.

We can quickly trace the proliferation of this process of devaluation of anything that is not readily rationalizable to everything from our everyday industry to mega-corporations that affect the collective in general. Lip service is paid to clichéd notions such as "out-of-the-box thinking" in popular pedagogy and psychology, and predictably, this never gets deeply personalized in a way that a grandmother's tale does.

---

1   I have adapted the above passage from my notes I took from one of the essays on pedagogy and teaching. I am unable to trace it but remember taking notes which was an adaptation from the points I read from the essay. Neverthless, I am deeply indebted to the impact of that reading. Even some points mentioned in the next point are from that reading.

Hence, the pre-knowledge of the Mahabharata ensconced in the psyche of an adult through no rational thinking or effort is anathema to any extendable business of the mind today.

2. **Obsession with legitimate knowledge:** *We engage with legitimate knowledge of every day, like clothes—they are extraneous, unnatural, artificial, and yet, life without clothes is inconceivable and we cannot legibly imagine a time when civilized humans went about their lives without clothes. Legitimate knowledge takes the shape of bureaucratic licensing, traffic signals, user manuals, application process in a court of law, certification systems and similar civilizational inevitables that structure particular forms of knowledge.*

The urgency with which legitimate knowledge becomes a compulsive disorder in the modern culture can be seen in this example. I remember listening to a speaker in a conference on educational philosophy say that Harvard with an annual budget of 100 billion dollars is the repository of legitimate knowledge. Such institutionalization of "legitimate knowledge" often automatically delegitimizes traditional webs of knowledge. The speaker went on to subvert this kind of legitimate knowledge contrasting it with the 'stupidities[2] of the Nyamgiri hill tribals in Orissa that have 'saved our earth'. Forget the 'superstition' of the tribals, even classical reading and philosophy are depleted and weakened due to a lack of sufficient space in the academic timetables.

All this seems a bit strange. Some of the finest minds in the history of humankind, like Newton, Galileo, Einstein, Copernicus, Francis Bacon, William Blake—all of their thoughts and knowledge processes can be traced to esoteric knowledge like traditional and subterranean religious studies, occult and alchemy. Our modern-day cognitive anxieties stem from an unknown fear of an imagined disassociation

---

2   "Stupidities" - In a talk on "Education for the species" Nirmalangshu Mukherji says that legitimate knowledge will not save the earth, but the "Stupid" knowledge of the people of the soil can only save the earth. In saying so, he uses "Stupidity" as a desirable, necessary notion rather than in its conventional sense.

with and distancing from 'legitimate' knowledge. Look at an Indian mother's anxiety when her young kindergarten child is unable to recite the names of the months from the Gregorian calendar but is perfectly at ease while the ignorance of the very same months from the Indian traditional calendar elicits no such anxiety. And what is not deemed legitimate by the collective is passed on, lent out, outsourced and marginalized—not unlike housekeeping, security or the chanting classes for children beyond school hours or Sunday afternoon classes.

That which is not outsourced or marginalized is bundled into well-packaged and ready to use, pre-digested information nuggets that are canonized and blessed by the dominant legitimizing authorities of the day.

3. **Consumerism:** *How can one use the knowledge, legitimate or otherwise? To what use can this knowledge be put? As said in the earlier point on 'The Primacy of Cognition', reading and stories tend to be geared towards acquiring more information. And without the complex intervention of the grandmother, and combined with the need for 'usefulness', the didactically shared information we are left with is flat. Even voracious consumers of knowledge find such sharing unimaginably tedious. When knowledge is not considered fit for consumption—like Astrology that describes planetary influences on our current state or History of Ancient India from the Indian schoolbooks—they get laughed at, smiled benevolently, sympathized ('when will these poor chaps learn!') and there is a felt need for civilizing these poor folks!*

In a culture that values only that information or narrative that helps individuals 'get ahead in life', what we urgently need is a healthy dose of subversion. We need to provide individuals with a variety of experiences and stories that have ostensibly no immediate useful purpose—other than the pleasure of being in the midst of a conversation.

The Lure of the Ceramic

That is all good, but what is the real reason behind this spectacular depletion in the life-sap of enthusiasm in grand narratives, all of a sudden? On a human historical timescale, the time it has taken for this erosion seems like a flash.

We are enamoured by the 'ceramic'. We have come to worship conclusions. All conclusions and forms are always deceptive but very convenient to deal with in practicality. Let us look at a piece of advice given to young spiritual seekers, a quite well-known aphorism in popular culture—"Burn the Bible and kill the Buddha if you find one on the road." The implications are pretty obvious—carry no conclusions. However, since we are enamoured by the 'done', the 'ceramic', the 'tangible' and find it convenient to deal with, our tendency is to limit to what can be handled. To keep it portable. If the individual is powerful and focused enough to make whatever conclusion that is possible as the 'end of everything' for the entire community, the entire community carries only conclusions—no confabulation ever.

Yet, we are deeply convinced even if we don't allow ourselves to acknowledge openly—conclusions do not allow for accommodative nurturing.

This is quite similar to our own current circumstances. What we generally deal with is the moulded plasticity and 'McDonaldization'[3] We have been driven to deal with standardized, easily installable, manualized and emotionally dis-invested structures. The 'McDonaldized' modern world is much easier to be surrounded by and transacted with than the immense possibilities that lie dormant in the confabulated grand narratives and accommodative nurturing entwined with deep emotional investments. Irrespective of the economic framework in which these structures of

---

3   [From Wikipedia] McDonaldization is a McWord developed by sociologist George Ritzer in his 1993 book The McDonaldization of Society. For Ritzer, "McDonaldization" is when a society adopts the characteristics of a fast-food restaurant. The process of McDonaldization can be summarized as the way in which "the principles of the fast-food restaurant are coming to dominate more and more sectors of recent[quantify] idea about the worldwide homogenization of cultures due to globalization.[1]

moulded plasticity operate, our risk-averse and profit-maximizing culture embraces them because they do not evoke the dangers of the unknown possibilities of the grand narratives. It is not a binary moralistic judgement call to say that this moulded plasticity is either all good or all evil. It is just so as our world around us exists. And our concern here is to unravel the 'Buddha', who is ever-present but has been engraved in 'ceramicity' of conclusions, binary possibilities and the limits of moulded plasticity. Akin to the larva feeling the freedom within its cocoon without exploring the possibilities of being the Butterfly. Without this explosion of the myth of the cocoon's freedom, the Buddha refuses to speak, or speaks only in ritualistic practices and appears devoid of any practical connection.

Our contention in this book is that when whatever is left after the depletion and abandonment of the grand narrative, is only within the confines of the 'prescribed' texts and the textuality of legitimate knowledge. Society just seeks blind mastery without the life-assuring playful application. The problem with 'legitimate' texts is this—even when mastered, it remains slippery and flippant; lack of mastery further creates an insatiable urge for even more mastery and legitimacy of knowledge.

As an example, take an Indian school student's anxiety in not being able to memorize the answers and facts on say, Buddha's life. Even after memorizing, the student makes it doubly sure by having it 'engraved' into his memory by sufficient rehearsal. The student finds it safer to 'know' the answers about Buddha's facts than just floating in the stories on Buddha, and these facts represent the narrative of purport on Buddha. This problem persists in various ways—damned if you know and damned if you don't know it. Knowing this legitimized Buddha, we ignore it, or in not having mastered it, we are in perpetual anxiety of somehow mastering it.

Danger of a Single Story

'**Buddha, The CEO**' is an attempt to inquire into the conundrum of life within the confines of organizational excellence by examining Buddha in our incessant need to make decisions in the actual circumstances of life.

The authenticity and the strengths of our decision-making process come from how we allow the 'complexity' of a given circumstance to work even in the simplest decisions that are made. It is reflected often in how far we can see the impact of our decisions. Buddha, it seems, could see Angulimala[4] in all his dimensions—his previous births, current tendencies, previous dispositions, life constraints, etc. This ability to see the 'complex' network in one single action is seen as the core of leadership, and **'Buddha, The CEO'** tries to address this in the following pages. Angulimala is just a case in point. Buddha had the same complexity in every story he moved through. Every human being as a story. This is reflected in a poignant talk by Chimanda Adiche, the Nigerian writer, who calls it the 'danger of a single story'.

'Buddha' is the metaphor for the collective wisdom that we have, always had and always will have. And **'Buddha, The CEO'** is an attempt at the examination of this metaphor.

How is it Relevant to the CEO of Today?

Just as Buddha is a metaphor for the whole wisdom of the age, CEO is a metaphor for the modern executive—any modern executive who has to govern, execute, engage in the relevance of the real world with an abstract promise, pitch, sell, make money and feed families. Wrapped in one acronym is a multi-layered fold of ideas, services, products, promises, morals, skills—and time itself. At the centre of it all is an engagement with the world that continuously extends an invitation of contract.

The truth of any modern executive who is laden with the responsibility of leadership is that she has to deal with an inconclusive two-way truth. A

---

4   Angulimala's story is well known in the popular culture. Anguli is the fingers and Mala is the garland. So Angulimala terrified the community and occupied a portion of the forest waiting for someone so that they can be killed, and his garland can be extended to a thousand fingers. And as the story goes, Buddha accosts him and for the first time, as the story goes, Angulimala is unable to react. Buddha's peace transforms him, and he is accommodated into Buddha's monastic tradition.

persistent question the CEO has to grapple throughout her reign of work is where is that fine line that divides the realms of her identity into an individual personality and the extended self that represents the company or society or the larger wellbeing of humanity. Both sides of the line are equally real. A CEO intuitively knows that just being that at work, both self-preservation and the welfare of everyone (however limited or expansive) are forever entwined.

Inheritance of the Things Past

The moment we become part of an organization we inherit its past. As said earlier, one brings both personal past of one's identity and also the past of the organization's expectation and practice. A CEO (CEO isn't a position but a metaphor) inherits the complete spectrum of the past—both the organization's and her own. And it depends on the CEO how meaningfully she inherits the past, iteratively. An 'iteration' is to reuse knowledge in much more functional and meaningful ways by integrating new experiences into the past of who we are or who we have become. The significance of these formulations—the way they are formed—is amplified in and through the work we do. So that we 'see' and 'know' as we go.

And CEO's of modern organizations, including slightly predictable ones like schools and very open-ended ones like a space agency handle complex organizations. Complexity is a function of the number of data sources that determine actions. Like markets, uniqueness of upcoming organizations, cutting edge research, emerging end-user requirements, dispositions of new generation staff, customer demands, styles of leadership, technology, social needs, demands of affiliated bodies and many more.

It is a no-brainer that every organization, even natural ones like a beehive or anthills have to perform to sustain and stay relevant without any incentive of artificial markers of growth and development. So, suffice it to say that any human organization—whether a school or a corporate company or a government agency—with all its entanglements with growth, progress, development, value propositions, markets and such, is forever adjoined with the spinal cord of performance running the entire length of its existence.

Performance means to be immersed in the entire 'ecosystem'. Every individual is an 'ecosystem'—a miniature cosmos. The CEO, the book proposes, when attains the 'Buddhahood', is the ultimate expression of this understanding.

Why a Buddha But?

Anything a society can look at collectively, even a romantic idea or a narrative, attains the status of the mainstream. Buddha is part of the global mainstream—the epitome of the popular mindfulness practices and numerous spiritual sayings ascribed to him. These narratives of spirituality are available for consumption in the form of references and legitimizations. Capsulized references that are extraordinarily popular in the modern pop-spiritual landscape obviate the need for looking at anything deeply and sufficiently. And when we start looking at what is referenced deeply and seriously enough, we also will start respecting its limits and will not make it thin and frivolously suggestive, such as the ones that assert that India had developed aeronautic technology or bio-genetics long before the West had popularized it. When we are keen on knowing and have the capacity to reflectively develop a narrative as we go ahead, we also recognize the entire process of creation and development. The more, the deeper and broader one's experience and skills are, the more readily evident are the limits.

To be able to see the limit of knowledge respectfully also means a chance to expand it beyond the limits. It may no longer remain a limit but a fractal of the entirety.

The book also will exhibit that fractal—the entire round of the layers of growth and development, from conceptualization to auto-renewal. Each point here is an exercise in humility, i.e., acknowledging what can be never known and to call it a day—recognizing that the end of each learning is the beginning of another. In that sense, learning is like the 'death' of what existed before and whose limit has been respectfully identified, and to constantly keep the process of 'dying' alive is the ultimate transformation. To love and to live wholesomely as individuals or as organizations, which is what the project of existence is all about is a constant movement of 'dying' to the known.

Hence the book is co-written, written as it is read; causing a narrative as we go ahead—to add to what was missing, only to see that what was added to the missing is a rhythmic iteration and not a tangible absence. Hence, the whole book is an enterprise in 'unwriting'.

We should be in the centre—neither in the extremes of celebration nor in the cynicism of its absurdity; which means we invite critical insiders.

The Organization of the Book

There are three sections each elaborating a different strand and a conclusion—

Section 1—The meaning of organizational 'Buddhahood' is explored. The organic way in which organizations are built and it explores, through some diagrammatic models, how organizations could aspire for 'Buddhahood'

Section 2—the 'present' as a transformation of an 'impeccable past'. Organizations and organizational leadership inherit a past—in fact, it inherits the whole humanity. 'How does this function in the organization?' is the essential question here.

Section 3—starts looking at how leadership can be a function of 'commitment' vis-à-vis 'attachment'. Given the pan-presence of such words in the organizational lingo, the section investigates the reality of these high lingo motivational words. Looks at how great leadership is all about consistent 'regeneration'—a metaphorically expressed absence of a 'stable self' and how it plays out in the mechanics of organizational excellence.

SECTION 1

CHAPTER 1

Organization's Buddha-Hood

Mind, driven by fear goes to many a refuge

To mountains, and forests, to groves and sacred trees

That is not a safe refuge, that's not the best refuge

A man is not delivered of all pains after having gone to that refuge.

– Dhammapada

One has to be cautious in beginning anything on a rather grim note. The context sometimes becomes compelling, as I see in this case. I am giving in to my temptation. More importantly, I deem a quick canvas to see events as a rich interplay between abstractions and its real-world implications!

As I am writing this, Indian actor Sushant Singh Rajput's suicide is making rounds in the media. Wild speculations on the reasons for the suicide and direct accusations of nepotism on social media have become our new national pastime. Some have even taken recourse to 'channelling' and such other means of establishing communication with the departed soul; 'truth will prevail'—every fan appears to feel. More than anything else, a sustained campaign for justice by another actress, endorsed and celebrated by the media for its sensationalism, has made everyone believe that the 'system' has become totally corrupt; it needs an overhaul. As the case spirals out of control, it turns into the new discoveries of several caches of drugs in many actors premises and sucks in several other parallel industries and rackets; and an urgency to overhaul the system.

Somehow, the whole idea stems from the fact that any system can be overhauled and there's someone, who can really do it. There definitely is a possibility of resurrection and permanent reparation. And hence, the urgent need to get to the crux of it and quickly come to conclusions about who would lead and who the protagonist of this 'overhaul' will be. The observation that the system is corrupt, coupled with the belief that the system can be overhauled generates a fascist impatience for quick foreclosure; that impatience cannot afford a peaceful coexistence with imperfection. The urgency is to fix.

This leads us to a quick **lesson number 1**—nothing needs to be fixed.

That is the way of things—to be in flux. This is an opportunity for the discovery in the possibilities of action. It's good to believe temporarily that there's a solution so that action happens but the wisdom is that we are all grateful that there's something to be done!

Sushanth's death rightly demands action!

Not just action but it demands quick action. There's no time to lose. Like the American system that has fast-tracked police officer training to 278 hours from the mandatorily needed global minimum of 1518 hours for some professions including that of a barber's. This is unbelievable truncation. This will do if the police officer training requires one to just shoot and kill. It may have done away with sensitizing on human rights, the surreptitious play of prejudices and many more. I recorded this data on hours of police officer training in the United States from a newspaper article analyzing the consequences of such knee-jerk reaction in public policy, in the context of 'black lives matter' movement; and the consequences have been clearly distasteful.

I surmise the fast-track police officer training is itself a product of an over-paranoid security system that experienced 9/11 tragedy. The logic is simple—one can never be over-prepared, and the preparation is simple— 'teach the folks to shoot'. As Noah Harari argues in one of his books (I think it's in '**21 Lessons For the 21st Century**') the response to a terror attack is not in proportion to the loss caused; not the way one would respond, say, in the case of a pandemic or fire emergency. The response is far beyond the impact of the attack because it involves national pride—an emotionally charged equivalent of personal honour at stake. And hence, the response comes from a sense of hurt. The problem with an emotion like 'hurt' is that it's impossible to see the phenomenon as something more universal and historical, generated at a time long before the present circumstances that apparently caused it; it is this refusal to see the historicity and humanity of it that we tend to see happenings phenomenally and objectively. The human penchant for a drama!

I had heard from one of my friends that police officer training in India, despite the nation's abysmally low per capita resources, involves an understanding that's just not limited to 'shooting a firearm'. I was told, and I had envied that then, that the trainees watch **'Crime and Punishment'**—a film based on Dostoevsky's famous novel of the same name, probably, as part of examining the psychology of crime; they also undergo sociological lessons, instructions on cultural diversity and gender sensitivity. For instance, how can a trainee be sensitized to deal with a society where polygamy is illegal but certain tribes are neither shy of the practice nor are they accustomed to the law? A sensitive police officer would know that it's not just implementation of the law but community sensitization and education while also recognizing the importance of homogenization for a modern global economy. And also probably knows the ill effects of such homogenization and the action that is needed within the parameters of 'reality'. Actions that stem from a complete acknowledgement of what the whole affair is and also actions that filters down to the question of what's at stake obviates disproportional collateral damage. Intelligence is to minimize collateral damage. Quick-fix solutions and event-based-reactions would hardly do.

The challenge is the belief that there's a solution and that it can be permanently overhauled. The actress campaigning for justice to Sushanth appears to believe so and the general public has found a sudden hero amidst the lethargy of a national lockdown. There is a justification for a demand to probe the incident but to hang on to the narrative is yet another kind of suicide—by all of us getting entertained by this.

Somewhere, an urge, and a fondness, to fix comes from a never-ending training for improvement that we are all familiar with. The constant urge to keep the feet on the 'pedals of improvement' on is well portrayed in Arthur Miller's **'Death of a Salesman'** where Willy Loman is hysteric and has turned into a burdensome lunatic with a dream that has no logical connections.

There's no argument against the fact that institutionalized responses to fix are a necessity. Instead, our argument will be to see how leaders can have a canvas, than an event, for holistic action!

And that takes us to **Lesson no.2**—every action has a spillover!

Spillovers cannot be controlled but an awareness of it helps recognize quality action. It, at least, helps in placing appropriate control mechanism and coolants in case of a backlash. More importantly, knowledge of spillover helps one reflect—is it worth it?

Sushanth's suicide has spilt-over. Sushanth was by no means a pushover. Having given blockbusters like **M. S. Dhoni—The Untold Story** and consistently growing in stature from soap operas to the status of the nation's heartthrob, Sushanth has had his full circle. There was no reason for the suicide. That could have been easily explained away had it been a struggling actor who is at crossroads.

Such is the interest that Sushanth's new film Dil Bechara, released posthumously, has seen ninety-four million views in four hours. That's staggeringly high even for an actor of Shah Rukh Khan's stature. The tragic demise of the endearingly gentle actor appears to have generated far more interest than the sum total of everything else happening in the industry right now. Such is the sensationalism.

In the life of The Buddha, a time comes when he has to ordain Maha Kassapa, his disciple, to lead the order after his passing.

Maha Kassapa is on a mission to compile Buddha's teaching and questions the Enlightened one why all this knowledge should be codified. The Buddha replies thus:

"so it happens, Kassapa, when beings deteriorate and the true Dhamma vanishes: then there are more rules and fewer Arahats. There will be, however, no vanishing of the true Dhamma until a sham Dhamma arises in the world. But when a sham Dhamma arises in the world, there will be more rules and fewer Arahats."

"….and (there are) five reasons for the deterioration: it is the lack of respect for the Buddha, the Dhamma, the Sangha, the training, and for meditative contemplation."

Knowledge is codified when there is an imminent danger to the order but, as Buddha says, these codes take one further away from the Dhamma but is essentially protective in nature. A community needs codified knowledge but can an individual function on codified and impersonal knowledge?

On human Potential:

In the same tradition of the story Maha Kassapa ordained by the Buddha to succeed him has a pre-ordained life that leads him to the Buddha.

As Adhidhamma mentions, Maha Kasspa born earlier in the birth of poor Brahmin during the time of Buddha Vipassi shares a cloth with his wife. They attend Buddha Vipassi's sermons by taking turns to use the same clothing. On the last day of the sermon, the poor Brahmin donates this cloth. And having donated rises his hands and shouts, 'I have vanquished' which is noticed by a king listening to the Buddha from behind a screen. The king sends his royal men to donate even more clothing to this venerable Brahmin who seems to know what should be donated to the Buddha. Even those gifts are given away. The poor Brahmin is then appointed chaplain in the royal court and his poverty ends thus.

In his later birth, born as a wealthy Brahmin named Pippalahi he marries Baddha Kapilani, his former wife in the previous birth of poverty. This time both find the ephemeral nature of existence and its sinfulness in similar kinds of incidents: when their servants mention that the worms being eaten by the birds and their suffering are eerily the sin of the masters whose orders they are following.

The revulsion takes them to the Buddha Sakhyamuni. Human potential demands full expression and we repeat in actions till we have expressed it out with total compassion

WHY IT FINDS A PLACE HERE?

Because we are seeing what an event is! Why do so some events, like death, takes precedence over other such events—other deaths here? What makes us look at some events very seriously while ignoring others?

Human beings have a span of life and degree of potential to be fulfilled (this also has a tangential reference to the life of the Buddha[5] which is put the adjoining box. I recommend a cursory glance at that). Fulfilment of potential, like the list of things completed on a day, is gratifying. Just as something remains incomplete when our 'to do's' are not fulfilled, life apparently blown out before its time creates a vacuum that sucks in what was never sought in the first place, sucking in even those that are to be avoided.

That's what has happened in Sushanth Singh's death. Several directors are being accused of nepotism, there's an ongoing demand for CBI inquiry, a First Information Report against an actress has been lodged, old footages of an innocently done fun at an award function is being invoked to show the humiliation of starlets in the hands of Bollywood biggies, the naturally and obviously condescending and life demising principles of the industry are being vehemently deliberated upon and many more such interesting and related developments occupy our prime-time screen today. Considering the current imbroglio in the industry due to the Covid-19 lockdown, this was the last of the things that the industry would have wanted.

The thirty-four-year-old actor, with immense demand, suddenly ceased to exist. The stains of death have smeared everything else including the dent on the finance or balance sheet of some production houses who may have signed up Sushanth Singh for their ventures. Probably an auto accident or

---

5   accesstoinsight.org - I happened to comes across this while browsing for some information while working on this book

plane crash may also have created all such conspiracy theories but suicide is particularly poignant.

Such is the nature of anything that's not meeting the perceived potential and its perceived logical end. It spills out, mitigates other possibilities, diverts energy and is hugely wasteful. This is not just about what ends abruptly, but also of those which strive towards a narrow aspiration without consideration for the immense potential of the endeavour; ending up in looking for more productivity, profit, better balance sheet or cash flow.

Lest it appears the book is about some culture-mongering, didactic lectures on the ethicality of an organization, let me quickly add that impact, productivity, efficiency and profit are the most important reasons for the functioning of an organization; just that it's an outcome, as the book intends to show, of all the other things done within the organization. I remember a popular anecdote of my friend Manoj Lekhi here who used to quote Rudolf Steiner's description of a kindergarten. According to Steiner, Lekhi would say, children are like saplings in the garden. No amount of direct pull on the plants would help it bloom but earnest work on what surrounds the plant would. This is too popular an example (almost a cliché as I realized later and ascribed to many other theorists) to be explained further.

But how is it relevant to organizational excellence or, even more broadly, how we handle our lives?

Like the tragic death of Sushanth, organizations, even when surviving, may just be bracketing out the huge potential that subsists it. A formula that appears to work is embraced with scant regard to the wider dimensions and subtle learning that could make it a world-class organization. Organizations (and also individuals including leaders) become neurotic identifying with a narrow interest. Narrower the interest, deeper the mediocrity. Neurosis is the bases of mediocrity! I know the statement appears unaesthetic and judgemental and the utter lack of evidence is a cause for concern. It may even generate suspicions whether it's worth pursuing it any further. All that I can do at the moment is to seek patience

The description aptly suits schools in India constantly worried about a narrow interest in producing '100% results in the board—exam'. Not wrong. But neurosis about being right all the time in getting 100% results in the board exams doesn't allow the schools to see what's really missing. When what's missing is acknowledged, there's at least awareness and a possibility for growing beyond the parenthesis of what's considered important! Only schools (organizations as well; 'schools' is a collective term right now representing all organizations) can escape mediocrity by recourse to PARAMAHAMSA Intelligence. (We will examine PARAMAHAMSA INTELLIGENCE vis-à-vis PUROHITA INTELLIGENCE in a short while from now after we take a small digression). It's akin to a person travelling all the way to London from New Delhi to buy chocolate. It's laughable. A chocolate purchase isn't wrong or denigrating but that the whole lot of work that forms its background is absurdly asynchronous and that begets inefficiency.

On the other hand, a world-class organization, while clearly focused on the blunt ends like profit and money, knows the fundamental and the inherent need of its work for the world; not just in the products or services it offers but in creating an outstanding model that's an answer to the new age—an age that is ever changing. Like the famous anecdote of a mason working on a building when asked about his work says that he is building a world-class cathedral, the nature of each person's in an organization need not be limited to the narrow grinds of fitting a bolt in the long chain of the assembly line. It lacks meaning!

I am reminded of Prof. Krishna Kumar's (the former director of the National Council of Education Research and Training) recent article in The Hindu (27th August 2020). He deconstructs the celebration of the New Education Policy (NEP 2020) of India heralded as a beacon of hope in the popular imagination for the imminent need for a radical change in education. He particularly makes note of the middle-class urgency for literacy and numeracy, and interestingly subverts the notion by pointing out how the ability to read may happen at the cost of meaning. Meaning is sacrificed at the altar for an appearance—in this case, the mechanical reading of words happens at the cost of comprehension and appreciation of a text.

In my own experience as a volunteer with the Art of Living Foundation, I have experienced a story—a tacit one—that surrounds all of us *'sevaks'* (volunteers). We go out and register people into courses, generate programmes, clean the area and serve (we do have our own internal dialogue, of course; just that it doesn't matter what my mind appears to be telling me). But the point is the immensely credible *Guru Puranam* (*puarana*—is a collection of stories pointing to an ideal) surrounds us. Stories about the immensity of the *Guru* surround us. There is a *purana* that surrounds us. Not like general awareness but more intimately as a fact that 'we are out to transform the way the world works and the way the world sees spirituality' and 'it's indeed a great gesture by the master to have allowed us to partake in this great journey'. It's nothing related to how good a volunteer I am or how easily I could meet the targets. The same rules of the game apply here also. Those who are doing extraordinarily well are given better responsibilities of area coordinator to national coordinator to several kinds of instructorships. All these happen within an extraordinary amount of integrity; there's no imposition of rules and regulations but just the intimate presence of the *Guru* essentially drives us.

Art of Living Foundation today is a world-class organization. The organization itself doesn't matter, as *Guruji* himself has said sometimes. He especially mentioned this during one of the many conversations the foundation held with people all across the globe during the recent lockdown, in response to a query about the organization. The organization is decorated because of the work it does and by itself has nothing to offer. We will explore this with another metaphor in a while from now!

We can, right now, consider a few questions before exploring the relevance of an organization!

How about building an organization that generates unprecedented profits while nobody feels neurotic about competition? Can we see the fun of creating an organization where profits don't mean stressed out slogging employees who slog because they are afraid of missing out on the elusive success? Why don't organizations strive to unite, what in Kantian perspective, otherwise, would never meet—knowledge and reality? How can organizations be fulfilling in its humanity?

Without easing out into readymade answers like Corporate Social Responsibility and such, there's a possibility in viewing the huge potential of being in a world-class organization.

HOW RELEVANT IS AN ORGANIZATION?

Not at all. Instead of being this blunt, let's make it a point to observe this.

When there's an 'A' and a visible 'B' that one can move into, forces get organized. An organization gets into formation. The idea that there's a 'B' and the consideration that it's worth pursuing is what evolves and organizes itself. The organization is formed out of an idea worth its salt.

Almost like the organization of a 'human being' evolving from a mere multicellular non-entity to feel-able, discernible identity. Man proposes a more complex 'topographic iteration'. Neuroscientists and evolutionary biologists would agree that the human body cannot be decoded but can be maintained and periodically overhauled. Unlike the simple arrangements of the constituents of a pen, what comprises a human being and how the arrangement is caused is a far more complex question than the most complex and sophisticated robot or space technology ever produced. Does human life begin from birth or conception? Hard to answer! Can the same set of activities done by different sets of human beings result in the same outcome? Our experiences easily deny this as well!

Beginning to question the origin and purpose of an organization is by itself a complex endeavour. Like the inconclusiveness of any anthropological exploration, which seemingly hasn't been able to make a cohesive sense of as mundane, but an arbitrary entity as language, organizations also defy a logical paradigm while describing its origin and function. More than the complexity, it offers a functional disequilibrium because every time a question is answered, it keeps on gyrating out of context. Rather than checking into the question of sounds and syntax in exploring language, it branches itself out into other innumerable, equally complex inquiry like genetics, evolution, karma, destiny, mythology, holy scriptures and new search for witnesses; and probably develops into a whole, yet another, branch and method of study, gyrating out into a complex web of arcane academic activity. What has been a series of effects ultimately leads to another effect and we stop only when we are forced to stare at a blunt end where we are unable to find another cause for the effect.

Since 'effects' are all that we have, it makes sense to see the whole question form the effects caused.

Humans organized into an organism produce results and they perform. These performances are the result of totally untraceable number of causes. Any organized entity is such. One can be happy or sad about it, but no way to trace back its entire trajectory—except in broad narratives like the description of a battle in the history textbook; or the way we make temporary breakthroughs towards a global health issue. Summarization offers good entertainment and temporary stability but not the entire truth. So we are all dealing with an unanswerable question. We had better acknowledge this before we proceed further!

Why are collective human activities organized into businesses, organizations and such? Is it anything more than a club or some such entity? Since it's going to be incomplete, we as well can explore an angle and probably get temporary answers—establishing provincial equilibria as we go along and explore the entire cartography!

IS AN INK BOTTLE ALIVE?

Let's presume for the sake of argument that life forces are organized into a human body for a purpose. Without the body, it would be just not possible and there's no meaning as well for the body without having to do something with itself. Like an inkbottle placed on the worktable, organizations themselves do not have anything to do with what they are supposed to do. An inkbottle has no idea as to why it should continue its existence except for the fact that it has preserved the ink within it. The ink is exhausted and the bottle becomes useless. Dispose of the bottle within the known parameters of disposal. Even an empty bottle disposal not cared for causes damage and collateral effects. But the damage is more if the inkbottle breaks accidentally or out of deliberate human act.

The usefulness of the ink comes within the very organization of the inkbottle. Without extending the metaphor to include the more complex organization of production houses that produce ink and marketing teams that take care of the communication and its dissemination, just the 'ink bottle' alone provides with sufficient archetype of the inherent quality of an organization. Secondly, as we had seen, the relevance of any organized entity is in its 'effect'; without the effect the organization is invisible. Like the human body is largely invisible to us except when it causes an effect on the human mind through some pain, an ink bottle is invisible except probably when it causes an effect. Let's examine this.

An inkbottle by itself has nothing to do and causes no visible impact on our businesses or lives but its inept handling will. The inkbottle broken or mishandled has the potential of untraceable damage—spoilt walls, stained floor, smudged paper, discoloured table, etc. not to speak of clothes and the complex changes within human emotions and relationships. Not just that, the ink that's spilt can never be traced back to its originality as the washed water gets into gutter, the sink, etc. carrying traces of ink; and if at all these traces combine back by sheer providence, it's not going to happen in the immediate next millions of years. Since the ink bottle was organized to keep the energy intact and to be of use whenever needed, it is the whole gamut of ideas—from manufacturing to maintenance and manuals to reliability of the user—which are organized into one whole to care for the inkbottle. The idea 'ink is useful' has manifested into the organization of the inkbottle and the necessary paraphernalia around it.

I know I am probably extending the metaphor a bit longer than needed. This dilemma by itself is the 'ink-bottleness' in the present writing. There's an idea worth exploring—that's how the book is resting on your hand or screen; this idea supposedly has a potential that should be explored exhaustively. And the idea by itself means nothing unless the forces of the market, aesthetics of writing and editing and every other entity required in its production is taken care of. A job well-done morally and meticulously is all we have in the present moment; somehow this simple task of writing something I believe in is all that I can do and the forces that create an entity out of it is a product of this intention (also intensity!). The idea that the ink bottle, if mishandled, can cause potential damage is at least as important as the idea about its use is. That's the difference between a view about what we do and hold valuable as part of our worldview altogether vis-à-vis a view that encompasses human life as a set of activities. Both are valid and equally valuable. The former is a classical viewpoint that we are interested in **'Buddha, The CEO'** while the latter is the commonsensical viewpoint that explores the right processes and methods in accomplishing anything. The background of activity, how holistic or fragmentary, as a reflection of organizational relevance and legacy is what will be explored!

Organizations exist because there's an idea behind it and the idea itself has its traces. An easy lineage can be established—the idea, technology to test the worthiness of the idea, the best way one can allow the idea to blossom and sustain itself, aesthetics of its arrangements and so on and so forth. The tracing of this lineage and complexity are proactively forward looking. In the sense of creating value chains and a set of necessary activities to sustain the value chain. There's a lineage that is also comprehensively in the background. And to the ordinary eye, this connecting link between stages of lineage is at most a wafer-thin, logically deducible reality but not an existential one; and it's not surprising to see sometimes even the total absence of awareness of even the logical connections!

When one looks at the organization as the whole—a completely organized self-expression of an intention—it cannot but realize its objectives. When it's the *'purusha'* and the *'vishwaroopa*[6], it just doesn't fail. The proposition, as we proceed through the book, is the opportunity of 'being whole and complete' at all times as we process in our endeavours of leadership. And, by the way, it is supposed to cause extraordinary performances. Buddha, you will discover, was always a peak performer because he had the complete understanding of the entire lineage!

* * * * *

Examining Conundrum

In the *puranic* narratives that largely reflect Hindu philosophy, evolution is summarily a ten-stage process[7]. It is the Hindu equivalent of *Genesis,* and the ten *avatars* are the manifestations of *Vishnu*—the Hindu deity who maintains order. There is a small description of the process that will ensue but before I jump into that, let me explain my present conundrum as a writer in the following lines.

The temptation to explain it all away is irresistible. Every time my ten-year-old son comes seeking something, say an automobile mechanism, I am tempted to tell him everything I know—constantly fed by the anxiety that any explanation is not complete enough and sometimes its opposite—superfluous information. A deficit explanation may still work as he looks for not all the data but only what is relevant to his current conundrum. His query about how a car runs doesn't need the principles of Thermodynamics or Carnot cycle but the exhibition of the sheer, gross mechanics of the push and pull that creates movement.

---

6   Purusha and Vishwaroopa are generic terms to indicate the eternal principle that runs everything and also through everything. In the spiritual traditions it's the all pervading subtle presence in everything we do, are, produce, think etc.

7   the stages of evolution is quite popular in the mainstream culture. Beginning from fish and evolving through the transition phases of tortoise, pig, Narasimha (a half-human, half-beast), Vamana (the dwarf), Parashurama (the wielder of axe), Rama (Lord Rama), Krishna and Buddha to the ultimate form of Kalki. For our modelling here we have just taken the 9 avatars only. The *Bhagwatha* also counts the incarnations to 24!

So is true of organizational leaders and business heads. When they look for knowledge, they look for everything that would help their businesses grow, make their workplace much happier, create a workspace that dwells on innovation, an organizational design that is sleek and lean and so on.

That is the conundrum in my writing. What should I say and how so that business and organizational leaders take home what would be valuable for them?

Right now, sitting here, I am bombarded by thoughts. I am unsure which thought is valuable and which is not. I am thinking about the book, on how to make this sentence even more appealing, of tingling pain in the right ring finger and so on. There's an improbable order to these thoughts. These thoughts are involuntary a product of sustained improbable order for millennia. All that we can do is to re-arrange this improbable order and make it more predictable—something that wouldn't happen by itself.

That's why a tangible intention is more important at this juncture. This kind of focused attention is both an opportunity for growth and a necessity for knowledge to function. Since knowledge happens in epistemological breaks, like the serendipitous discovery of penicillin, focusing on one or two 'tangibles' could be necessary for a paradigm shift in the whole organization; because a shift is serendipitous, a focus on the tangible can make it earnest. We are at the brink of such an exploration; at least the aspiration is—earnest to sense order and openness to serendipity!

Like the process of evolution itself, each of the *avatars* is a finite rendition of the whole. Each time the expression is limited to the requirement— the way we draw money from the ATM to meet our requirements. The finite rendition is itself a function of what's at stake. A powerful a small boat or a life jacket, or even a powerful swimmer, is all that's needed to save a drowning man while a flooded town would require coordinated efforts of the entire system—the navy, police, medical personnel and the officials of the place. Hence, the question of what is relevant is from a close examination of what really matters at the moment.

A PEEP INTO THE EVOLUTION OF GREATNESS

Why should organizations and companies understand this enigmatic performance? Newtonian Mechanics and consequent specialized diversification have compelled us into a precarious belief in the autonomy of 'excellence'. The 'truth' is that 'excellence' is inter-dependent.

The fact is that every point is a point of transition—a junction for an improbable order. Though I will be very happy if this book hits a best-seller list and makes good returns for me, I can never be sure of it. What I am sure of is that these thoughts will have an impact in the long run. It's not pride but a matter of fact that any idea gathers momentum and significantly changes the way people do things. We will never know how; that's why whatever is being done should be done with utmost care and devotion. That's what Buddha and Patanjali emphasized so much on the ethicality of work!

To work ethically and with utmost care is greatness. There's nothing else that needs to be done. 'How do we go about doing it?' is an exploration we are committing ourselves to.

Unlike growth and change that can be either measured or perceived and is relative to at least one previous stage, evolution is a continuum. Evolution is so 'all pervasive' that it's impossible to notice. One has to just 'know it', like the day-by-day transformation of a child into an adult—generally visible only to an acquaintance visiting after a considerable time but absolutely indiscernible to the familiarity of the family members. Growth can be shown but not evolution and transformation. Even in the *Dasavataara*, the dissimilarity between the fish and pig or between the semi-human beast and a fully evolved Buddha are too obvious but are hard to recognize in the actual process of transformation. In any case, even if we were to see it historically, phenomenally, it took aeons together for a shift from one to the next. They are available to us only as summaries and are connected in this mythological narrative.

The concentric circles that spiral into several identities of 'progressive' evolution in the Hindu mythology are in a way totally unrelated to the previous one—except as in a concentric circle, with the locus intact. Only the patterns of the equidistant periphery from the centre are constant. The constant centre in the evolution of the *avatar* is the need for order and stability so that work can happen. What is the work, then? Not to disturb an order; order is disturbed when there's excess or when someone or something in the connecting link is not working in symmetry. There's 'noise' and the 'noise' has to be reduced or removed. The principle of re-arranging the symmetry for a workable order creates successive *avatars*.

There's a symmetry and structure to the whole but formed of dissimilar intermediate entities. The principle of both genesis and evolution, in that sense, are integrated into one whole here. Anyone familiar with these Genesis stories of Hindu mythology would know each stage as a response to the performance demand within the context of sustenance of order and homeostasis. Since I will only be able to just describe it quite succinctly here, I advise the reader to make a quick reference to the evolution process in separate readings.

The evolution process gets interesting—something that naturally stabilizes the ever-gyrating entropy of a creative process in particular and of an earth that blossomed into newer realms of its expression in general. Fish evolves into other different species to save the creative process and helps see the value of sustaining what was created, albeit in a different form[8]; the tortoise stands a fulcrum to an unstable world being churned towards creating sustenance before other forms take over in newer stages.

The principle around which evolution happens remains constant—creating successive stages of homeostasis. Transformation is not another version update but a paradigm shift to look into a wholly new challenge. Even then the principle remains unchanged. The principle around which evolution

---

8   In the first stage, a fish tugs Manu's ship to safety from a pre-warned inundation. And Manu helps preserve the creative elements of the epoch—the seeds, animals and other items of the previous creation cycle.

happens, in this scheme, remains constant—just a settled beginning, a point of stability untarnished by any outward expression, that one can return to. Returning to the core principle provides an opportunity in expanding the possibility of life. Just survival and sustenance, to begin with, expands to some act of creation in the second *avatar;* to one of struggle into expansion in the next while the fourth looks at resolving a new ambiguity in growth and so forth.

Stories have been anthropoid as much as it is of different species. The process of resurgence has always existed; reestablishing the ambience so that performance can happen. Each of these evolutionary stages is focused around the principle of performance itself.

We could as well examine it here a bit theoretically.

When we look at an organization, we get access to three things—

1. *The constituents of the organization*

2. *How it's assembled and*

3. *The intended performance of the organization*

A perfectly performing organization is well synchronized, placing all its constituents right. 'Performance' is the organizing principle. When organizations don't perform, doubts are natural to be raised about, both, its constituents and the way it is assembled. Is it not so? When organizations flop at the stock market, everyone including the CEO and the whole rank and file is under fire. Demands at revamping the order or dismantling it totally, the very focal points of the organization and everything else that constitutes the organization is suspected. The reverse is also true— stock market rise and the CEO is elevated to the status of a super-hero and everything else is forgotten, almost investing dictatorial status to the leadership.

Maybe it's a rather abrupt beginning but apt to the course of reading into performance and its ramifications. This brings us to some important questions—are such general attributions of success to events and individuals ideal measures of success and performance? How will we ever know that the current performance isn't hiding future ruckus or vice—versa? Sometimes valuable wait time due to a deliberate delay may appear like under-performance!

So, performance has to be understood. When it relates to performance what matters is—

a. *Obstacles to PERFORMANCE.*

b. *Symptoms arising out of these obstacles; symptoms that you're stuck.*

c. *Actions based on a certain understanding.*

BUDDHA AS A PEAK PERFORMER

Buddha belongs to these stages of evolution described above. And Buddha represents a state of auto-renewal.

*High Performance Organizations are in a state of auto-renewal. This ability not to be stranded—in either success or failure—is 'Buddhahood'. **Buddha, The CEO** has this consistent auto-renewal mechanism.*

Buddhahood stems from an understanding—an understanding that's not stranded by finite stories. A finite story, like a closed-ended question, forecloses possibilities and playful permutations that are necessary for cognitive diversity. That's where Buddha excels—being able to transcend the finiteness of stories. When one develops the capability to respond to Angulimala, you're a Buddha; or vice versa, once you are a Buddha you can respond to even an Angulimala. Angulimala had stranded in the process of evolution. He had reduced the question of life to an easy identity—someone who had accomplished the acquisition of 1000 thumbs—well almost; a trophy of 1000 fingers that made life meaningful. It required a Buddha to help him crossover this fetish.

Angulimala was stranded, not in the realm of performance, but in the meaning of performance. So, when Buddha meets Angulimala, it's two peak performers meeting. One was floating in the freedom of absence of a stable identity and another was fixed in an identity.

As the story goes, villagers advise Buddha against the journey, warning against not only heinousness of Angulimala's acts but also in the despicable nature of his dictatorial urge. Conversation was impossible; it was not a theatre of improv but one of a monologue.

As the story develops further, Buddha didn't listen. Went ahead and created a new story within the form of Angulimala.

In that sense, Buddha was a peak performer

Buddha transforms Angulimala. Like all apocryphal anecdotes, this is credulous and has mythical proportions associated with it. The anomaly here is that the stranded Angulimala became important to Buddha. He shouldn't have. Buddha already had a functional organization—fully equipped with an army of followers, disciples and second rung leadership. In a way, Buddha was 'sorted'. But Buddha did respond and the legend is available for our appropriation. God knows what divine cog Buddha found in the wheel of Angulimala!

To a fulfilled organization like the Buddha's, even Angulimala mattered. Angulimala was a part of humanity even if he represented a dysfunctional part of it. Buddha didn't decide to respond to it but it was a natural choice[9] in being a Buddha. It was automatic. Buddhahood does it

The diagram below is a schematic representation of the two phases—the phase of growth and one of performance. The diagram represents the nine stages of the popular *Dashavatara* (the ten transitional stages of the complete expression). Before we get into the description of each of these

---

9   Choice is distinct from Decision. Having come across this in an insightful talk by Rishi
     Prabhakar where he explains how life is nothing but a series of problems we keep on solving. I
     have tried retrieving that conversation but couldn't. It is available only in my notes now.

stages of growth it makes sense to see, at the outset, the position of Buddha in the layered representation. One can easily misconstrue the construct to be hierarchical as is wont in the Newtonian-Mechanistic models. Instead of privileging one expression over the other, it makes sense to see each as a transitional stage of the full expression of the Buddha; and it's hard to see, as explained earlier, that the fish and the pig of the earlier stages is the very Buddha that we are considering now. In the Hindu Mythology Krishna is the *Poornavatara*—a completely expressed potential. That's a state where no more has to be achieved—nothing more has to be delivered.

The expression of the ink from the ink bottle, taking from our earlier metaphor, is the organizational evolution Krishna represents.

Can organizations attain Buddhahood?

YES—in case it develops an ability to respond to human conditions and human existence. Even an Angulimala matters. Organizations are a partial aspect of what humanity is connected to—including, as a deputy director in an organization I had worked for used to say- 'the dust on the blade of the fan and the crumpled tissue paper in the toilet'. The leap may be too big as it appears impossible to respond to but is much simpler than what it appears like. And the statement, if unqualified, would look like a continuous mechanism of correction. But that's not what is meant. Instead, it simply means adherence to the principle that responds appropriately to what's needed; and what's needed is always fluid, not a rigid set of prescriptions!

NO—if it's terribly limited by its own stories; limited by its own understanding of its vision! A vision that's not discretionally accommodative but brackets itself into suffocatingly narrower domains as it progresses.

The corresponding diagram is representational!

The diagram is inspired from the Drexler - Sibbet Team Performance Model in 'The Decision Book - Fifty Models for Strategic Thinking' by Mikael Krogerus and Roman Tschappler.

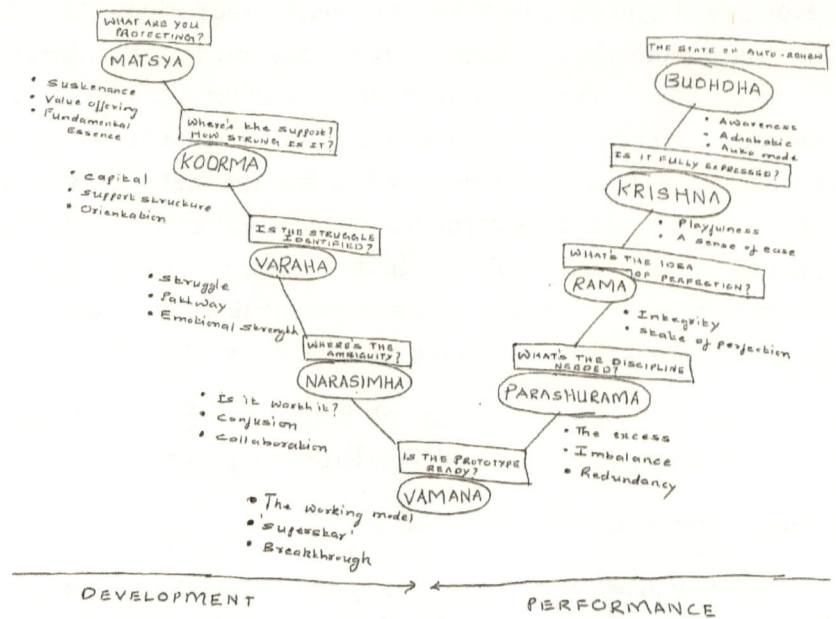

LEGENDS TO REFLECT ON

Sometimes, legends mark a company more than the actual prosaic work within it. One such legend of a company is Infosys in India. I have zero experience with the IT industry but Infosys stands tall amongst the legendary stories of Corporate India. It's a story built around its founding and its phenomenal success. So, even when one's not a part of the organization or the expert that reflects on the principles of organizational success, Infosys provides sufficient data and a legendary status that is conspicuous.

One such legend is about the ambiguity that the founders encountered way back in the late eighties and early nineties. The legend is so popular that it doesn't even demand authorized sources. Hence, I put it here for consideration as is known about Infosys—co-founders of Infosys approach Narayanamurthy to rescind the company; 'nothing is happening' was a terrible feeling that the board may have encountered. That was after making attempts for more than a decade. So it's rather natural to question the very existence of the company—especially when it's stranded and going nowhere. The question of whether it was worth continuing at all is indicative of the ambiguous state. That's when Nandan Nilekani, Chris Gopalakrishnan and other board members approached Narayanamurthy with the suggestion to rescind the enterprise. I may be forgiven for any inconsistencies. The intention is the concept.

As the legend goes Narayanamurthy offered to buy back all their shares. They chose not to sell and stay put with the prevailing ambiguity. Transcending this ambiguity, they went on to create a legendary company in the form of Infosys.

The question of ambiguity is something that companies will face. Ambiguities crop up only when there has been something on stake, something that the companies have struggled through—may be financially, or in the amount of time or knowledge expended on it. In other words, ambiguity is an important milestone only if there has been something on stake all the while. Not just the ambiguity arising from the existential question of whether 'it's worth it', but every important organizational question also passes through ambiguity—whether to go public or not, whether to raise debt or equity are all questions that demand a Faustian bargain. The term comes from Dr. Faustus, a character in the play by the same name, who sells his soul to the devil in exchange for universal power. The bargain costs Dr. Faustus dearly.[10]

Infosys's adherence to value doesn't come in stand-alone strands. Steadfast to the value of ethical business isn't a simple model—it comes as a packet like a pill that comes packaged with its sugar and adhesive elements making it into a full tablet. What was created was a prototype of excellence—unequivocal adherence to its values. Infosys went from strength to strength—listed in NYSE, extraordinary share value growth, social acknowledgement and respectability and high level of accuracy in its business projections.

Once an entity transcends ambiguity, a prototype is made and if strict adherence to its core values is sustained, it expresses itself. Not only in its chosen business line of software services, but Infosys also expressed

10   the character or Dr. Faustus is immortalised by Christopher Marlowe, Shakespeare's literary mentor

and influenced the social sector through its foundation and several other businesses apart from the employees who participated in it, innovative employee welfare options—it was fully expressed, what in our model is 'Organizational Krishnahood'.

Buddhahood is a state of auto-renewal. The founders no longer were limited to the enterprise. Narayanmurthy is a much sought after adviser for many government projects. He headed Karnataka's first task force on knowledge way back in the year 2000; Nilekani spearheaded one of the most ambitious projects of the Government of India—UID, an Identification of Indian citizenship. Once an organization attains Buddhahood, there's a systemic renewal of excellence in every enterprise the creators take on.

This is true of all organizations.

A DIGRESSION BUT WORTH IT—

Let me stray into one a much smaller, not well-known organization now!

This is described in some detail in the description of **Satpuda Valley Public School** in the subsequent sections. I would like to briefly describe the way the whole school began to expand the point here and also to indicate that, irrespective of the social impact, organizations will have to encounter its Buddhahood periodically. To explore Buddhahood is to meet an Angulimaala head on.

Satpuda Valley Public School began with the ideals of a democratic Organization, freedom to the people operating in it, burden less learning, integrated classroom practices and community learning initiative. When we started this in 2005, these ideals were very important for us. For instance, democracy was an important ideal; it manifested in the way we looked at our curriculum. Without textbooks, we created intense consultative groups to consider what is worth being taught. Democracy also meant being humane and hence, from our understanding then, desisted from anything that would mitigate human value—including not drawing agreements and contracts of work. So, in the year 2007 when we were to hold our annual parent meeting, an important ingredient of schooling then, we faced our first challenge of what it means to be senselessly democratic—12 of our teachers either had left without even notice and some had gone on leave.

We had to quickly revisit our value of 'democracy'. Lama Surya Das in '**Awakening the Buddha Within**' describes how they had to revisit the value of non-violence and non-killing in the Monastery built in the US. Cockroaches played havoc and that was the chief hindrance to the seekers attending monastic practices. How to deal with this? Without hurrying and paying full attention to processes of life, Lama had to consider pest control agency to take care of the roaches. Similarly, my meaning of democracy expanded in several conversations with people around me and the challenges that stakeholders posed from time to time. There was no definite meaning to rely on but one confabulated through out!

We also had to revisit our value; we had to renew it for our practical purposes!

The very reason why we were formed had to be protected—the 'mitochondria' of the organization was to cause quality learning and create appropriate accountability with the parents. Equally important was to identify the DNA that would replicate itself into excellence in every area of the enterprise. The DNA was also to ensure a level of learning that would replicate itself in everything our learners may choose to do later in their lives. Every value had to be re-visited in its peculiar circumstantial contexts.

Hence, the chief questions any enterprise will have to encounter are— where is the respiration happening and what's the DNA?

Buddha as a Junction—Melting Pot of Geeta, Patanjali and the Scriptures

A younger colleague of mine, who had started translating the *Gita*, had argued about maintaining sanctity in translation—translating exactly what Krishna had said on the battlefield. This had both—value in seeing texts as they are and also the provinciality of demands each situation puts on a text—a problem of scholarship, in the presence or absence of interpretative discretion! Both arguments were equally valuable.

Let's take the first one—the value of seeing the text as it is. The modern penchant of seeing every text and narrative in allegoric forms robs one's ability to visualize and remaining with an understanding even when no evidence shows up for it. So, by depending too much on interpretation we will be endorsing the fact 'what cannot be expressed has no value'. More so today when we are dabbling between the materialism of our knowledge and the unverified esoteric spirituality—sometimes portrayed through semi-formulated ideas from Quantum Physics.

At the same time, any knowledge needs the discretion of the consumer. Riddles that have been captured in pragmatic, actionable collective knowledge require interpretation and flexibility. The book probably uses this form more than the former. And that's what happened in my conversation with this young colleague who had countered me with the 'sanctity of the text' argument.

I had countered him in turn. There's nothing called a 'sanctified text'. It's always inter-textual; which means, no text including this writing, is a stand-alone model. There can be unique expressions and creative output but to claim originality is just not possible!

So, what we know about Buddha is also inter-textual. Equally important and true is the other way round as well!

Though texts indeed emerge into maturity through these inter-textual elements, the penchant of reading everything as allegory means the perceptions (we will deal with this in a later chapter 'WHERE ARE THE GHOSTS?' In Section 2 which sees perception as a starting point of growth) are yet to be built strongly enough. Retaining the pristine quality of the text is as important as a mature revisiting of the beliefs; this parallels with a revisiting of the beliefs and ideals that formed the enterprise in the first place. Just as to have uncompromising elements engraved well into the cultures of an organization is as important as certain values that have to be periodically reconstructed and reassembled, the principles of the book have to be used discreetly and 'inter-textually'. It need not be a literal text but the text of life and live experiences—the conundrum of our everyday life that appear to contradict and question what any text says.

Not revisiting it amounts to 'stuckiness', a concept which is dealt with in the next chapter within this section.

This 'inter-textuality' will be visible in the numerous escapades that we will indulge in throughout this book into Patanjali, Ashtavakra, Bhagavadgeetha, Buddhist Thought itself and several verses and anecdotes from the *Vedas* and *Mahabharata*. Right now, Sage Patanjali is explored!

> *Why 'will Buddha' be read allegorically here? And why is Buddha again and again subjected to this kind of utility?*

FROM THE SAGE PATANJALI

A *Yogi*—a seeker aspiring for complete union—faces nine different kinds of barriers according to Sage *Patanjali*. 'Union' could be too esoteric a term in its connotations and hence, we may make-do with many mundane expressions like 'completely expressed organization'. Though Sage Patanjali speaks about individuals and seekers, organizations and companies are not any different. Attaining Buddhahood meant going through the entire range of the evolutionary process. As the diagram suggests, organizations also undergo the same—just that some do it fast and others take time and yet others appear to just eternally exist somewhere in between. For any of these entities—individual, company or an organization—there are barriers to be surpassed for the full mastery! What are they?

There are nine obstacles[11]. We may examine what that means to organizations—

1. **Struggling**—financial issues—badly leveraged; legally insecure. Doesn't appear to have a substantial reason for existence. Unarticulated aspirations or aspirations that have been incorporated because they appear fashionable. When clear 'A'

---

11 I heavily imbibe talks by Guruji Sri Sri Ravishankar in these explanation. To the really interested I would recommend Guruji's talks. His slow, steadfastness by itself is a great experience to be with. The intense silences that it caused for me were magical! More than what the message and its meaning had on me.

and 'B' are not identified, if the required pain of finding the direction and its appearances is not factored in, the organizations struggle to fulfil every aspiration that it finds attractive. Krishna in his philosophical exposition to Arjuna in the Geeta speaks about *'vyavasayitmika buddhi'*—the focused mind - as a necessary ingredient for action and redemption. Struggling is a revolving door movement without ever entering the arena of action.

2. **Inconsistency**—The assumptions determining the cause of the organization isn't uniformly clear; inconsistencies in approach. Inconsistencies are hidden. Many a time these inconsistencies are in the form of silences or gossip.

In his now-famous talk on the Golden Circle, Simon Sinek narrates about the discovery of the aeroplane and Samuel Pierpont Langley's abandonment of the project midway—when the news rolled out of the innovation by Wright Brothers. It's not consistent with what was expressed, to begin with—the project on-air flight. Instead, being a pioneer dominated Langley's mission. The same was true of Wright Brothers themselves who compromised on their value when another 'competitor' appeared on the scene.

This is partly an affair of the Human Resources department. Indian philosophy uses 2 terms—*Shreyas*—long-term welfare and the welfare of all and *Preyas*—the limited welfare of oneself. Many times used in the description of the cycle of life and death like the one that happens in Chapter 6 of the Bhagawadgeeta when Arjuna seeks Krishna's clarification thus—what would happen to a *yogi* who has to abandon the path midway; won't he[12] be stuck midway without having enjoyed material benefits nor having completed the Yogic journey? Krishna responds thus—he continues the same journey in another body. Likewise, Human Resources department is interested in logical continuities and in determining where

---

12   the masculine gender is deliberate to reflect the spirit of the Geeta

to begin the process of integration of the new staff and also the older ones into a new process. Kindergarten may not be a great beginning; re-inventing the wheel is a cumbersome process.

3. **Panic-Driven**—panic that drives the process. A 'pyramid of panic' is at work! In the book on 'Insights' published by Landmark Education Worldwide, there's a reference to Joseph Heller's novel **'Something Happened'**. The protagonist Bob Slocum, a mid-level executive, narrates his life in an unconnected stream of, what in the end he calls hallucinatory, revelations. In the novel, Bob Slocum describes the pyramid of panic built within the company he is in. Every person is afraid of five persons and each of these five is afraid of another five and it goes on till there's a pyramid of panic. Instead of its full expression, such a 'Pyramid Company' is instinctively under the influence of 4 C's—Competition, Comparison, Compulsion and Compromise; the 4 C's are according to my spiritual teacher friend Vilas the limitation of mortal beings. These are certainly not the hallmark of a great company.

4. **Compulsively erroneous**—lacks the spirit and ethical bases (see TRANSFORMATION IS A DESIGN, Section 3). This is quite easy to get wrong! It's so slippery that most of the times it exists in mere rhetoric or grand narratives. Since, it's possible to feel good in clean chambers, coffee corners and water holes in the utterly clean and uncluttered office spaces, this many a time is a substitute for the lack of real spirit behind the work. Modern organizations cocooned in 'space-time' pigeonholes are under a constant urge to protect what's valuable, dispel what's excessive and outsource what's not relevant. In doing so the basic ethics are intact while many a project happens by cutting the corners and without a deep insight into the implications on everyone in the organization.

5. **Flabby**—Not sinewy and supple; not lean but heavy and complex. Complexity is '*karma*'. Let me explain with an illustration—food is

necessary for survival. But our food is not just that. There are side dishes, nutritional supplements, enhancers and a whole package that accompanies it. This whole paraphernalia that constitutes food is complex—a far cry from the simplicity of filling the tummy! Systems and processes that an organization employs may not be a straightforward connection between 'A' and 'B'.

6. **Narcissism**—with beauty and preparation; turning in a 'single loop'—lacks innovation. This is where excellence, used again rhetorically, is seen in the externalities of the organization. To package things well and to look neat for a purpose and yet be in constant reflection of what's valuable is pertinent to the point here. One cannot be spontaneous but be rehearsed; yet all rehearsal is to feel the utter simplicity of it all. To 'look good' and 'be right' squashes out a vibrant possibility.

7. **Obsession**—Obsession with uniqueness is a huge deterrent in remaining unexpressed. Uniqueness is natural to the design of any entity but making up one is a huge complexity. It's an extension to the last point.

8. **Stagnation**—Feeling or in a state of being stuck; appearing to reach nowhere. Employee boredom, the tyrannical sameness and the terrible monotony of everything are largely pervasive, not only in our lives but also in the tacit understanding we all share, that it's irrelevant to express or discuss it. And hence, the 'stagnation' is wrapped in silences.

9. **Chaotic**—too many changes—too many directions! Unstable.

Symptoms—

1. DUKHA—sadness; grief stricken. Frustration, weariness and anxiety—unsure of its direction and destination! What's the point? Was there not an easier step? And doubts—'maybe we should have brainstormed a little more before doing this'. Leaders, many a time, share how sleepless they get because the direction of the company

doesn't appear to be functional. I had an experience where the principal of the school I worked with constantly complained about how she is being spied while referring to the appointment of a vice-principal by the management without consulting her; and the chairman of the school experienced sleepless nights as the direction was consistently missed.

2. DHAURMANASYA—bitterness and hatred; manipulation, contrivance, gossip and backbiting; allegations and counter-allegations; complexity and opaqueness. Mostly visible in the form of silences in the organization and the amount of talk time hogged by the leaders, based on the power hierarchy, in any meeting; bitterness exists. Acknowledging the existence of bitterness by not sanctioning oneself a divine authority of leadership is a great step at resolving it. More on this in the subsequent sections of the book.

3. ANGAMEJAYATVA—lack of coordination, multiple demands and pulls and coteries; mismatch between what's desired and the manifest! Getting things done involves politics and if all that the organization is intent on doing, at every level, is to get things done then there's a clear case of 'absence of coordination'. A chain of schools I have acquaintance with practices values as a way of educating the children and growing along. The principals of the school hardly find anything valuable in the Chairman's dicta. There are Value-Heads in each school to coordinate what the Chairman believes in but the principals find them another instance of interference and as totally unnecessary to the project they are in and the demands the customers subject them to.

4. SHWASA-NISHWASA VIKSHEPA—income -expenses out of control; consumption and productivity out-of-order. Lack of efficiency, quality mismatch. Again in both Indian traditions and mythological references, some certain beings and animals are sacred while others are not so sacred. The sacred beings called the

'*devas*' are characterized by their sense of giving. All rituals to the 'devas' are towards fulfilment of a desire. '*Devas*' in that sense are highly efficient and they give off, just contribute while '*asuras*' feeding on heavy food and liquor are energy inefficient. Cows in that sense are scared because they are highly efficient—hardly consume anything and are contributing without being territorial. Cows are sacred but are also heavy—unlike the suppleness of a tiger or any other carnivore. Even in efficiency, there should be something missing in the chain of evolution that it has become so. This itself is an interesting allegory about being efficient yet adaptive and sinewy!

Remedy—

Patanjali recommends an easy one.

Get back to your focus!

'Beat the bush' and 'don't beat around it' as Sri Sri Ravishankar refers to in his commentary on the Yoga Sutras.

Patanjali calls it as '*ekatatvaabhyasa*'!

Buddha recommends it in His first of the Nobel Truths—life is suffering; we are eternally stuck in suffering with a 'hope' and 'desire' - with an expectation. Many a time, to meditate on the first of His Nobel truths is enough. Its contemplation draws attention to the core—where did it all begin?

When we have not paid sufficient attention to the beginnings, or don't revisit the beginning as often, we tend to be 'beating around the bush'. The organization may become an activity galore, a lot of operations but doesn't generate any satisfaction! (Quite incidental to refer to one my younger friend's complaint about the 36 to 40 hours he spends as a senior manager in meetings every week in his organization. He works for a global corporation with revenue and profits in billions and not one that can easily be dismissed as a start-up.)

A PEEP INTO THE *GEETA*

These formulations are not different from the 'Bhagavad Geeta'. The chapter 13, for instance, enunciates '*Kshetra*' and the '*kshetragna*'—the field and one who is cognizant of the field! These enunciations have repeatedly appeared in the Indian texts as in from many others from across the globe. In a way, this is also a reflection of what was referred to as 'seed' of excellence earlier—the seed that runs through everything that forms the organizational excellence.

In lyrically beautiful Sanskrit verses, Vyasa has compiled what were supposedly Krishna's utterances in the battlefield egging on a reluctant Arjuna to a fight. According to my friend Vilas, the beautiful verses are original literature—not original in thought. And he further elaborates in his talks that what Krishna recommends is to surrender to him so that there is a purification of the mind for appropriate action. A mind that is biased towards a goal is hardly of any value, Krishna says.

The question remains—how do we clean that up? How will surrender help in doing it? In any case, how do we surrender? That's why in Shankara's commentary later in the 12th century, especially the *Vivekachudamani* and *Brahmasutra*, are largely necessary to compliment this succinct text of the Gee*ta*. Shankara is rightly called a pseudo-Buddha, not derogatorily as some sections do but as a form of profound erudition that linked it to the *Sanatana*[13]! Shankara Meets the Buddha, as many scholars would agree.

The mind can't conceive historical figures as a continuum; as an accumulation or as a cumulative effect. An age that celebrates even children's cartoons in terms of good-bad, villain-hero binaries (exceptions like 'Wreck it Ralph' exists), an individual isn't a product of an ecosystem but an emergence that is a mechanistic genius or spoilt brat. Hence we need to put Buddha in a context, as done above in the *Dasavataara*.

---

13 ever existing could be its meaning; unlike the belief system that all religions and spiritual order degenerate into, Sanatana is the eternal presence that is constant

We will examine later in Chapter 2 how Buddha celebrated 'stuckiness' and why being stuck is the most important quality in catapulting into world-class organizations. Buddha celebrated 'being stuck' by his famous refusal to answer some fundamental questions—soul and God being two very pertinent ones in his list. In that sense, unlike the discourse-based analytics and the rituals of the *vaidik*[14], Buddha transformed it into a popular movement of 'knowing'. While Buddha himself acknowledged the lineage of his knowledge and the cumulative essence of *vaidik* knowledge, 20th-century political polemics largely placed it again as a binary opposition to the *vaidik*—chiefly representing the *Brahminical* dominance.

That is not the reason for the choice of Buddha here—to appropriate Buddha as a practical figure who democratized knowledge. The opposite is. Buddha is the fullest expression, democratically renewable, widening participation and making things happen even in 'stuckiness'.

The theme referred to above will continue through the book. For now, we can just summarize the chapter.

* * * * *

To summarize the whole chapter, we could begin by looking into the key questions and some key points. In case these thoughts have excited you, you may refer to the conversations on 'TRANSFORMATION IS A DESIGN' and 'SHOULD AN ORGANIZATION BE PROTECTED' which come in the later sections of the book right away. For now, a few questions should suffice—

1. *How will the organization last? What's going to sustain it?*

2. *What will 'transform' through the organization and by its perseverance throughout the organization? What paradigm shift or worthwhile breakthrough will it cause?*

---

14 Pertaining to the *vedas*

In other words—

1. Have you discovered the mitochondrial bases of the organizational DNA? Have you discovered the '*SANATAN*'ic element?

    Both 'DNA' and '*SANATANA*' may represent the same entities externally. DNA is what's physiological and characterized by the dynamic mechanism of genetics while *SANATANA* is the root— the evolutionary spirit one may arrive at by continually regressing the genetic code. In a way, '*SANATANA*' refers to the ultimate cause.

    Organizational DNA largely expresses the processes and systems that sustain life. These systems and processes and their connection to the organizational web are illustrated in Chapter 3 of this section to an extent that's relevant for the point at stake. Sufficient here to observe that there's an underlying energy that drives everything in the world—even a mediocre organization has some sustaining basis. Something appears to be clearly at work. Likewise, DNA in an organism represents the four fundamental C's—Compulsiveness, Compromise, Competition and Comparison. I owe these terms to my dear friend Vilas for his extraordinary erudition on Indian scriptures and their practical bearings on life. A wolf, for instance, knows the survival instincts; there's a mechanistic determinism about it. It's not creative pulse but momentum that sustains it!

    The *SANATANA*, on the other hand, has something at stake! It's not sufficient to act but be fundamentally aware of the entire range of 'butterfly effect' generated along with the realm within which an act happens. It requires successive regression.

2. Are the nuclear strands clear to you? (LOOK AT THE DIAGRAM OF ORGANIZATIONAL DNA—CHAPTER 3)

Companies transit from a state of 'sustenance' where the real questions pertain to 'what really needs to be 'sustained' and 'incubated' to a state of

'Auto-renewal' where the real enterprise is at work and the soldiers are on retreat!

This wholesome transition has intermittent points of transition. These 9 phases have the perfect 'V' shape—4 in each arm and one in the centre. On the left, the four stages represent the phase of development and the one on the right represents the performance.

WHAT DO THE POINTS ON THE 'V' DIAGRAM REPRESENT?

The phase of development (the left wing of the 'V'). This is a version of the broad narratives of the organization. A similar 'V' will be encountered later in Section 3 of the book. Since it's not a linear text one may refer to these back and forth for appropriateness. Here each stage is explained briefly for the practical necessities of reading further.

1. *At the stage of 'SUSTENANCE'—the avatar of fish—brainstorm, intense discussions and being settled about what it takes to achieve is registered. What's the value proposition? Is it worth being protected? What's getting sustained?*

   The vision statement, target and the impact each of these goals have on the organizations come into picture here. The needed impact of 'velocity' and 'momentum' stems out of the perceived value creation. So the whole question boils down to pure 'perception'—untested and not having undergone the rigorous test of logic.

2. *At the stage of 'SUPPORT—the avatar of the tortoise—creating the rule book, the agreements and contracts, clarity of execution and reviews, funds, training, etc. are identified. Where's the support? Is the support credible? Have the fundamentals been cleared before the support system is taken?*

   Investments and plan for returns, plan B's and the necessary training and development of the required resources are the players here. Also what support exists for the manifestation of value proposition becoming a lived reality of the daily transactions.

This is a significant step. The fundamentals matter a lot here. Are the stakes put rightly?

3. *At the stage of STRUGGLE—the avatar of the pig - the most important thing is to follow the principles of 'excellence'—doing everything extraordinarily well—housekeeping, maintenance, hospitality, meetings, documentation. To recognize the nature of excellence becomes the key here. Do you recognize the struggle? Where's the pathway and what's the pathway?*

   Is the product, marketing, sales structure, brand value or the leverages that matter?

   Being able to recognize the stepwise growth, the phases of growth of the organization become important. The process of recognizing what comes first between say human development and research; products or producers and other binaries cause stress and havoc. But an important phase of growth for the organization.

   It's critical, at this stage, not to hanker for clarity but excellence; since it isn't clear what shape it would take, despite the well-known optics of 'vision building' and intentionality, the point is to feel committed to doing everything to the best. To a large extent, this book and my new enterprise of writing for the market stands here. It involves reflection for all of us venturing in—to be reflective and constantly examining the bases of our work!

4. *At the stage of AMBIGUITY—the avatars of the Narasimha—the ability to manage toxicity. Creating appropriate rituals to flush out what's unnecessary and a commitment to discovery. Whether there was exhaustive brainstorm in the first stage matters. Where's the ambiguity? And how are you ensuring that the whole organization is being straight about the ambiguities?*

   The phase where there's hope but also fear that it may not turn out as planned. The ambiguity is seen in the variations between declared quarterlies and the actuals, between intended performance and the actual performance of the CEO or in the constituents of the board!

These 4 phases need nurturing; this is the set of phases where huge gaps start becoming visible. Without ignoring any, nor being overwhelmed by any requires the '*purohita*'—the priest! (PUROHITA—the priest—is described in relevant details in the later chapters of the book. Particularly Chapter 3 of the current section describes it quite exhaustively and illustratively)

The job of the '*purohita*' is to look for the stages where you are stuck and keep on generating appropriate measures and remedies!

And the *purohita* helps you recognize the actual work that needs to be done before the organization proceeds to the next!

Only when the entire set of the above stages are managed well, do we have an opportunity to move to the next stage—stage 5—PROTOTYPE!

At the stage of 'PROTOTYPE' is the avatar of Vamana, the dwarf—creating congruency models that generate the product or service; every point of delivery is a miniature prototype and the 'difference' the product or service is. Every link in the chain is a self-similar fractal of the whole.

Being able to see the entirety, as a miniature at least, is to see the 'VISION' of stage 1 in some kind of tangible form. An important stage of growth! In fact this is the beginning point of growth. All the previous stages provide for the strength and nurture for this MODEL PROTOTYPE to bring itself to full expression—STAGE 8.

THE GROWTH PHASE STAGES—

The important questions are—

1. *At the Stage of DISCIPLINE—the avatar of Parashurama—What's excess? Where's the imbalance? What discipline is necessary?*

Clarity about what's really unnecessary and what is needed to make it work well. There is a balance at this phase between all the components that have helped create this model—the market requirements, communication, package, etc.

Attention is to the noise; generating a deep listening and being focused; listening for the unnecessary noises and damping it further or eliminating the discordant ones through observation for imbalance and excess. In the actual legend of Parashurama, he went on killing the Kshatriyas—the warriors—as they bred inefficiency.

As a parallel to the same thought process, which will be considered in relevant detail later in Section 3, we could as well examine the penchant for the 'asura-daiva' [15] *conflicts in the mythical narratives. Even now in the Indian traditions, the cow is worshipped: feeding on grass and contributing to the sustenance of a community. It hardly occupies space and consumes resources and hence breeds super-efficiency models, unlike the territorial predators that ensure absolute protection over their territories and thereby breed inefficiency. The metaphoric predators of Special Economic Zones of the modern era have hit the real-life predators to such an extent that it requires statutes to protect them from being endangered. Parashurama removed such excesses back then!*

2. *At the Stage of IDEAL EXPRESSION—the avatar of Ram—has the prototype evolved to a perfect model? Is it disciplined enough that everybody knows what's the ideal?*

   The key is consistency; the uncompromising adherence to what is really valuable—a decision to remain consistent even when the existence of the business itself is at stake. This is an extremely demanding situation and generally, organizations budge and give up here.

---

15 Functionally 'asura-daiva' represent the angel-demon binary.

At the stage of 'IDEAL EXPRESSION'—the avatara of Rama—entails the examination of the fundamental wastage—compromise, compulsiveness, comparison and competition. These 4 Cs don't allow for consolidation. Human life is entirely about these 4—survival and continuation. It is not difficult to see why so many compromises are apparently compellingly 'practical' and 'existentially necessary'.

Rama characterizes benign dissatisfaction—hungry for the full story he experiences a benign dissatisfaction with an already functioning—apparently fully functional—business entity.

3. At the Stage of FULL SELF-EXPRESSION—the avatar of Krishna—Is it completely self-expressed? What is still blocking the full expression of what the organization is about?

A stage of perfect synchrony; absolute integrity and yet playful. There's joy all around, a sense of lightness and aesthetics, and is breathing life!

staff and their growth; full realization of each individual's performance and growth. What projects should be taken up so that not just the island of the company or organization but the whole ecosystem is owned? Take on more, participate 100%, examine resistances and use the same for full expression. The point where excellence is morbidly infectious—everything connected to the company is 'expressed'.

4. At the Stage of AUTO-RENEWAL—the avatar of Buddha—Are you free from it? Can everyone rest—be peaceful? Can it recreate itself? Are the seeds right?

The ultimate question is faced—'how does it matter?' Not from one of an arrogant and cynical dismissal of 'who cares' but a genuine wonder: 'how did it all happen?'

What is happiness? What exists even before anything really happened? Buddha, in terms of Will Durant, represented a flux that was authentically continuous. Buddha contradicted easy sloganeering of 'aham brahmasmi' ('I am that' kind of rhetoric) by a profound *acknowledgement of 'grief' as existential and crass materialism of Charvaka[16]. It's fundamentally innovative, refreshingly straight and complex revision. What's the point and is it worth it? Buddha in this lineage is the potent stage of auto-renewal and continuous regeneration—fully evolved yet in flux.*

And recognition of actual work—

Buddha also represented it in his policy structures. He simply refused to answer some questions, which included, as said before, ones about God and *Atma*. The model of growth and development that's illustrated, likewise, is 'stages of transition'. Reducing its esoteric aspect, the emphasis is on the allegorical quality of the narrative, which many a time is dissatisfying and highly personal. That's probably the centrality of the whole proposition— the personal and subjective taking precedence to the objective and impersonal.

This is not what the finest expositions form the *Puranas and our* scriptures are meant for. They have been appropriated here, quite symptomatic of the primacy of the intellect in the present age. At the same time when we jump any of these transitions, we may have to revisit at an extra cost and amidst disharmony. Transiting from mere models of sustenance to being world-class is something we will ponder as we go about.

---

16   another school of thought generally equated with the Epicureans

CHAPTER 2

An Aspect of 'Stuckiness'—
The Realm of Buddha-Hood

He who knows that this body is like froth

And he learnt that it is unsubstantiated as a mirage

Will break the flower pointed arrow of Mara and never sees death

Death carries away a man who's gathering flowers

and whose mind is distracted

– Dhammapada

STUCKINESS

When Maulvik Bagga (name changed, of course) walks, he strides. His massive frame at 6'2" gives him an air of authority—unintentionally; and sluggishly glances, askance, through many frames in front of him—his CEO's reports, vendors waiting to receive money, suppliers waiting for an appointment, an employee wishing a furtive benign glance at himself and many more in the motley town with a two hundred thousand population where his stature is too immense to be ignored. He can afford to ignore each of those and be bored—choosing to attend or not based on his fancy and the state of lethargy. He forgets things, gets impatient with long reports and wants to quickly jump into 'so tell me now, what' mode!

This is the story of that burly businessman who is endearingly simple, and so clever that it's hard to distinguish whether he is shrewd or innocent; whether he is too detail-oriented or extraordinarily uncomplicated and ultimately whether his promise is a promise or a carrot to the onlooking hare who will perpetually wait for the carrot. Let's have a peep into this business structure that he has crafted so meticulously—lazily and organically.

AN EXPLORATION OF 'STUCKINESS'

I remember the growth of this company called LifeBliss. I witnessed it first hand, beginning in the year 2005.

Maulvik Bagga, the shrewd businessman in his late 30's now, listens to me for what he calls 'insights' in my conversations with him. He doesn't appear to implement it but participates wholeheartedly in the conversations with a keen interest for insights and avows its application to varied aspects of his life, if not all. Hailing from a Marwari[17] business community, well connected to the roots of the place in terms of its social and political life, Maulvik finds ease in working with the bottom line. Unencumbered by the burdens of formal education and fancy ideas, or the need for sophistication in interaction, he brings ease amongst his staff and is at ease in everything he does. Very organic and participative, Maulvik has created systems and practices that appear extremely humane in his tiny functional office, devoid of any excesses. It looks sinewy and sophisticated in that.

Maulvik takes pride in the efficacy of the method that created the company—organically. The company began under two interrelated things—a desire to expand and involve in the family business and another—a conspicuous opportunity.

In what is described by Maulvik about LifeBliss was 'an opportunity' that was 'unmissable' in his words, and with attention easily opened an obvious

---

17   A Community known for the entrepreneurial talent and known for their business acumen. The name comes form the region they originally hailed form - Marwar within the North-Western state of Rajasthan in India

business opportunity. According to him, the major clients for the farmers' seeds in the predominantly farming belt was the government agencies and the 'mandis'[18] and the farmers transport their products to the godowns on their own at a cost. In addition to these farmers' heavy dependence on private money lenders rendered risk to their profitability. In summary, it offered an invaluable business opportunity, which would also contribute to the lives of people.

Maulvik saw and participated with unequivocal robustness in this opportunity. With a whirlwind tour of the countryside, exploiting the social connection and the political clout, Maulvik met all the farmers in the region. And the offer was mouth-wateringly unmissable. Maulvik began the offer smeared with a benefit—

1. *This better price made better sense, which even otherwise LifeBliss would have had to pay to the Government's official agency, which buys and stores seeds.*

2. *And the extra cost, in any case, would be lesser than the margin that would have been paid to the agency. And also saves the company from unnecessary heckling with the government agency, notorious for their show of strength to hapless company officials.*

3. *The farmers won—as they get extra cash; and LifeBliss won—as it got its priced products at a lower cost and signalled an easy monopoly given the strength of capital and social connection that formed the promoters' background.*

4. *Besides, that helped LifeBliss establish its brand value as a single-window destination—transacting at convenience and freedom.*

What else, even transportation was offered. This was a simple, logical extrapolation and easy—even otherwise transport would have been

---

18 Generally a farmers' interface with the general public where the produce can be sold. Run as cooperatives, government regulators manage it and is chiefly the trading centre for the Indian farmers.

necessary to transport from the government *mandis*. Instead, the transport was offered to the farmers and farmers' profit margins expanded further. Even more, money was offered in advance for the seeds that should be anyhow lent. This was a welcome offer to the perennially cash strapped Indian farmer. The lending of advance money foreclosed any other agency playing in the field. Again the clutches of money lenders eased on the farmer's pocket. The whole package on offer was irresistibly mouthwatering.

It was an instance of vertical integration—commodity, logistics, financing, research and help, seed business, etc. Being primarily from an industrial family that produced edible soybean, the whole scheme was tailor-made for success.

The above description is a simple model of business, which catapulted LifeBliss to one of the leading seed companies in India. More than anything else, the perfect and easy business model provided the right impetus to the young business initiative in Maulvik. Maulvik believes in the ease of his business so much so that he is extremely fond of his favourite line—'right is easy, easy is right; be at ease, you'll be right'.

Luckily the story doesn't end here allowing for our expansion into a valid theory of 'stuckiness'. The story begins with his 'stuckiness'; now he feels terribly stuck and that's the reason for taking his name here!

A Background To The Story—

To explain its relevance, I will have to describe Maulvik's other businesses and enterprises.

He is involved with Pyramid Valley International and was responsible for the beginning of the Satpuda Valley Public School, both of which are described in the book specifically to discuss the 'stuckiness' amongst the several aspects of organizational challenges through them. He also participates in another electronic company—popular for its goods—with a controlling stake.

Recall Maulvik's favourite line—'right is easy, easy is right; be at ease, you'll be right'. That's one of the operational philosophies of Maulvik. To be at ease. He is so fond of that he still senses the feel of a business by what he calls 'simplicity' of it all. Whether we have discovered and can articulate it or not we all are driven by such myths. So, it makes sense to ask ourselves some questions at this juncture—

- *What dysfunctional myths are driving us?*

- *Taking a good look at our lives, can we discover what wrong wall is our ladder of 'success' leaning on?*

- *Where are we doing well and where do we feel stuck?*

- *What are the ones we conveniently consider unimportant that may be influencing the way our organizations perform?*

You may pause a bit and ponder on these questions, which will come handy as we progress to the next levels of the analysis. If you have done it, we may progress to the next few descriptions.

Now, as Maulvik converses with me on several aspects of business and its 'stuckiness', we can unravel some 'wrong walls' his ladder of success leaned on. Predominantly Maulvik had dealt with the businesses that dealt in products with shelf value and one that wasn't virtual but real.

Let's Take the Example of Life Bliss

Seed business in India is utterly fidgety, heavily dependent on the unpredictability of rains. That makes the products of seed business not only of extreme low shelf value but also volatile in its dependence on the monsoons. To sell within the expected rain periods is critical. Even the mother business that provided both the seed capital and a playing field, Metul Oil And Flours Limited, a soybean extraction plant, produces edible oil with a shelf value. In other words, every business Maulvik was involved in, experienced and became successful in was based on volatile inventories.

So, the model, the ladder that worked for Maulvik leaned on the wall of 'push'. Push the products, people and inventories as far as possible. Creating capital and quick purchase of seeds, providing capital to the farmers in advance and quickly occupying the market was the ladder that worked.

In summary, some of Kaushik's ladder of success leaned on—

- *Push. Push is the only way businesses work. Work harder, harder still and even more. Struggle. You have an Elon Musk here.*

- *'Paise se hi sub kuch chalta hai, saab'—loosely translated, 'Everything is a play of money, sir'. Dependence on capital influx.*

- *Independence and control. Elon Musk again.*[19]

Did it create auto-renewal? Was their discovery of an eternal element that would have run any business or life?

To somehow push the products into the market and have the inventories dissolved appeared to have worked; LifeBliss made substantial profits. What probably is of more interest here is—what didn't work despite this 'success ladder' and where was the company stuck, whether noticed and cared for by the promoter or not?

As is described in the last part of the next chapter, what the company couldn't discover was the larger organizational or human crises, which would have made the company eternally functional and relevant instead of being just a more convenient agency of exchange. As a seed company LifeBliss had to put all its energy into making profits within the known confines of the region—Metul (a real place but given a fictitious name here), a provincial district in MP and its surroundings. What human crisis remained unattended to and largely impacted on the other playing fields? I will enumerate two such global crises in and related to the field of agriculture with its ramifications—

---

19 These ideas and semblance with Elon musk emanates from my reading of Ashlee Vance's biography 'Elon Musk'

1. *Increased conversion of agricultural lands into more profitable industries or more convenient real estate. Agriculture is neither glamorous nor profitable. Even in smaller towns the agricultural land is either abandoned or converted into colonies. And the abandoned farmers throng the already crowded megacities for the cheap labour force or debt-ridden cabbies for Ola and Uber. The cycle is a never-ending loop, which now appears, only a COVID—19 kind of disaster would stall, of course with its own set of unpleasant ramifications*

2. *Decreased land but increased food production has resulted in the lower nutritional value of food products and hence a huge impact on the health of humanity. India is the 'diabetes capital' and not very far behind in cardio-vascular and other hormonal related diseases. (For instance in the Nutrition Club I go to I have learnt that Potassium that was once sourced from a single banana, maybe a few decades ago, requires at least thirteen bananas today. I cannot verify it but have witnessed pleasantly surprising results that a small change in nutrition brings forth).*

It may appear slightly digressing but I appeal for patience for a while.

The above 2 may not appear directly linked to the avowed business model of LifeBliss. Agreed. But the point is not that, nor is it an off-handed recommendation as to what LifeBliss should have done. The simple point is—a model that was good enough to sustain couldn't sufficiently open up the complete possibilities of the business. Whether the company participates or not, the complete array of possibilities is an important ingredient for growth. And, like Infosys and its leadership which participated equally well in other avenues of social contribution, the seed of excellence thus discovered through fully expressive enterprise will replicate itself in anything the leadership of the company cares to enter.

The question here is one of expression. While Krishna was fully self-expressed, he generated surprises by marrying apparent contradictions. One such I will state as a case in point—while egging Arjuna to war, he carefully places the nest of a bird stuck amidst an impending danger of civilizational fight. Bheema is intrigued—how relevant is it to save a nest when the whole clan is at the brink of destruction. Krishna famously replies that your fight is your *karma*—your doing—while installing a bird to its safe place is a natural outcome of observation. This small incident is not to be taken as a sentimental assertion but as what it means to respond to the crisis on hand. Later on, even when Krishna eggs Arjuna to fight it's based on this simple logic—you can never know the consequences of any action; and to be able to fathom the depth of action is by itself an act of extraordinary perception.

What I am trying to assert here is more than a few set of actions missed, which is clear only in retrospect. The point, instead, is the dimensionality of possibilities that we have access and exposure to.

Maulvik missed the metaphysics of agri-business. He had an advantage that even Elon Musk didn't. Even for the eminence of M S Swaminathan[20] Green Revolution only bought some time; what was really required was the Evergreen Revolution. Did Maulvik invite all of the past in generating what had been generated—the easy availability of irrigation, pesticide usage and the entire machinery—including the government subsidy? Did he participate towards totally inheriting the opportunity of an evergreen revolution? Partial inheritance, like in this case the business instincts, generated profits—nothing more!

Applying the principles of the diagram described at the beginning of the previous chapter to LifeBliss, it at its best shuttled between Sustenance and Prototype—a prototype that worked well re-living itself in its numerous recurring ambiguities, struggles and in the successive re-creation of support systems. What couldn't be done was to build an ethically resplendent, ever-

---

20 Renowned scientist in India who was instrumental in bringing about the green revolution of 1960's which was largely responsible for the self-sufficiency food in India. Though the Green Revolution was a national necessity for a congenital food deficit, Dr. Swaminathan is also known to have been an advocate for alternative practices to agricultural including his foundation's research on sustenance in agriculture. Personally speaking Dr. Swaminathan is himself a case of extraordinary work who evolved and re-invented himself constantly and thereby the way he saw and mentored Indian agriculture even after its Green Revolution.

responsive, humane company that would have not only been a torchbearer in its idealism but also would have fully expressed and renewed itself automatically into different ventures that Maulvik wanted to participate in. Shuttling is a euphemism for the states of iterative 'regression-progression' couple!

To have engaged in the more complex aspects of discipline, ideal-hood, full self-expression and auto-renewal would have required a little effort beyond the generally known ways of responding to a company. What did it result in? Without auto-renewal can companies be happy and fulfilled? Was Maulvik's sense of 'easy is right' translated into late-night partying and long overseas vacations, really 'easy and right'?

'STUCKINESS'—AN INQUIRY

What is *stuckiness*? As I type the word 'stuckiness', the red underline that focalizes the error refuses to go. Even after several rounds of contemplation and conversations with many of my friends, I could not get an alternative term for it. So, 'stuckiness'[21] sticks! And by this term what I mean is a sense of being stuck into something—like a boulder being pushed on to the truck by a group of exhausted labourers; neither can they drop it midway nor have sufficient energy to execute its completion. It's a point of intense conundrum. Since I am unable to use a better term, I am sticking to it for now; I am 'stuck' to it.

Buddha, both historically speaking and as a lineage from a system of thought, emerged out of particular traditions of knowledge, which was visible in several parallel philosophies including Shankara's Advaita and was philosophically an extension of *Charvaka's* materialism[22]. We currently

---

21 I found the expression 'stuckness' in 'Zen and the Art of Motorcycle Maintenance' after I had used this expression here. I have used parts of the book in many conceptualisations later on. Wish I had read the 'Zen Book' earlier!

22 Shankara is a 12th century Indian mystic who is chronologically later to Siddhartha, the Buddha. Renowned for intellectual as well as spiritual acumen Shankara is known in the popular culture as the rejuvenator of the Rishi (saint) culture within India. His strand of spiritual thought, summarily known as Advaita (non-dual), rejected the appearance of apparent reality of the manifest world. While Buddha is the hero of the mass with its simplified commandments and practice, Shankara is known for his intellectual rigour and sharp analysis.

don't have time and space for exploring this nor is it the intent of the book. Again there is a danger of having summarized all these too narrowly.

But the point is this—whenever we encounter 'stuckiness' in an organization—at any level—be it HR and recruitment, lack of innovation, growth challenges, attrition or a feeling of being too scattered, the beginning point of such 'stuckiness' is somewhere amongst the nine layers of manifestation described in the diagram of Chapter 1. It doesn't mean that we should press ourselves too hard in discovering it all by ourselves. As the chapter later explains and as cross-references throughout the book are explored, the understanding through an organizational mentor (the *purohita)* would go a long way in explicating this.

This aspect about 'stuckiness' came out when my brother Umesha, himself an organized speaker with substantial erudition and experience in corporate restructuring processes and liberally uses key texts of Indian esoteric knowledge, asked me what the 'purpose of the book' is while reviewing my writing. The question troubled me. Of course, there were easy answers—making more money; an idea that I wanted to expand; safer ones like 'absolutely no purpose, revolutionizing the way corporates run; to communicate so that I don't have to rot with my knowledge' etc. None of these motives appeared appealing. The dominant feeling was that this book has come out of a naive idea that 'esoteric' knowledge and subjectivity play a big role in transforming the way we work collectively. I call it naive not in a derogatory sense but with a sense of danger in over-simplification that we all indulge in sometimes; in fact, it's the opposite

---

His Bhaja Govindam', 'Vivekachudamani' and 'Bhashya's can be looked into for a more elaborate description.

Charvaka on the other hand is both an esoteric figure as well as historically recognised and precedes Buddha chronologically. Comparable to the epicureans, Charvaka advocated primacy of the senses in the complete expression of life. In a way appears to be a logical transition between the already established elitism of the Brahminical practice and experienceable mass practice of the Buddha as Historians like Will Durant have portrayed.

I owe this connection to the long remembered notes from Historian writer Will Durant's description of the logical evolution of Buddha in his world history series!

of being derogatory—naivety is eminently useful. It fuels easy propulsion without the intervention of excessive thinking.

To be good-heartedly naive is stupendously beautiful. Because it presupposes goodness without evidence. This is explored later in one of the chapters (**Transformation is a Design**, Section 3). But the book was stuck! It appeared rudderless without a stated purpose. Though begun innocently, I was stuck at the point of executing the book.

To be 'stuck' means an opportunity to explore not only what went wrong or was missing but also to explore the meaning of it all. On a more personal note, I remember one of my middle-aged colleagues who lost her husband felt stuck and her constant refrain was—'what was my mistake that I lost him?' Not only was she forlorn but felt compelled to find imaginary reasons for an apparent mishap in the natural death of her spouse. She has sufficient material means, had grown up children and her lament was not really about supporting sustenance in the absence of an earning member. But the question remained—neither was it related to her material conditions nor a cognitive inability to fathom the depth of her situation.

To search for meaning beyond the immediate is obvious in human endeavour. And the perspective of the end—a total perspective of the ephemeral as limiting is the real issue—brings forth a feverish search as to what the meaning of our experiences and endeavour are. My colleague's search was probably guilt ridden but it also could be an extraordinary learning tool when we take happenings—including mishaps—seriously. That's what this book is set out to do—to explore the 'stuckiness'. The danger is that many a time we don't feel stuck as we find it extraordinarily useful to somehow engage in what we have been doing all this while in our life and also in our position of leadership within the organization.

When 'stuck' somewhere within the nine levels described above, and acknowledge it, we have an opportunity to distil the meaning of it all. Mark Booth recommends a thought experiment in his **'Secret History of the World'**—to put all great literature into a giant computer and ask it to distil out what deterministic laws about life these great works suggest.

Likewise, if we subject all our great esoteric knowledge it would distil out into somewhat these aphorisms—

- *There's no way to avoid what has to be completed. To remain incomplete means to have found the edifices of mediocrity. What has been avoided has a way to find you back!*

- *To feel stuck at a point is an opportunity to see the whole. Feeling 'stuck' is an opportunity to put the dots together.*

- *It's irrational to bifurcate into rational dichotomies—important— unimportant, small—big, impactful—non-impactful, useful— useless and so on so forth. Not that we should avoid exercising discretion in determining our priorities, purpose and vision but just that these bifurcations require attention. (You may recall the story of Angulimala in the beginning; responding to humanity means to respond to everything humanity is connected to).*

- *Our fears are like pits into which everything we do is drawn. Greed is a form of fear!*

- *What was wrong, even if evaded, will have to be paid for.*

There's a pre-supposition of such knowledge in the general naivety of conversations seen amongst our elders and the simple folk who work for us. Religions are filled with technicalities of confession, effect diminishing rituals for wrongs done and rites of passage as graduation from a set of inconsistencies. In a way to remain dynamic, to avoid 'stuckiness', is the very edifice on which human knowledge has built itself.

One such 'stuckiness' the book itself tries to escape is the conceptualization of 'Buddha'! To make Buddha fluent with everyday events of life and see the porousness of him is the endeavour.

ORGANIZATIONAL IMPLICATIONS

Let's look into the other ventures Maulvik was involved in—Satpuda Valley Public School (SVPS) and Pyramid Valley International. Both depended heavily on building social capital, educating and influencing people and constantly listening for what is needed. SVPS was a school that began (repeated in several sections later in the book) with a vision of revolutionizing the way schools learn and evolve while Pyramid Valley International (PVI) is part of Pyramid Spiritual Societies Movement, created with the mission of spiritualizing the whole world.

Unlike almost barter like business systems built in the LifeBliss what really mattered here was to invest sufficient time into the understanding of what it means to educate in the former or the meaning of 'spirituality' in the latter. The question was—how will a better educated world operate and a spiritually evolved world function?

Satpuda Valley had to be conceived in terms of what it means to educate, how learning should happen, radically different review mechanisms on progress and investment into ways by which parents—our customers here—were to be oriented to see the value of the system. Push would have been counter-productive. Unequipped with anything but 'push', I have personally experienced the paranoid that Maulvik experienced during the initial years to finally, under enormous stress both due to his new business LifeBliss and also because of the unemployability of 'push' as a strategy, abandon it totally as a real venture. Of course, it became another family wing for social involvement.

Again the possibility, of a school that began with the aim of revolutionizing learning itself, of creating leadership in the entire community of schools in the region and would have probably catapulted itself as a pioneer in the very ways in which stakeholders learn in a school. Who knows what would have been the implications—may be India would have been counted amongst countries that exhibit extraordinary sensitivity towards learning and children; maybe our Programme for International Student Assessment scores would have bettered or we may have led appropriate assessment tools for growing economies. More pertinently these had implications on the way Maulvik ran his other businesses or the other ventures he loved being a part of and make a mark in. But it's not just a matter of speculation!

School did not figure well in Maulvik's list. With a very low operational leverage, and being too open like the defence sector or the railways, it doesn't offer a controlled system of a business; certainly not to the scale of his agri-business. The school, instead, added a vaguely portrayed image of Social Responsibility especially when Maulvik's family attempted being enlisted into the market. There was no other reason why the school should be really cared for, work with the complex variables and face the conundrum of an enterprise. Contrast this with Buddha's encounter with Angulimala—there was no reason to establish yet another contact, that too with an outlaw, when the organization had well-oiled processes and was deemed to have produced successful models!

There was another—and a much stronger one at that—reason for marginalizing school in the priority of activities.

Unlike seed business which needed 'push' and a focus on the bottom line, SVPS as a school needed attention—being attentive to learn and discover. Any discovery would obviously demand steadfast attention and multiple conversations. Unlike a boardroom discussion where the talk time is hogged by certain articulate and dynamic individuals, conversation involves an ability to allow for 'silences' to show up—teachers' frustrations and stress under the new system, confusion amongst the consumers in the ways of the new system and many more.

Bottom-lines requires information—on volume, on margin, on expenses, plan for the day and estimation. Discovery requires showing up. To show—up means to just 'be there' and being there allowing yourself to be pulled by what is required. It requires one to drop the privileges—all kinds of privileges. And when one doesn't show up, there's stagnation and violence. As we will discover partially in the next chapter, violence happens when there's incompletion—stoppage of something from its natural flow. In the real absence of the promoter who should have participated in the collective resolution of the lived realities of 'revolutionizing the way children learn', what ensued was multiple versions of education that contested and contrived for their own space—ranging from strong opinions about meting out punishment to children to the drill work that's necessary for mastery—contradicting the very edifice in the first place.

Showing—up is not easy. It's a reflection of 'stuckiness' because nothing visible happens due to participation in conversations. Volumes don't move, margins are not bargained, predictions are not discussed and no worthwhile transaction can really be observed. This reflects in the many training programmes that are either considered waste or a necessary evil to keep the semblance of a responsible organization. Because, apparently, things are working!

Pyramid Valley happened at a later part. Formed of trustees, and with the declared intent of spiritualizing the world, creating meaningful action plans and patience to guard the growth of this venture into an organic enterprise required education and deep insights. 'Push' again would have been impossible but 'push' that was exercised was counter-productive as will be explained in the relevant sections as we progress.

Just like LifeBliss where, though successful, full self-expression wasn't touted as the rule of the game, SVPS and PVI also didn't turn out into fully self-expressive entities. Having attained mastery and the stage of auto-renewal in any of these ventures would have auto-fed any other taken up.

And Maulvik's most recent adventure (which I find too amusing to miss a mention here) was when he asked me recently to log into a session his brother led in an international conclave on science and spirituality. His brother is carving a space for himself as a spiritual teacher and he had sponsored himself into the conclave. I had no interest in it but I obliged—just as I, like all of us in the modern world, participate and involuntarily witness a plethora of activities that I am hardly connected to or have any control over. I had logged in when he again called me to request to pose a question in the chat, which was happening online; he further requested me to pose yet another question—this time anonymously. I laughed and obliged yet again. His reason was clear—to extend the session by another half an hour and to have a particular number that would prompt the organizer to take these sessions more seriously for an easy invite next time.

Habits die hard. Maulvik was again at building another enterprise through push. Forget Buddhahood, the enterprise lacked even the basic lyricism of commandments. As I browsed through I found a lot of questions like mine that had been posed in proxy! 'Stuckiness' isn't something Maulvik is used to! And given his deep pockets will hardly ever be able to see its implications.

ASPIRATIONAL MATRICES[23]

Look at the illustration here. The illustration is suggestive and is linked to the later illustration called **'The Inter-Connected Web'** in Chapter 3 and the **'Web of Excellence'** in Chapter 4. Organizational and individual aspirations can be categorized into the four elements and each one represents particular features of humanity.

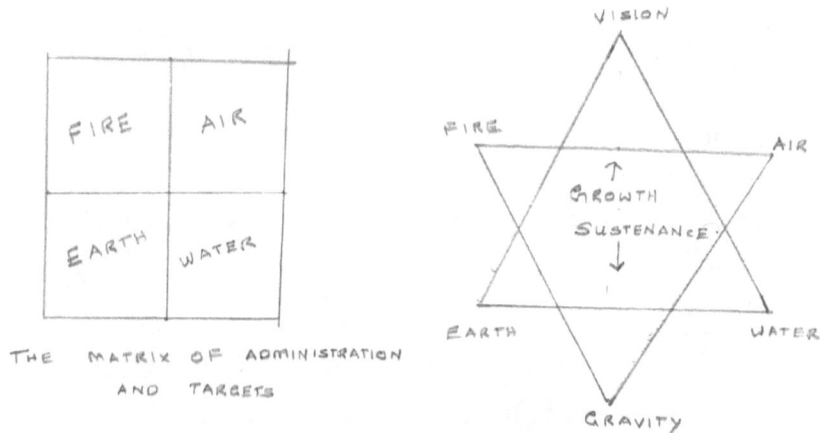

And there are the axes on which lives revolve. No single axis but multiple axes is complementing each other but, unfortunately, humans pose each other into a contest! Regular Euclidean Geometry, like the regular frameworks of our language and concepts, will not be able to show the possibility of several parallel axes drawn on different points. Just as Quantum Physics

---

23   I came across the expression 'matrix organisation' from Ravi Venkatesan's 'Conquering the Chaos'. I have just used the adaptation of the term and in no way relates to the concept he describes.

and Relativity demands a new Geometry, this conceptualisation requires a newer ways of portraying our space.

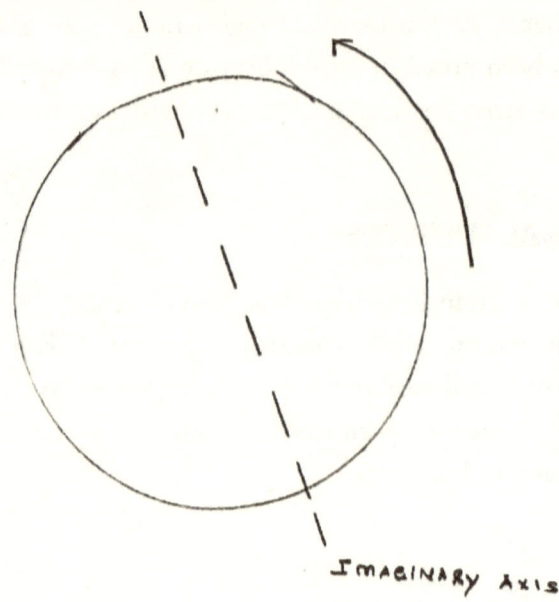

IMAGINARY AXIS

Organizational leadership and executives also revolve around these axes. What are these axes? How can we revolve without ignoring any, being partial to just a few and packing up ourselves with activity towards 'numero-uno'?

In the Bhagavad-Geeta, Krishna declares himself as the 'cleverness within the dice', 'intention in deeds', 'Arjuna amongst the Pandavas', etc. Krishna explains to the confused Arjuna how the subtlest expressions are not noticeable but what fulfils everything we do. In complete self-expression of Krishna—a perfected model, the very element of *sanatana*[24]—is the seed who helps create everything else. Quality happens when leadership attends to what's really needed—business, society, wellbeing and nature! That was the 'seed' LifeBliss missed—altogether.

---

24   *sanatana* refers to the eternal element that is constantly present and transcends time. This is the
     element that always has been. Just as the whole book rests on the element of evolution and the
     expansion of meaning of every term, *sanatana* also expands in its meaning; it doesn't stagnate

Elsewhere in the Bhagavad-Geeta, Krishna also promises his own appearance whenever there's stagnation; whenever there's a 'stuckiness' that has to be resolved. Access to the seed resolves it!

Revisiting STUCKINESS

The modern world is solutions oriented. Most organizations experience 'stuckiness' as either a general mismatch between prediction and what 'is' or when it's impossible to predict. The 'stuckiness' is an important phase of excellence but is ambiguous. Besides without connecting to the 'seed'—the question of humanity—most 'stuckiness' questions are reduced to trouble-shooting and operations. 'Stuckiness' is not just boredom; like a bored teenager cannot but indulge in something, at least shake his leg restlessly when even a mobile phone is proscribed, ambiguity isn't something individuals and companies are equipped to handle. The penchant for solutions and beliefs induced by scientific knowledge that there should be a 'solution' doesn't allow for appropriate elongation of 'stuckiness'.

When one can act within prevailing models of management and leadership, which the modern scientific materialism and phenomenology are prone to recommend, appropriate prolongation of 'stuckiness' is not one of them; 'stuckiness' isn't even a possibility in the modern super-mart of unseasonal vegetables. The wait time for a seasonal vegetable for over a season or two allows for sufficient practice of wait time, which modern super-markets and refrigeration system have done away with. Should we really do away with this ambiguous wait time?

The penchant for solutions, and to be at ease at the earliest (Maulvik's unexplored single statement) doesn't allow for appropriate wait time—so that deeper patterns emerge.

The biography of Elon Musk describes how even as a company Ford Motors was stuck. Ford Motors was naturally nervous. Without extricating from a 'mess of complexity that Ford has evolved over time' responding to a new contender on the block, like **Model S** would be impossible. The surest way was to dismantle the company to renew itself into a new set of realities. It would be like asking an adult to change her height.

That's what the Buddhahood of an organization is and what Buddha CEO's do—to stop and reboot. In ultimate terms, the act of regeneration is possible because there is no stable self, no sense of deep identity and moulded plasticity. Krishna, as per the legends, could do it. Krishna was an identity that was so flexible that he simply evaded war against *Jarasandha* (a fierce opponent of the *Yadava*) and Krishna comfortably took on the title of 'ranchordas'—a fugitive coward. Choosing what battles to fight, Krishna escaped the world, which in any case is a fabrication.

That means an organization that is porous without an identity functions well—like the *avatars* that emerged as required but didn't stick to an identity. Their identity was not something to be defended but a gift to be shared. Though romantically appealing, it still doesn't appear a practical tool to implement valuable ingredients into our models of work! I recommend allowing ourselves to be suspended in this new possibility till we explore its sense in the next few chapters.

It may make sense to explore different dimensions of 'stuckiness' and how one can be with it. One was in the form of *Patanjali Yoga Sutra, which* was explored to some detail earlier in Chapter 1 of this section. Another can be seen in Chapter 2 of the Bagawadgeeta.

Chapter 2 of the Bagawadgeeta, described as '*Sankhya Yoga*', logically disentangles Arjuna's fallacious riddles on violence, war and sinful action. Arjuna's scholarship is immaculate. In one of the discourses that I came across, the speaker paralleled Arjuna's scholarship with modern-day corporate seminars and training and banged the table in mock imitation of the motivational seminar industry. It was fun, of course, but had a semblance of an insight. Knowledge that Arjuna had acquired hardly related to operations at the point of a crisis, and handling the ambiguity of an unproductive workspace is one of the deadliest crisis. Arjuna's mastery yields nothing. He is stuck without the guide Krishna. Krishna is the *Purohita*.

What happens when leadership doesn't fathom the dimensions of 'stuckiness' and ambiguity?

There are two possible answers form my contemplation on the question—

1. *One of them refers to one of the rituals for the dead in the Hindu customs. On every anniversary, the dead, referred to as **pitrus**, are offered food and energy to pursue their existential limbo for some more time. Without this offering, it is believed, the pitrus languish in the corridors longing for a body. The longing is such that they may tend to jump into any form of existence—including the lower births of animals and other 'lowly' creatures.*

   The reader doesn't need to take the custom seriously. We will also not develop the argument as that's not something we can verify the veracity of and neither is the concern we are addressing here. The point is when hung in a labyrinth, or the survival is in question, or when the conundrum of the spare time is too intense we tend to do anything—even in high-stake businesses and many a time with life! As the suggestion here goes, one may not mind doing something that hardly has any value and many a time contradicting the very base on which the edifice is built.

2. *The second is in the form of Krishna's discourse to Arjuna amid war. In this 2nd chapter itself, Krishna describes the strength of poise and the importance of equanimity in wholesome action. It's similar to Buddha's description of '**Kammapatha**'—the path of wholesome action. In the ultimate verse of the chapter, the 72nd, Krishna uses the term 'brahmi'—a state of absolute tranquillity—as the source of all creation. 'Brahmi Muhurta' also refers to the 90 minutes before sunrise. This duration is considered auspicious for great work. It's not the time itself but the logic of a creation process, as some scholars point out, generating anything of value only during the last one-eighth of the whole process. So, 'Brahmi Muhurta' of 90 minutes is the last one-eighth of the entire duration of 12 hours from sunset to sunrise!*

The remaining seven-eighth part of the duration is where the creative process is subjected to action, confusion, struggle, searching for sustenance, etc. and the only way one can tide it is by realizing that there's no way but to keep treading with happiness and tranquillity.

This is not to say that one should get into metaphysical exploration. That's not the point. There is a word Thich Nhat Hanh's comments on the 'Parable of the poisoned arrow' through which Buddha dissuades seekers from metaphysical speculation. One should not handle 'ambiguity' with such sterile statements as 'life is full of up's and down's', 'every dog has its day', etc. They may be true but as per the tenets of 'ambiguity,' they are also matters to be subjected to inquiry and deconstruction. The important thing is to get rid of the restlessness of 'ambiguity'. And collective practices established and embedded in the learning of the company can make it happen—to be able to withstand 'stuckiness' and ambiguity.

I am tempted to insert a small personal anecdote—one of our favourite family pass time during our childhood days was my little niece's habit of pushing a chair till the wall blocks it and crying out loudly. She didn't know how to come out of the 'stuckiness'. Being unproductive is worrisome!

CHAPTER 3

Brand Value of a Buddha Organization

Let's live happily then,

Not hating those who hate us,

Among men who hate us,

Let us dwell free from hatred.

— Dhammapada

For thousands like me in my home city of Bangalore, the most precious destination is the Art of Living Ashram. The ashram doesn't need a separate introduction—such is the popularity and acclaim that this organization has exhibited through its demonstrative accomplishments over the years. The organization is so resilient that even during these testing times of lockdown there's a huge surge in the number of activities it is participating in and there's new vigour in its courses; I repeated a programme recently where a staggering 8000 other people were my co-participants—while many were fresh participants, some of us were enthusiastic repeaters. And newer and fresher courses have been added to its already existing list of highly effective programmes.

The huge popularity of the destination has been well capitalized by the real estate businesses by marketing their colonies with reference to its distance from the ashram. Such is the dense vibrancy of the ashram that restaurants, transport services, massage parlours have all been thriving in its vicinity. The Art of Living offers a huge plethora of courses—more than 60 as enlisted on its board in the campus—apart from the several humanitarian projects it is involved in. The question is—did Art of Living succeed because it has diverse and wide-ranging offerings? Or did it diversify because it became successful in its primordial offering? These fundamental questions take to something more general—when is it the right time to cross-sell and expand the product base? In other words, when can we be sure that our brand value has better bandwidth? How do we know that the existing product needs consolidation and better packaging? When companies and industry leaders recommend 'Blue Ocean Strategy' and successful companies appear to offer wide-ranging products is at best confusing.

The core of the Art of Living Programmes is the *Sudarshan Kriya*, a unique breathing exercise that participants majorly report as remarkably transforming. I took the programme in 2003 and till date consider that the finest moment in my life—a moment of undeniable freedom. We can't delve into it as, right now, our interest is the organization itself—the ashram is a vibrant space of creativity and enterprise. An international Ayurveda centre, Ayurveda Pharmacy Research and Development centre, Ayurveda Medical College and Research hospital, courses that are always full, a *Vedic pathashaala*, rehabilitation centre for over 2000 cows of indigenous breed, an established software firm that has created the Indian equivalent of WhatsApp and several humanitarian agencies including *Dharma Sthamba Yojana*, Gift a smile, etc. The list is even longer but sufficient here to indicate the vibrant relevance of any work done well or something that stems off a fundamental innovation—*Sudarshana Kriya* in this case. Not just this. The internationally renowned Master Sri Sri Ravishankar (who we all lovingly and affectionately call Guruji) has been known for the hugely relevant and internationally acclaimed humanitarian work towards peace and stability. The soft-spoken, lovingly gentle Guruji doesn't speak in rhetoric or emotionally charged language. His soft-spoken lingo utterly shorn of jargons and complex expressions is what appears to have worked for World Economic Forum, UNO General Assembly, WHO, India's Ayodhya Panel and many other agencies of change.

At the core of every Art of Living activity, as said before, is the *Sudarsahana Kriya*. Whether one goes into the Advanced Courses or the DSN (another advanced programme) all of them are initiated by connecting back to this core practice of *Sudarshana Kriya*. Added to this are two important elements—a consistent practice which is also its brand image and the Guru stories that surround us all—volunteers—in dedicating ourselves (time, money and other forms of commitment) to the work! Anyone who undergoes the Art of Living basic programme which is now popular as Happiness Programme has free access to Sunday 'Follow-up's' where the participants not only undergo the breathing practice in Guruji's voice guided by a trained Art of Living teacher but also has a chance to straighten up their practices. This is beside the weekly congregation called *Satsangh* wherein, again, one has access to the relevant information for advancement.

This is what sustains the organization, but that's not the strategy for sustenance. It's a structure that allows for an enduring practice that otherwise may be forgotten in our daily distractions. When a sacred practice is preserved, the shape it takes is of stupendous value. But the challenge is we quickly shove ourselves into another methodology as strategies are bound to show up a lacuna. Improve on the lacuna, and restructure if necessary, but it's critical to begin to 'show up' reverentially. That creates cumulative value as Art of Living has shown.

Another popular master Rishi Prabhakar used to say how a '*Sanyasi*', by sheer dispassion, brings prosperity all around him (her). That appears to be evident with the Art of Living. The new Metro line is drawing close to its completion in the city with a destination stop at the Art of Living Ashram. A general visit to the ashram is rewarded with an experience of happy and beaming, radiant and extremely successful volunteers contributing to its operations. A traditionally built ambience exhibits simplicity but is very deep and dense in its offerings. Art of Living has never desisted from its practice—*sadhana, seva, stasangh;* and the dispassion is in not debunking it because it's not towards an objective in the first place. Being in *sadhana* itself is the objective!

This takes to another organisation as a study in contrast!

Not very far from the Art of Living Ashram, around seven miles ahead of it towards Bangalore suburb, is another spiritual organization—Pyramid Valley International. Smaller in size and operations than the Art of Living, this was founded in the year 2003 as the headquarters of the much larger Pyramid Spiritual Societies Movement. Pyramid Meditation is its unique point but Pyramid Valley is also a place that can be hired by teachers and spiritual masters for their own offering and seekers for their own practice learnt from different teachers. Promoting all spiritual practices and encouraging all seekers is its mantra!

Though Pyramid Valley and the Art of Living have the same avowed interest their organizational make up has marked differences. Unlike Sri Sri Ravishankar, Brahmarishi Patriji is hard spoken and is a maverick and his followers commit to this style that they fondly call as 'scientific'; while the Art of Living bases itself on the traditional practices of the Rishi culture of India, Pyramid Movement is more based on *Anapanasati* meditation more common to Buddhist traditions (both organizations respect every other practice).

There's no way to judge spiritual practices nor is it the intention of the present work. In fact, it's spiritually counter-productive to indulge in such comparisons because one is sure to get caught in a maze. Our clear intention is to see what makes a difference in the way organizations create role canvases for themselves, what their sense of success is and how they measure their accomplishments.

Though both Pyramid Valley and the Art of Living are spiritual organizations, the comparison ends there. Without a clearly identified market and without having created a felt need for its offering - a desire that that was never felt - Pyramid Valley, as an organization, still struggles with sustenance and is constantly involved in knee-jerk reactions towards improvising itself and I was also a part of such a change as a learning consultant to the organization. Again, as a reiteration, please be reminded that we are not talking about the spiritual principles that the organizations adhere to but use the organizational systems to explore the core ideas on which an organization thrives and grows. To summarize this comparison and to delve what is important for us, we may look at some key points here—

1. *Ambiguity isn't a state an organization aspires for but an outcome that inadvertently happens.*

   The roles in AOL is crystal clear. It doesn't work on ambiguity nor is there any pressure—perceived or obvious—to create results. As far as my observation goes, most of us who are ardent enthusiasts know the roles we need to play—to be a volunteer once and to be a disciple in the next and to become a teacher in yet another. And, ritualistically at least, we add no meaning to the work—it's all Guru's work we say—happening through the Guru; the Guru Purana surrounds us. Such roles don't exist in PVI though the sense of service is starkly visible.

   Instead of making the philosophy and values intermingle and be porous with the questions of sustenance, statutory regulations, social norms and public order PVI took a more convenient route of appearing democratic—by making porous the roles and identities. No wonder, without a gradient and appropriate inquiry, Pyramid Valley has never expressed itself fully.

   It doesn't mean to say that the organization doesn't add value. It does. It's not fully expressive and at most floats at the level of struggle—the Varaha in our Dasavataara.

2. *What is the yardstick and what is the practice?*

   Yardstick and practice both go together. The practice an organization recommends, values and strives is the same as the tool used in measuring its own evolution. Pyramid Valley recommends meditation, reading and congregation as the key to the problems of life and leadership amongst many but the practice is hardly seen integrated into its own system. AOL makes it damn interesting with structures in place—cooks, volunteers and even the external agency of security practice Sudarshana Kriya. Satsangh, the congregational practice in AOL, is a celebrated affair.

As long as the yardstick can gauge that what is intended is not achieved, there's space to practice what is recommended; and as and when the intention is accomplished, the yardstick gives a shape, form and transactional element to it. AOL does it so beautifully. I should mention an incident I remember—I attended the first Advanced Meditation Programme in 2006— 3 years after my basic programme. During the course, we participants were playfully initiated into yoga sessions in AOL's beautiful lawns. It was fun and humorous to practice those beautiful asanas which were led by Kashi Bhayya, a senior faculty of AOL. The success that came from that playful contribution was measured by people's enthusiastic participation and what later came out was a beautiful programme by itself marketed all over the globe and gratefully consumed by thousands of AOL devotees. The yardstick and practice had intermingled so well that it was hard for us to distinguish between the two.

3. *The characteristics of the attained are the Sadhana for the aspirant.*

Delusion is a stage for theatrics. It's easy to be really serious about what we are acting out. it's like a teacher who should exhibit some clarity in showing that the Physics she knows is good enough for the students to help themselves with eligibility tests. But to believe that mere rehearsal of numerical for years on is real Physics is to be deluded. Such delusions drive Organizations especially when they are at the stage of STRUGGLE—the Varaha!

Delusion is when characteristics are presumed to be a possession of the practitioner. This also explains the relevance of the Buddha. When the Sanatanik Vaidiks believed that to be able to shout out 'ahambrahmasmi'—I have attained—is a reflection of their own sublime nature, someone like Buddha had to come and wake them up. Some refused to wake up; some did wake up.

During a conversation with a senior there, during my consulting days with Pyramid Valley International, we had an interesting altercation. We were discussing problems of finance and sustenance; challenges to be resolved and projects to be accomplished when he had impatiently dismissed my appeals to be 'practical' saying that he can solve all the problems, personal as well as professional, by the 'power of meditation'. It was amusing at best. It prevailed all along the organization and that was a practical barrier to excellence there. And equipped with only such knowledge and without rigorously established systems for learning and inquiry, the organization went on collapsing continually. Such differences of looking at problems and solving them do exist. What was different in PVI, however, was to use a repressed statement as an escape from real work on improving the state of affairs!

But the organization has an energy that runs it—Patriji's steadfastness to his vision has held the organization together. Patriji does his work totally involved and brings an unmatched freshness to his vicinity. There are two issues with energy—one is that it's subjective and that it needs a direction. Without objectivity, and consequently, without a direction, there's not much within that would help it self-propel and thrive. Threads are too loose!

4. *Organizational health*

Feelings and emotions are to be expressed—it is believed; if unexpressed it leads to physiological issues—it has been substantially proved. Suppression of the lacunae by everyone by convenient usage of 'I am not the body', 'every solution exists in meditation', 'I am pure consciousness', 'we are unique', etc. are not just false and cause physiological injury to the organization, but also are anaesthetic and lacks hygiene.

Pyramid Valley practices this too often while in AOL there's clarity about when to express it and when not though a spiritual organization cannot entirely do away with such subjectivity. What is important is the appropriate expression of these terms and not to use them to silence whistleblowers (which I witnessed when the main players on the board silenced the organizational auditor when he expressed doubts about the debt in the balance sheet and many including Patriji replied to the effect that the questions of good and bad, right and wrong should never affect missionaries of spirit).

The human fondness to 'look good' is too fundamental to explain it away. It can turn anything into an apparent positive trait. Angulimala celebrated his ownership of 1000 fingers. There's futility ingrained in our fascination to 'look good' because that's a vortex that pulls everything within it. So when the fundamentals and truth of the organization aren't explored enough, it may tend to put everything as a characteristic to be proud of—including those that are totally dysfunctional!

What actually burns the organizational fire cannot be doused! Let me just be as cryptic right now lest more explanation would drag us further down.

We will be delving into the details a little later. Right now, sufficient to mention how Pyramid Valley as an organization grew into unnecessary entropy and litigation—all because of not being absorbed by what's unique about the organization but busy constantly trying to express the uniqueness. A complete explanation will have to wait till Section 2 of this book. Pyramid Valley didn't celebrate 'stuckiness' but looked for easy routes out of it and, as we shall see later celebrated appearance than really worship the core (recall Patanjali's barriers to growth; narcissism is one). Some of the key players with Pyramid Valley openly made absurdly irrelevant statements about how they are different and not some kindergarten spirituality like Art of Living, etc. They would claim that they belong to the 'University' of Spiritual Sciences while other spiritual traditions still subsist on the rudimentary. This sentiment is starkly visible in Pyramid Valley. While Pyramid Valley is stranded, great work continues to happen with the Pyramid Spiritual Societies Movement—the mother movement that was primarily the source for Pyramid Valley International! And in the recent lockdown, it's evident in the numerous online seminars, meetings and discourses that have happened through Pyramid Valley International—a work that was primarily a work of the movement has been smeared on to the Pyramid Valley International.

It doesn't mean that organizations don't experience internal contradictions. What we are trying to indicate here, instead, is the importance of meaningful expression of an organization as an organism by itself. Without full expression, taking a cue from our 'ink bottle' paradigm of chapter 1, Organizations tend to become moribund in spite and because of thousands of iterations resulting in multiple strands without a centrality. How does a centre actually guide all the outer manifestations is a question we are going to spend time on a little while later!

This obsession with appearance and a narcissistic craving for uniqueness can be explained by an analogy to a traditional practice prevalent in South Indian temples. In the South Indian temple traditions, the deity to be taken on a procession is never the statue located in the Sanctum Sanctorum but another statue meant for processions. Even photography is not allowed of a deity, which is under worship. The logic appears to have been deduced from the point that a photograph can never capture the subtle realities of a deity;

a static image of a photograph cannot capture the subjective dynamism of the deity! It has always been so—the core is to be never compromised while appearances can be varied all the time. Appearances have boundary conditions and are just a replica of the unchanging core. There's a page on the lesson of organizational excellence here!

What asymmetric brand images troubled PVI—

- *Google review ratings of more than 4.5*

- *A destination that charges no fee*

- *We are liberal*

- *Asia's biggest meditational Pyramid*

- *Host to India's only Global Spiritual Congress*

These appearances are important but as stand-alone images, they don't form a brand but personal hubris! The fondness to look good, to appear healthy at the cost of exploring how the core value expresses itself in varied facets of realities is a lot more destructive than doing anything good.

So, that logically takes us to our next question.

HOW SHOULD ORGANIZATIONS LOOK?

Since we have looked at mythological angles as a way of penetrating the path of the Buddha, there's yet another story that comes to my mind right now. The story of Mahabharata is quite well known; what is not common, however, is the finer stories that happen in between the whole narrative. Such subtle stories placed within the main narrative is called *Upakhyana.* One such is the story of Vidhura's[25] attempt to pacify the warring factions.

Amongst several strategic interventions by Vidhura to save the Kuru clan, one stands apart. This is when Vidhura approaches Dhritarashtra, the blind king, to desist from the despicable act of waging a war against his

---

25   Vidura is the uncle of the Kauravas and the Pandavas

own nephews. He suggests, instead, giving away the part of the kingdom which was legitimately theirs. Duryodhana who was close by reprimands his uncle in unequivocal terms. Duryodhana accuses Vidura of being a dog who feeds on their bounty but barks on behalf of the opponents!

Vidhura, in fact, is the only one amongst the Kauravas to defy Duryodhana's unethical manoeuvring. He does so even when Draupadi is pulled into the courtyard and disrobed; Vidhura helps the Pandavas when they are trapped in a burning house. Despite Vidhura's wisdom, Duryodhana doesn't find it logical enough to follow the advice. The grosser gains of a wider territory and the possibilities of victory (because he has a bigger army) in case of a war attracts Duryodhana logically. To accommodate Vidura's sentiments appears non-sensical to Duryodhana.

Organizations can supersede the highest priority based on what the leadership finds fit. The leadership has the prerogative on what should appear to be the organization at the forefront. Many a time, it's the grossest and the most visible that tops the priority list and not the most important. We will examine this further in the chapter 'Transformation is a Design' later in Section 3. Right now we can rest the case with a statement by Roger Martin, the former dean of Rotman School of Management at Toronto University, that I came across in 'Creative Intelligence' by Bruce Nussbaum—"If you can't measure it, it might be the very most important thing about your business." This is a double-edged sword—one may turn it either way!

WHAT'S VISIBLE IN THE ORGANIZATION?

The ancient hymn of *Purushasukta* from the *Rigveda* there is a division in organizations and societies based on the work we all perform. Since it connotes class of people based on the professions they are born into, it has been rejected by many as divisive. And many scholars protest this irrational opposition stating the evidence to the fact it's not divisive in terms of class. The apologists look at these not as a human class system based on labour but more as different attitudes we exhibit in the way we perform any action.

I am largely subscribing to the latter understanding and meaning here. These attitudes are a continuum of a range between happiness in being part of a virtuous cycle of contribution and anxiety-driven tactics of survival. One may experience these emotions in any work people do.

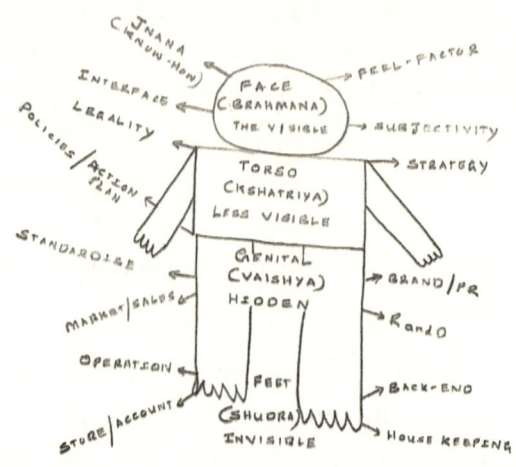

Much like the 'centaur' of Greek mythology, it represents the eternal debate on the primacy of entities between man and the man-made. Mary Shelley's 'Frankenstein' represents one such and more prevalent in the even more openly expressed anxiety about technology replacing human jobs. Technology will replace jobs but the anxiety is misplaced. Like the 'centaur' with a head and torso of a man leading the body and legs of a beast, man will constantly lead technology. In other words wisdom leads the processes and systems - spirit thrives!

Brahmana generally refers to a class of intellectuals and one may find dilettantes here. *Shudra* on the other end of the spectrum refers to labour and one may find sabotage and rebellion here or vice versa. What is visible to the world outside is largely dependent on the context of work that's happening. It is sometimes the CEO who becomes the face and other times it could be the legends that circuit out; yet other times, it could be the happiness that the company exudes.

An organization has an inbuilt mechanism of making sense of what should really be visible at different points. At different times and space, the organizational segments inevitably behave differently, and intelligent leadership is about aligning the appearances to what is needed. Like Pepsi, as a company, showcased its manufacturing processing unit on its advertisements instead of the romantic imagery of the earlier commercials, when the soft-drink's quality and ethical drive were in question when traces of pesticides were allegedly found in it. The liberal humanistic practices, environmental friendliness are all part of many commercials today including the latest ones that look at being politically right—to showcase gender sensitivity and equity; or in removing incorrect undertones like 'fairness' as an aspiration for humanity in its communication.

Not just in its communication with the outside world but also in the communication that happens within a company. The accountant, for instance, may have a detailed outlay of the entire finance in front of her but may not be able to draw inferences in terms of what needs to be varied in the capital structure and revamping the leverages in terms of debt and equity. The sales graph, dues and liabilities, purchases and requests are all visible but don't make the whole sense. The sales head on the other hand recognizes the array of potential clients that can crossover; the marketing team looks at the intersection of creative expression and the promise of what's on offer.

Not any different, the housekeeping staff may see the different things to be done with the computer screen, the toilet, the floor and the rest of the hardware. But none of these ever have to bother what the real brand value of the company is. The work that is to happen is exclusive to the brand value of the organization or company. The repetitive processes will continue irrespective of what and where the company is!

It is certainly not mandatory to be scrupulous as to how the housekeeping is doing its job! Probably an investor may not directly look into how good is your refrigerator or the kitchen cabinet. (As a matter of 'excellence' it matters but not as real brand value. I am a bit ambiguous about the term 'excellence'. Hence, it will come in quote till it gets resolved!)

'What appears is not actually what is!'—something that's familiar to today's world of hyper-communication. Some statistics that I have come across says that we are bombarded by a bewildering eighty-two thousand bits of information every day. I am not sure whether that number is accurate nor is it necessary for us to verify the veracity at this point. What we are much more familiar with is that we have learnt the art of ignoring advertisement communication between our TV or YouTube programmes. However subtle or iterative, advertisements are hardly noticed in the general viewing except when, as Al and Laura Ries argue in 'The Fall of Advertising and the Rise of PR', the 'car salesman' syndrome strikes the advertising industry with a vengeance. So much so that my friend Ravishankar, while reviewing this book's introduction, simply struck off the word 'salesman' I had used regarding the work of a CEO.

The anomalous behaviour is too stark to be missed. Stakeholders, including the intimate employees of a firm or an enterprise, hardly believe what the leadership says. Of course, there are exceptions to the general rule. TATA, Azim Premji, Narayana Murthy amongst many other industrialists are highly valued. And I have already written at length about everything that's offered in Art of Living is grabbed by thousands of followers all across the globe.

Brand value cannot be a direct exhibition activity. One cannot brandish, as some schools do, the qualifying percentage in the standardized tests or board exams. It's too obvious. No amount of quarterly figures would ensure consistency and quality. What can be exhibited can always be excelled and hence loses its shine; if to keep shining is the chief activity, there's a problem!

Probably a unique enterprise will look at a unique brand value—the way everything within the organization functions. As was seen in the 'V' diagram of the first chapter, the principle around which evolution happens remains constant—just an ever-settled beginning point; a point of high stability but dynamic, an untarnished space that one can return to.

This kind of search for the consistent principle that transcends apparent difference in manifestations keeps happening. In one of the conversations with my friend Ravishankar, with more than two decades of experience in the IT sector behind him, (his callousness towards the IT sector becomes evident in the conversation. A philosophizing, extremely well-read Ravishankar sees himself a misfit in the sector—a sentiment that's quite frequently reflected for different reasons amongst many of my friends) he had referred to the organizational strategic cascade that happens in his organisation. The example he gave me was how the head determines a value or a set of values that act as a theme for the company to function in. I am not sure how it works but from a cursory basic observation this kind of cascade is basically a 'top-down' flow and it is reverse 'Buddhahood' (Refer to 'Yoga-Kshema—Organizational Welfare' in Section 3)

WHAT DRIVES IT?

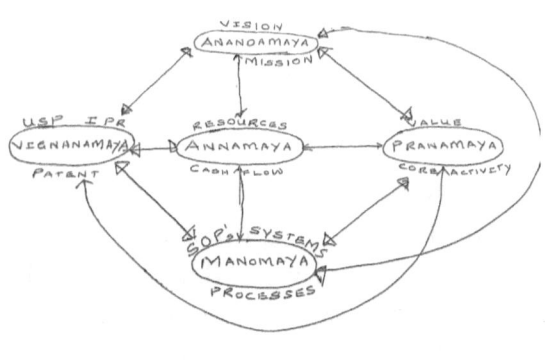

THE INTER-CONNECTED WEB

What ultimately drives an organization? It has the same architecture that relates to what drives a human body. The adjoining diagram represents one such here. The diagram represents the five *koshas*—the five fundamental elements in the description of human life—*Anna, Prana, Mano, Vignana and Ananda* loosely translated as food, energy, mind, intelligence and bliss.

Anna, or the food, has central importance here—something that drives the interfaces together—the interface of sustenance amongst every entity that has caused the body. Looking plainly at our own lives, our body is the interface of all relationships that we have. Similarly, an organization or a company is an interface between the value that the company adds with the entity that is receiving the value which itself requires sustenance, partially provided for by this company.

Resources are sourced from everything—the value proposition, process that sustains the value, uniqueness of the offer and the vision that drives it. Likewise, each entity connects to the other four organically into a web. In the previous illustration of the *Purusha*, the different categories are formed of qualities, commonly referred to as *gunas* and their permutations and combinations. There are three gunas—*Sattva, Rajas* and *Tamas.* the combinations of these in different entities in several proportionalities cause a particular form of expression. And as per Krishna in the Geeta, this belongs to a cosmic order—a definite method of work.

This fundamentally drives the organism—its metabolism, predispositions, culture and the 'fundamental act' of its existence.

Let's find a proposition to begin with at this juncture—'an ideal company is one where nothing needs to be sold'. Since there are no such companies in reality, we may just as well keep it aside for a while and look into other pressing matters.

Let's also face it—no amount of bragging by a salesman would help a conversion of a potential into a customer. It's in the subtle stories that the company creates for itself that a sale happens, just pitched in as a matter-of-fact by the sales guy. (It's not the bottom layer SHUDRA work that generates sales and interest in a prospective client). Of course, a sales pitch reduces ambiguity and creates another dimension of truth through the service or product.

There's an inter-connectivity to the whole affair! There's a mutual-nurturing that sustains excellence. The whole organism moves in unison and the 'cog in the wheel' could be anywhere. Even unverified mood swings, cluttered workspaces and brittle 'likes and dislikes' at any point in the organism could be the bottleneck stalling the conduction that's necessary for balance and health. That's more so in the modern age where everyone is in some other's place. No role appears to be complete.

To make it easy and conversational I am taking an example of a salesforce's work and the market that exists outside. Let me repeat—this is just an illustration and doesn't pretend to canvas without care for subtleties. Therefore I request the reader to read and drop!

> *When a customer rejects a product or service on offer, is it just a rejection of the pitch? Or is it beyond it? How much of the customer does the salesperson represent to the company and how much of the*

company for the customer? A salesperson is an inconclusive two-way truth!

That's why it's difficult to describe the difference between 'truth' and 'strategy'. A politician's language, for instance, is strategically alright but not trustworthy as it's unambiguously false. Winston Churchill is said to have described an eloquent politician as unafraid of risking ridiculous predictions and is equally eloquent in explaining away why they didn't turn out to be true! A sales pitch on the other hand should be trustworthy and strategically inviting!

A successful company intuitively knows when to 'kiss' or when to say 'I love you'! Too early expressed intention may kill all possibilities while too much of explanation and extended courting will never make the intentions clear. This knowledge is intuitive. And right now the suggestion is take everything seriously—including the 'Angulimalas' within the organization. One never knows. Developing the organization's sixth sense is when the culture values humanity to the extent that what matters is just humanity—nothing else.

So, what's the prescription? There's no prescription but a hell amount of reflection.

What are the resources and what's sustaining it? What's the USP that sustains the process that helps build the resources? Is it discovered/given/adopted? How indigenous is it? (Examine the chapter on 'AN ORGANIZATION IS NOT ELEPHANT DUNG'). How dynamic is the vision and what's the amount of ambiguity associated with it?

The corresponding illustration that follow shows this dichotomy between work and the spirit that drives the work. A small description from Buddha's life should demonstrate it succinctly.

In fact, Buddha's historicity is testimony to the fact. Buddha lived and became relevant at a time when knowledge didn't find its utterance in the lived realities; and vice versa when each *Shudra*[26] worked 'laying a brick', as the metaphor goes, 'without realizing the cathedral that was being built'

Such stories of organizational pride and how workers have felt a sense of ownership abound the 'motivation' writings on leadership. I am not referring to that kind of 'pride' and sentiment though certainly, those have their own utilities. I am not referring to such motivation, however valuable they are, nor even hinting anything against or for it. Instead, I am impatiently hinting at the full glimpse of the work and vertically integrating it to the purpose of existence itself. The rationale is simple but ubiquitous—how much ever is achieved in health, stock value, market share, etc., it still remains just a leaf in the Amazon jungle of life!

We are here examining a different kind of ambition—the ambition of catching life itself, calmly and serenely and knowing that that's all that matters!

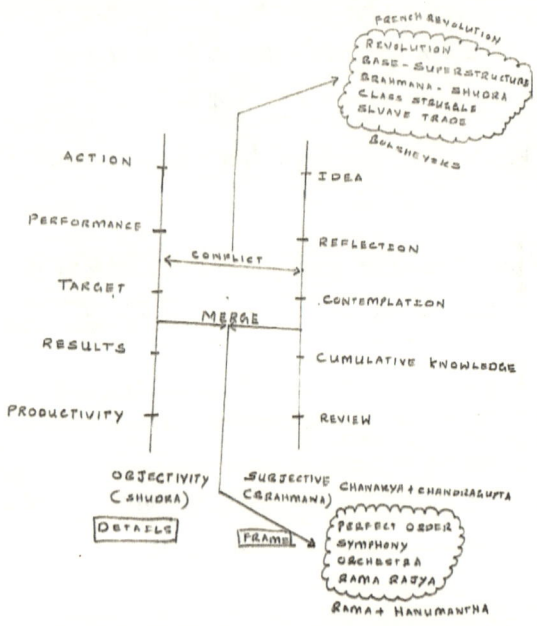

However, each CEO will have to indigenously discover the ways of doing it!

The Perfect Coexistence

As seen how organisms move as a whole, we can also see how perfection is a coexistence. It is not an individual act but an

---

enterprise of the group! It's an ecosystem of creation, sustenance, processes and directionality.

The basis of unity is in the marriage of the 'shudra' and the 'brahmana'!

Conflict between the two is a revolution, class-struggle and the eternal quarrel! FRENCH REVOLUTION and the SLAVE TRADE!

In my work as a consultant, I found this conflict in leadership. For instance, in schools I worked with, I found the principals in panic while the teachers worked in the classrooms in relative peace. Without a need for real hands-on work, principals tend to worry while teachers were liberated in action—however rudimentary and problem-solving actions they were. Teachers appeared happy, peaceful and in freedom; and every time a teacher applied for an early exit or leave, the principal would panic.

> **This is not unusual.**
>
> In Joseph Heller's 'Something Happened', Bob Slocum, a middling executive, while preparing for his promotions revives his life in memories. In his reverie, he sees his life, failures, psychic escapades etc.
>
> In his dense imagination he even suspects his own sanity in being unable to connect one anecdote to the other. And Heller extends this dilemma to the novel also.
>
> The novel hangs up with the ultimate question: what's true and what's hallucinatory. A theme that is abundant in Ashtavakra Geeta.
>
> This is not unusual:
>
> We are pyramid of potent panic!
>
> Competition exists: hallucination or true?

This isn't unusual! In the absence of actual work in 'real' situations what principals pondered about was a psychological world—and unsurprisingly, their responses were psychotic; they were based on fear. See the box which offers a summary of a novel mentioned before that reflects this angst!

'Conflict' exists in the leader's psychosis.

D V Gundappa, one of the pioneers of modern Kannada writing, describes his contemporary writer B M Srikantaiah (BM Sri as he was known) in his 'Gnapaka Chitrashale' (Memory Portraits) as someone who could speak for

6 hours at a stretch and 3 hours of his talk would involve defending himself against imaginary critics!

Our actions may not be any different—they really do not merge into what is needed and may constantly miss the fundamentals! They may merely be a response to the imagined—fear in this instance!

Merger is about perfect order! It's an orchestra, a symphony! Chandragupta—Chanakya for instance. (described in the box)

The legend:

Chankaya meets Chandragupta

Chandragupta is a lower caste, ostracized, sub-human and a powerless individual. A Shudra

On seeing Chandragupta in a game, Chankya refers to him as 'samrat' - the emperor! Chankya's paramahamsa element transcends the limits of social reality and identities - appearance, illiteracy, a mere child and the lower caste.

This when Dhanananda, the reigning powerful emperor, mocks the 'sanatana', the ever-present principle. Dhanananda is unable to grasp the subtle nature of 'knowledge' and 'knowing'; Dhanananda derides it as theory. When 'sanatana' - the fundamental essence that feeds the organisation- is ignored, the organisation falls! (Such disdain for the abstract, sometimes valuable, theoretical knowledge is not uncommon especially in the industry)

In summary—

Shudra—ACTION, PERFORMANCE, TARGET, RESULTS and PRODUCTIVITY

Brahmana—IDEA, REFLECTION, CONTEMPLATION, CUMULATIVE-KNOWLEDGE AND REVIEW

THE UNIT OF LIFE

The perfect blend of these 2 cause the strand of the DNA! The double helix is the unit of any existence—the idea and the work towards it!

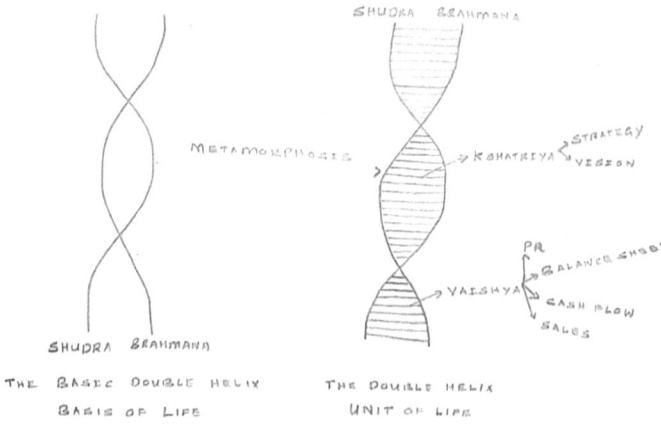

THE BASIC DOUBLE HELIX
BASIS OF LIFE

THE DOUBLE HELIX
UNIT OF LIFE

THE BASIS OF LIFE

To form itself into a basis of life—a way of self-sustained process, ever-growing—it has to accommodate the VAISHYA and the KSATRIYA; enterprise and the legal structures protecting the organization play its role. The intellectual property, R and D, the sales force and the PR provide the strands for the same!

Business, Sanatana and the Paramahamsa!

PROLIFERATION

There's an ethical element, a fundamental intelligence, that drives organizations. 'Sanatana' manages the ethics and when ethics take a beating, there's a struggle to hold together; and it's held by hook or crook. And 'hook and crook' becomes the game!

Sanatana is the ever existing; it doesn't cease to exist with the end to a prevailing order or belief system. It transcends the belief system and identity.

Ramakrishna[27] likewise transcends the identity of Vivekananda!

Can we transcend the identity of a company or an organization? Transcend from the state of actions and plans to the state of evolution; a collective commitment to 'evolution'—the fire of learning?

When we discover an ability to 'transcend', it minimizes violence; otherwise, the changes that organizations cause (as seen in diagram UNIT OF LIFE) brings violence, which is by itself a source for further violence down the line! And the cycle continues. (See the description at the end of the chapter about 'violence')

There's an ontology of violence that organizations should recognize. There's violence in an unexpressed - or incompletely expressed - employee as much as in an unexpressed company.

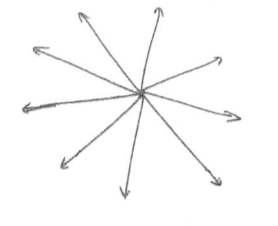

CENTER — SPOKE

Paramahamsa locates the centre by going beyond the obvious. Sees 'Vivekananda' in the ordinary 'Narendra'. Travels from '0' to '1'—creates out of nothing, sees what is not. This is an essential element of breakthrough business! (You may refer to Peter Theil's description of the same in his own words in his book 'Zero to 1'.)

But this also brings about the danger of 'redundant creativity'—like the unending interior decoration of an elite house! When 'narcissism' presses the pedal it becomes hard to escape the rut. It reminds me of my nephew's hilarious habit of de-cluttering his worktable to focus on his work only to procrastinate the work indefinitely!

Paramahamsa is all for innovation. A *Paramahamsa* may easily look at a future where innovation is indefinite. While *Paramahamsa* allows for all kinds of innovation, *Purohita* flags an activity down even if there's an iota

---

27   The 19th Century Indian mystic, the Guru of Swami Vivekananda. More popularly known as Ramakrishna Paramahamsa

of hazard. So, effectively, in real-life practicality, all *Paramahamsas* come with a *Purohita*. *Purohita* helps to recognize the limits of gravity—the limits of space-time condensate, so to say!

'**Purohita**' stops the redundancy; creates status-quo and in his *sanyasihood*, without a vested interest, creates prosperity.

Purohita stops the ever-gyrating anarchy and sublimation—a proliferation of the surface.

Makes 1 to infinity!

The STATIC QUALITY of the PUROHITA and the DYNAMISM of the PARAMAHAMSA both nurture 'quality'—an organization that's purposeful!

It could be interesting and informing to examine the ways of the Purohita within an organization because the question now revolves around a purposeful organization.

That explains why Pyramid Valley is more a monumental wonder, a one-off masterpiece—a product of *Paramahamsa* creation. It rests its laurels on being a public place that can thrill its first visitors. And nothing more than that as one of the senior trustees contended my criticism when I worked there about its dysfunctionality with the google review ratings! The subtler an organization, like a hospital or school, or a spiritual organization, the higher the ethical demand on its regulation; ethicality as a design that's a function of social apparatuses and necessary premises for a paradigm shift within it. Look at nuclear power technology for instance—it's safer (relatively despite popular protests against it), more efficient and environmentally more sensible (again despite the populist views; this is well described in Maat Riddley's 'How Innovation Works'). But why do people oppose it?

People's opposition may not always be rational. Though strong reasons exist in the form of worldwide activism against it which by itself is not based on sound logic, as many apologists of technology are bound to argue, there's something much deeper in reality about the way humans perceive the value of anything. One reason could be that nuclear technology has an element of incomprehensibility about it, a ghost-like eerie background to it—something that's beyond the control of the elements like air, fire, water and earth. Otherwise, it's a statistical paradox to oppose nuclear power; nothing seems to explain it well. As Maat Ridley says, 'We build nuclear power stations like Egyptian pyramids, as one-off project', Pyramid Valley was conceived like—a one-off project; a monument; a masterpiece that Google reviews stand testimony for. That's where I believe it goofed up!

What Pyramid Valley missed was an effective *Purohita*. When I had an opportunity to work I had presumed that I will act out the role of *Purohita* when probably the organization wanted me to be an estate manager. I may have misjudged myself or the organizational requirements. That's beside the point, but what I strongly see is that the organization terribly missed a *Purohita*—someone capable of turning out an effective 'learning organization'. In fact PVI, as an organization, never felt the need for a *Purohita*. It was enamoured by the proliferation of the surface!

Purohita[28] does two things eminently well—

1. **Recognizes that there's no static meaning. *Purohita* removes the definiteness about anything**

   When we ascertain a fixed value to anything around us and are unable to see that the definition is too temporal, we refuse to open up the domain. Either because of fear that it would be diluted or obsession with the preservation of what the present system has been yielding.

   Purohita recognizes both as true and valid—not to dilute what is already fruitful and established while constantly examining its limitation. Yet sees the 'what is' closely enough as a complex web

---

28   the expression *purohita* has largely stemmed from my brother's usage of the term. He runs his consultancy firm named after *purohita*. But the spin with which I have used the term is mine.

of conceptualizations repeatedly. A Purohita can locate how the values and vision of the organization is being deduced by everyone through—

- The boredom of sameness among employees,

- The complacency of nothing challenging,

- Safety of preserving one's emotions and

- A false persona that runs the show, etc.

They are shown to be manifesting into organizational lethargy and lack of perception to make a difference.

An instance—

Let's take the case of Satpuda Valley Public School again. You may recall how it was begun as an experimental school in a small town in MP with the hope of making a revolutionary difference to the way children learn. The small enterprise of a school, nothing compared to the modern conglomerates and specialized units of productivity, is easy and revealing in its factuality.

Amongst the several values in its conceptualization, 'democracy' (as discussed earlier) was an important one. To make collective decisions as a norm, to reduce hierarchy and privileging of any one, etc. were some of the new norms of excellence that we wanted to function in. To be democratic was the key to the process of learning.

For us then democracy meant being able to decide collectively and hence we had Saturday school parliaments to decide on some key issues and resolve differences ranging from unbearable noise in the corridor to an incomplete task that would impact children's performance. Added to that was to reduce privileging of individuals based on their ranks and qualification; of course, knowledge was recognized but not privileged.

Though 'democracy' was such an important ideal for us, we had to examine it in terms of what the 'customers'—our parents—really felt like. In fact, we were compelled to examine them in the light of our parents' complaints about growing indiscipline amongst children— chiefly the children 'talking back' to the elders in the family; secondly, the major part of our enrolment was from amongst the 'Marwadi' community—traditionally established in the goldsmith business. These businesses were strictly based on the principles of hierarchy and privileging of the eldest in the decision-making process; that was the way the businesses not only thrived but even existed. Our enterprise was a culture shock to the parents who fed the organization.

More importantly, some of our own teachers had started gossiping around these 'hallucinatory' and 'fancy' ideas. Their strong verbal, many a time boisterous, opposition in our regular congregation by itself deconstructed the very idea and was sanctioned by the value of 'democracy' itself.

We had a rational background and research to back the value of 'democracy' as an operational system. It was linked to authentic learning that can happen, the findings from neuroscience, etc. Nevertheless, our stakeholders compelled us to see the value from a different perspective.

'Democracy' had to be made more inclusive. The recognition that there's no static meaning led us to devise 'parental education programme' that would help parents see the significance of these principles in authentic learning. This resulted in several leaps of quanta—teachers turned to leadership and organization improved its capacity in putting up events day-in-day-out and, more importantly, in communicating in ways that would help the organization grow. And unsurprisingly many of these teachers turned out to be sophisticated ambassadors of children's rights and went on to lead several schools as leaders.

What entailed due to our attention to and the consequent expansion of meaning that ensued was the creation of staff development initiatives that we took upon ourselves seriously. A detailed Teacher Training Programme manual that involved conversations on behaviour, handling crises, teaching and parenting is part of the organization's intellectual asset still. It has evolved over the years into a comprehensive

15-day teacher orientation programme, 6 months of weekly mentoring and a booster programme of teaching mastery. The invaluable asset that Satpuda Valley Public School created for itself is the renewal of the 'teacher'. Probably, a practice of the same is much more relevant today when schools are simply closed due to the pandemic as I am writing this. The necessity of renewal in this instance is even more pressing.

The point is this—when you expand the meaning of what's presumed to be static, the possibilities open up. Our attachment to values (and sometimes processes) dear to us blinds us to the commitment to the value in the first place. *Purohita* expands the meaning and probably excavates the meaning of life itself through this!

2. **Purohita expands the organization's cognitive domain.**

Spirituality can be described as connecting the apparently disconnected and the disparate. Astrology connects your fate to the planetary movements, numerology relates your current state to the birthday, the gems and stones as a way of warding off a potential danger and so forth.

Modern organizational *'purohitas'* may have to take a leaf from it—to see organizational performance as a function of several apparently unrelated elements within and beyond the organization. In an expanded cognitive domain can one examine the sum total of several entities that is averaging unto performance.

Let's take the case of Pyramid Valley International[29] which is described in Section 2 and 3 to its full extent as far as the relevance

---

29 Lest I appear ungrateful I am repeating what I had said differently in the introduction: this is a beautiful campus on the outskirts of Bangalore and consider my years consulting with the organisation immensely beneficial and was full of life. Mandated to spiritualise the Globe, PVI appeared to have lost the correct drive and intelligent manoeuvring towards the intended goal. The years there was a struggle and was very hard to make a head-way. Some of these are later described in the text later. But the unmistakable quality was the people's commitment

for the present book goes. Sufficient here to refer to some instances to demonstrate how when we refuse to expand the organizational cognitive domain we tend to locate the 'solution' within the convenience of what we would like or know to do. In the instance of Pyramid Valley International the question of sustenance was answered by a simple logic—'let's have more accommodations and attractive facilities to have corporate training programmes, and let's popularize the campus by some means—print and electronic media with advertisements if necessary.'

The former led to huge investments even at the cost of making the organization dysfunctional with a huge debt leading to skewed financial leverage. This ultimately led to its current state of numerous litigations and distractions. The latter to a sponsored press survey leading to the declaration of PVI as one of the seven wonders of Bangalore and turning the 'spiritual' organization into a 'picnic' spot with sufficient influx of visitors. And invariably turned itself into a competitor to some very good parks in the city! Instead of managing what PVI was meant to, the shift, more convenient in many ways, was to enlarge the gardens and market the trekking around the surrounding hills which turned out to be another disastrous failure (recall our arguments before how when the centre is not held the danger is falling into the trap of anything and everything that appears attractive). And more importantly, as a spiritual organization meant to discuss knowledge, the easy focus was theoretical sessions on *Karma*, Past Life, etc. in the weekend afternoons without a mutual commitment and options to grow the concept to further inclusiveness. None of these examples is to denigrate the beautiful organization earnestly built by devoted meditators but to show that it wasn't enough.

and Patrji's joyousness. I wish everyone meets Patriji and examine personally how he stares at simplicity!

The focus should have been to look at efficiency and authenticity! 'Spirituality' being a dicey term lends itself to multiple interpretations. Rather than expanding the 'cognitive domain' of spirituality and terms like 'inner transformation' and revisiting it again and again, what PVI focused on was anarchical gyration far away from the centre; the tragedy was that even the centre remained elusive. So, organizationally, it remains irrelevant! The recorded transformations are too random, personal in nature and don't reflect auto-renewal or typical standards for the place.

A Few More Lines

A 'delusion' is what drives anything. The belief that one's work is a mission of humanity or the will of God has ensured the spread of religions and spiritual traditions across the world. The colonial enterprises were supported by the cultural delusion of the 'white man's burden' for a long time. A 'delusion' gives legitimacy to the work we do. Such 'delusion' is necessary for any work to happen and is seen even in the modern motivational terms like— enjoying one's work, passion for the job and such easy declarations. Such statements and artificial motivation appears to have lost its mission and furthers the 'delusion'. The limitation is that we don't see at as 'delusion'!

We tacitly accept it. Also, the investigation of 'delusion' is abolished or mockingly laughed at. Both modern management principles and science either do not acknowledge or resist to deal with this. I surmise sweeping off the reality of our collective 'delusion' is necessary to progress. Many a time, it doesn't even resolve anything but aggressively advertises itself to be doing so. I take a leaf of Peter Senge's argument in 'Fifth Discipline' and the one in Fritjoff Capra's 'The Turning Point' where we see an argument that every solution is only a future problem. Even innuendoes towards the falsity of such mega statements like 'passion for work' are met with 'be positive' kind of generalities.

But scientific principles of management and science itself cannot sufficiently explain why humans are really fascinated by certain things so much. 'The

Secret History of the World' by Mark Booth makes a detailed inquiry into this lacuna as to how even the Church dropped out a lot of its earlier esoteric practices to accommodate science and be consistent with it. The development of science isn't designed to deal with these intangibles. The recent struggle to make use of and appropriate String Theory - a rather new abstraction - stands testimony to this. Rather than encountering its inability to deal with these terms, modern science has done away with the question itself—the question of primordial motive, obsession, fetish, etc.

Our inquiry into these 'delusions' is an opportunity to look into the details of life—like a psychoanalyst can inquire into deep impressions of memory by analyzing peculiar associations between one's libido and feet as in the sterile obsession of 'foot fetishism'. In the same way, *Purohita* works with the leader and causes an inquiry into the avoidance, full-throttle exertion, diplomacy, silences, confusion and many other numerous strategies, organizations in their existence and its operations seem to exhibit—in organizational rank and file. It's not difficult to locate these in an organizational daily enterprises—one would avoid discussion of a compromised standard in finance or morality of an employee or defer it to a later date while emphasizing on quick service delivery to a client.

I am hopeful that the above isn't seen as a condescending summarization of the processes of business. In fact, as later described in a separate chapter, businesses succeed because they avoid or relegate certain questions well— the repetitive tasks and other waste. It's an important thing to avoid clutter and be focused. Though the constant refrain of the book is to see that we never know where excellence begins—sometimes, in taking seriously how dry and hygienic the seat covers are in your lavatories, for instance.

At no point can we endorse focalization of the non-essentials. Instead, I am trying to focus on the fact that these 'facts' of business provide for a rich source of inquiry. These inquiries cannot always be explained in case studies though careful research, I surmise, can certainly show that. One cannot examine 'delusion' with calculated rationality—it isn't a fixated and perfected model. So, one could examine the simpler expressions of the paradigm which, I argue, a *purohita* can do in the ordinary transactions of the company.

Again, it doesn't mean that rationality and rational systems (the ones that can be perfectly explained) aren't necessary. The objective rational world generates a degree of predictability so that all of us can work on and create. At no point can anyone deny the importance of logic and rationality. The only proposition at this juncture is this—rational systems that continue to emerge as models for our existence stops somewhere.

Back to Pyramid Valley...

Coming back to our latest example of PVI, the patterns created out of rational thought, as in the case of PVI, appear so perfect that even a dedicated group cannot see its limitation. Thought itself is such—one cannot see a thought completely from all angles. U. R. Ananathmaurthy's term 'critical insider' comes handy here. 'critical insider' is someone who examines the dominant process critically while remaining within the system committed to its wellbeing. PVI lacked that critical insider and what dominated instead were dominant silences, that were boiling inside. Opposition to a sentimentally held sacred belief is difficult and the critic may become bewilderingly lonely.

PVI leadership oversimplified their challenge—*more sophisticated construction as an anathema to its woes of financial sustenance; and elite seekers who would occupy these 'sophisticated' accommodation will cause not only financial stability but also a constant momentum for all time. Perfect logic!*

Instead of experiencing a flood of elite seekers and corporate programmes, PVI later had to grapple with multiple notices from the ministry for violating construction norms, litigation from one of its own trustees, the expulsion of a trustee unceremoniously, a sudden explosion of baiters waiting to pounce on the inconsistencies, still struggling with finances and board meetings characterized by boisterous expression of tiny differences. A potent organization had lost its—still undiscovered -centre!

Reiterating that the above description isn't about denigrating the well-built campus of PVI but to show how our own rationality and logic are insufficient tools. Predictability and features for organized work have to be built. At no point can this be compromised as that would signal peril and disaster. That's obviously intuitive. When this is being managed and constructed, which should be done professionally and with utmost attention, 'Buddha CEO' confabulates with a set of 'irrational' beings whose only job is to preserve a set of 'irrational' but metrically rhythmic and systemic formulations—an invitation to the subjective.

This illustration on Pyramid Valley may not be entirely a reflection of more objectively focused companies. Yet there's a substantial element of parallels one can construct.

More concretely speaking, the orthodox *purohita* in modern India is still invoked for special occasions—birth, initiations, nuptial rituals, graduation, marriage, death, and such other transitions. And each occasion is characterized by a particular set of lengthy metrically perfect expositions. *Purohitas* present it. Mere objective presentation as is in the scripture isn't enough but a Mastery is required. Preservation is an exercise in Mastery—retaining the content, rhythm and knowledge of the most appropriate time (*muhurta*) when it should be rendered.

Coming back to our point of the 'organizational purohita'—the preserver of subjective experiences—we may look at two important elements that we saw at the beginning of this exposition—

1. to recognize the absence of a static meaning and

2. expansion of the cognitive domain.

To expand the organizational dimension by examining its contours under a lens is to see the twists, kinks and the curvatures which otherwise never existed. When done thus, the contour isn't the same length as it appeared to be. Like the length of a country's border measured will not remain the same when we use a foot-long scale! Dimensions change. To examine and preserve this altered state of reality is a way to grow—holistically.

Without over-stretching the theme, it is still important to say this—Buddha never went into action the moment he realized what 'is'. He took several weeks to come to terms with the new reality and also the way it could be communicated; Gandhi waited for weeks together in silence, meditation and fasting to arrive at the thought of Civil Disobedience. To examine your experience and conceptualizations and to be with it long enough is an important ingredient of handling volatility. And without a mastery in handling volatility nothing worthwhile is happening!

Any other means is violence and the very opposite of what it means to exist. Buddha could not have forced through his way and Gandhi could not have remained non-violent in forcing an outcome—even in the form of a thought.

A DISCOURSE ON VIOLENCE—A stoppage or foreclosure to a natural process—an animal cut or a cockroach crushed on the ground is violence. It's delicate to be understood properly. 'ahimsa'—the equivalence of non-violence—is not etymologically a lucid concept; in fact, it's a pre-critical term and has to be personally discovered from the fundamentals. Organizational violence stems from a lack of awareness of what's on offer, the processes and the results caused—the sum total of all the results caused.

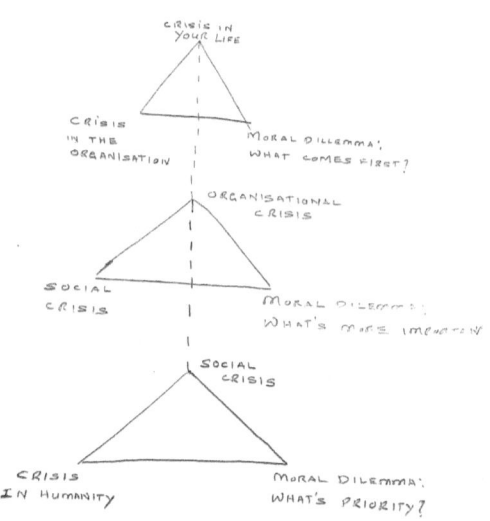

Buddha, The CEO will just not cause results but will be absolutely non-violent! And excellence takes birth in being non-violent!

The proposition—the real sustenance, or auto-renewal, is essentially a non-violent process! Inviting you to read through to discover for yourself!

In the adjoining diagram, each triangle is connected to the

other through a thin dotted line and each of the vertices in a triangle are connected. For instance, the organizational crisis and the personal crisis of individuals within it, along with a moral dilemma of prioritizing between the two for an individual form a central theme of post-mammalian evolution. Until the stage of mammals, a reptilian brain (metaphoric again, of course) doesn't even recognize the dilemma. To simply foreclose these dilemmas as if they don't exist is violence. My first Principal in a school I had worked for had oversimplified a philosophy—'my work comes first' and the obvious rationale was 'work is worship'. Since we are inundated with such atrocious readymade philosophy the *Purohita* is ever relevant.

The central thin dotted line that runs through the triangles is the '*sanatana*'—the principle that runs it all; the thread that causes the drama!

The Web of Excellence

The core of everything an organization does is rather difficult to find.

Many a time, nicely worded statements substitute for the real need of working towards the core. There are enough activities to play with and problems to solve that this exploration of what it means to run the organization and how it is relevant appears like a luxury to be indulged into once in a while in a retreat. And the proposition at this juncture to promote reflection is this: when we find the core, growth and social impact are phenomenal.

A story in *Yoga Vashishta* establishes this quite well. *Yoga Vashishta* is one of the most esoteric of spiritual texts. It describes Sage Vashishta's attempt to enlighten Prince Rama from a strange kind of depression that Rama finds himself in. Since the story is relevant yet off the course, it's in the box here!

The story is a chain of events in the life of Cudala and Sikhidwaja - the queen and king of a kingdom. The king Sikhidwaja is known for his extreme good governance and Cudala also known for her piousness.

As the story goes, Cudala gets enlightened and begins to converse with the king on diverse aspects of transcendental world and sikhidwaja constantly dismisses that as vain hallucination. Helpless but happy to be herself, Cudala continues her life without trying anymore to educate Sikhidwaja.

As time goes, Sikhidwaja also becomes intensely aware of the futility of things around him; he sees no meaning in anything and every loss and gain appear like a divine joke. Finally he decides to renounce everything and move to the forest, though his wife discourages him. She argues, 'retreat to the forest is important at a later stage in our life; not right now. You can still discover what you are looking for by ruling this very kingdom peacefully and efficiently'; Sikhidwaja refutes and even accuses Cudala of being immature in the transcendental aspects and moves into the forest in the thick of night when the whole city is asleep.

Cudala, through her divine eyes, finds out the whereabouts of Sikhidwaja but doesn't dissuade him from the enterprise. She just takes care of the kingdom with utmost efficiency. Later having waited for the right time to educate and enlighten Sikhidwaja, Cudala approaches before him in the guise of a young *Brahman*.

Enthralled by the divine guest Sikhidwaja asks the *Brahman's* counsel. Amongst the several things Cudala narrates, in the guise of the *Brahman*, she tells him the story of a merchant. As the story goes, the merchant is in search of the *Chintamani* (the philosopher's stone supposed to fulfil all of one's wishes) and when he finds it becomes utterly confused about its authenticity and discards it to continue his severe penance and other austerities.

As the time goes he finds another glass-piece and because of his continued hard work but now convinced about his own hard work, takes that to be the Chintamani. He discards all his belongings and goes alone to the forest to recreate his abundant world through this glass piece. And on account of that foolishness he suffers more!'

And Cudala (Brahman) concludes: 'likewise, O king, you also fell into the trap of these meaningless activities and austerities. Thus , you abandoned the jewel to pick a worthless glass piece in the form of these austerities and rituals.' Cudala explains how Sikhidwaja abandoned the infinite joy only to pick these austerities which has a beginning and an end!

Organizational relevance—

At the point of any creation—organizationally speaking or in terms of individual roles—something is dropped—a manager drops his previous style of paying attention to detailed execution and delegates instead; the CEO no longer sits on the finance team every time there's a glitch. And an organization may have to discard the belief in the paramountcy of the previous paradigm. When *Sikhidwaja* leaves for the forest, he had sincerely dropped the consideration that the kingdom was everything; and now with a new challenge arisen, he is still trapped in the same pit of scepticism!

And this is a delusion that we all face from time to time just as organizations do—

1. We throw what's valuable and retain the junk! Because it's easier to retain the 'junk' in the form of activities and operations, we have an easy substitute for the invaluable 'jewel'!

2. Having found a formula that worked for us once, we dwell in the same formulations again and again for a solution.

Please look into 'Necessity' in the chapter 'Two Pieces' in Section 2 and also 'Regeneration of a CEO' in Section 3.

An Experience in an Exercise of Organizational Transformation—

What happened in Pyramid Valley?

Pyramid Valley offers an interesting paradigm on how organizations function. And that's the excuse for repeating it so often!

Pyramid Valley International, called the New Shambala, is an impressive social not-for-profit organization located in the outskirts of Bangalore. Begun by a trust operating it, PVI has an expressed mission of 'Spiritualising the whole world'. This impressive structure, which provided for its '*annamaya*' was absolutely impressive.

Any organization will have to look at the question of sustenance (Refer to the Organizational Buddhahood' Diagram in Chapter 1 of this section) and PVI also did. Where will the cash come from? Is a question that had to be answered. This is where the organization came into an unusual dilemma.

Without breaking down the vision into a central process that drives and energizes everything leading, if possible, to a unique product, PVI pulled upon itself a self-referential dilemma characterised by a civilisational question—'who came first—the hen or the egg?'. Instead of allowing the process to play out its role, which is rather difficult, it was convenient to think of construction as a way out. More construction means more visitors and that's the surest means of sustaining ourselves and also doing what we want to do. This thought itself, as we are going to see, an egregious diversion!

Donations drove its construction. Once the construction was complete, there were a series of steps that PVI took—

1. *Create a PR campaign, as explained before, that ended up into positioning of PVI as one of the seven wonders of Bangalore and voted as the most exquisite amongst the 'wonders'. This was based on a survey by a daily in Bangalore (The Bangalore Mirror).*

2. *The popularity of this campaign resulted in a huge rise in the number of visitors. And Google reviews became the new shore. Managing excellent reviews was the key. And this was the first of the several digressions. An organization meant to spiritualize the world had to contend with the question of managing its space as the most exquisite 'picnic spot'. Meditation and Pyramid energy were replaced by the beauty of the hills and the safest spot for the privacy of young couples.*

3. *The quality of the campus became its primary focus and hence the expenses expanded. The expanded revenue requirements had to be fulfilled by some means. It was felt that more construction of rooms and residential facilities would bring visitors who would stay and will add revenue; better 'star' accommodations would be much better and hence more star accommodations added at a huge loss of 'equity'. Further, for the visitors to benefit from PVI, it was thought classes should be conducted and there comes up a 4000 sq. Ft exquisitely constructed Kabir Bhavan and the loan expands.*

4. *Classes to be conducted requires some sessions to be taken and 'The Law of Karma', 'Life After Death', 'Past Life', etc. crop up. By themselves valuable esoteric topics, but fizzled out due to the missing centre—*

'spiritualizing the whole world'! (Please refer to 'Yoga-Kshema' in Section 3).

Now let's look at another paradigm where the meaning of what's offered expanded.

Arohi Open School

The space is in the centre.

The jewel that Sikhidhwaja and PVI lost is what Ratnesh appeared to have stuck to!

Ratnesh Mathur, an alumnus from IIM Ahmedabad with an experience of over 20 years in the corporate world, one day decided to revolutionize the way children learn (this is my description. In fact, he doesn't even believe that there's anything to be changed. No delusion drives him! On my query during a visit to his 'open' school at Hosur, close to Bangalore, about what prompted him to take up this 'revolutionary' concept all that he had to say smilingly was, ' I am sorry, I have nothing interesting to say!')

As Ratnesh explained to me on my visit, he began a school to create a model that can be easily replicated and create a scalable business. I am unsure if Ratnesh agrees with it, but any endeavour, even Ratnesh's, begins because there is always an elemental entity that could be 'stored and shifted'— money, business, career, social contribution, brand value, etc. As explained earlier, without the 'delusion', companies can't move into newer domains, and enterprises don't last.

As Ratnesh began this, what opened up was a world of discovery of what's really authentic about learning, and what can be really valuable in the process of a school, etc. and he was no longer stuck in the pit of 'a great business model'. And these questions expanded into an open schooling environment, an open campus and training of thousands of parents on the intricacies of learning, emotional development of children, self-esteem, etc. Apart from these, he also conducts a variety of teacher training programmes and summer camps for children. I have benefitted from several of his interactions including one during my visit to Arohi Campus at Hosur.

Unlike PVI (I admit the scale of organizational visions are different), Ratnesh's Arohi is 'ergonomic'—it gently fits into what is a felt need! Of course, the scale is different but it implies something easy to connect here. Bigger organizations that require a high degree of systematization may tend to begin handling the 'systems' rather than what the systems were meant for in the first place. My friend Ravishankar, as said before, mentions his experience in one of India's IT companies where the managers spent most of their time managing systems and anywhere between 30 to 35 hours of his forty weekly hours would get into being part of the meetings.

Redundancy is extremely draining!

The point is simple—

When we happen to miss the centre, there's but anything what really sustains an organization! And the obsessions with the details and the 'sentiments' of the organization take precedence over what it is meant to do in the first place. No wonder, great companies and organization await another day!

But this is a rather difficult enterprise.

An Illustrative Explanation—

What's the most intangible in any organization? The vision of the organization. Because our lives are running and an undercurrent process keeps alive the organization also, the vision can either be conveniently forgotten or just used to embellish the board room wall.

Since it's so invisible, locating the vision (the primary reason and drive for its existence) in the daily activities and interactions is next to impossible. Even when compromised, it does not look like a compromise. The game is lost and the full possibility of the game remains unexplored. You may recall the illustration in Chapter 3 of this section where the different sheaths of the organization interact in a complex web amongst which 'space' is one.

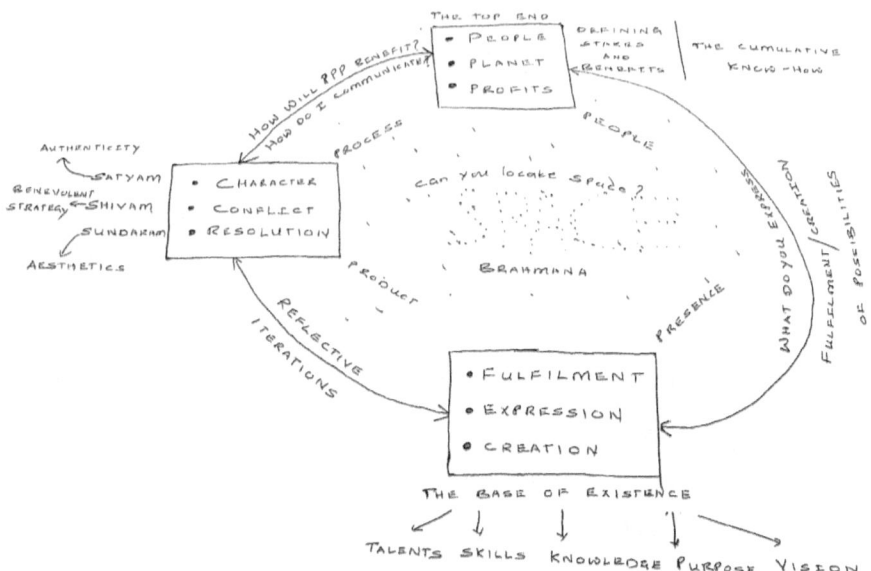

The idea is not to allow the 'space' to be spoilt. Because this 'space' located at the centre is so intangible (as the illustration itself suggests the difficulty in locating) that we don't even notice its dilution. We wouldn't accept a soup well prepared and garnished with a drop of gutter water (it's so tangible), but generally comfortable with toxic air. We do protest, of course, but air is certainly more intangible than water.

Spirit is the most intangible of all. And that's why we are at ease with the dilution of our spirit—'corruption and lower ethical standards are practical ways of handling business'. There's justification for diluting the spirit.

'Space' manages the organization's authenticity.

One of the ways of engaging the stakeholders into this 'value' perspective needs an enlightened HR. Look at the diagram on the adjoining page. An HR that looks at humans as a resource, for there is no better term right now, but the resource isn't limited to who works for the company or limited to just recruitment, policies, leaves, training, staff welfare and what is conventionally seen as HR work. HR in the scheme that we have pursued has a lot more to develop and offer than mere dry recruitment and database of annual performance appraisals. HR manages the space where innovation and qualitative work happens.

In Buddha's *shuddhashtaka*—the holy eight—the absolutely unresolvable is the final post. Because one cannot resolve it any further it stays there. The space is that!

THE Human Resources Department

Unlike a regular HR department, which may look at recruitment, training, appraisals and remuneration, HR can substantially create the fulcrum around which excellence revolves!

Not all information is always necessary for everyone! And not all 'go-getters' can be suitable everywhere. It requires for the HR to see without the urgency of the organizational leadership as to what it means to retain the value through its human beings!

It should begin by 'discriminating' (this doesn't relate to organizational fair practices and the value of equal opportunity that organizations are bound by) what information is valuable where! This is bound to boomerang if we have a hierarchical understanding of valuable knowledge—though the financial value of knowledge and skills are bound to be different!

As the 'funnel model' suggests, we may safely begin by looking at both information and human engagement at the four interrelated levels of Casual, Connected, Committed and Convinced!

Like all models, this requires discretion and reflection; more importantly, a commitment to the process of discovery! (It may be valuable to look at the 'Conclusion' at the end of the book). When different states of commitment within an organization interact, there's adhesion to what causes brilliant work—as a gyrating, mutually feeding organism!

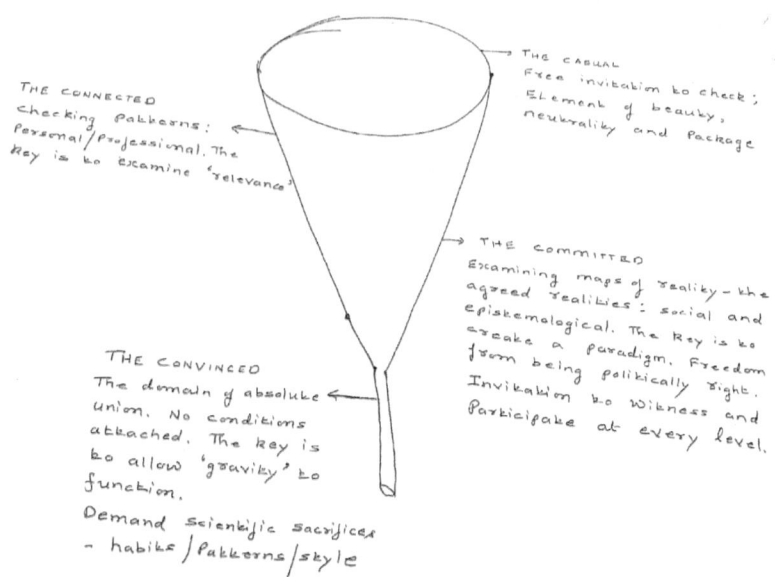

The diagram is labelled with:

THE CASUAL
Free invitation to check; Element of beauty, neutrality and Package

THE CONNECTED
Checking Patterns: Personal/Professional. The key is to examine 'relevance'

THE COMMITTED
Examining maps of reality – the agreed realities: social and epistemological. The key is to create a paradigm. Freedom from being politically right. Invitation to Witness and Participate at every level.

THE CONVINCED
The domain of absolute union. No conditions attached. The key is to allow 'gravity' to function.

Demand Scientific sacrifices
– habits/Patterns/style

Casual—how will anyone come to know who you are? What stories about you pervade the public domain that a layman can hold on to?

Connected—how can one get connected to you? What are the mechanisms for the quality of connection? What's the degree of authenticity—are you really who you appear to be?

Committed—what are you adding value to? What's the holistic stake for the one connected? What mentoring mechanisms exist? Is the lineage defined?

Convinced—a legend in creation; there's no gap. When there's no gap, no more story becomes necessary.

CATCHING HOLD OF THIS AT WORK:

WHAT WAS THE FUNDAMENTAL UNIT, THE CURRENCY THAT BEGAN THE PROCESS? WAS IT A GROWING MARKET OR SIMPLE BELIEF THAT A CHANGE CAN HAPPEN.

EXTRICATE IT AND EXAMINE WHAT IT HAS TO SAY; TEAM UP AND LISTEN TO IT INTENTLY. RECOGNISE THAT IT'S A RIVER THAT HAS ALWAYS BEEN THERE

SECTION 2

CHAPTER 1

Two Pieces

The thirst of a thoughtless man grows like a creeper,

He runs from life to life like a monkey seeking fruit in a forest.

– Dhammapada

PIECE 1

Necessity[30]

A Story...

This ascetic lived happily, on the fringes of civilization, bearing just enough to sustain—a begging bowl, a pair of tattered clothes and a hut.

That defined his existence as he focused on his transcendental limits...

It so happened one day...

A squeaky little rat had chewed off his already tattered clothes,

So, he thought of a cat to tame the rat

And to row the cat in the ocean of life, he got a cow,

And again, a wife to look after the cow's life,

Yet again, a child to mild the wild-wife,

---

30 I am aware of gender sensitivity but am using it just with the wish that poetic quality and the arcane element in it is not lost

And so it went on…

'turning and turning in the widening gyre,

The Falcon cannot hear the falconer,

> *The centre cannot hold,*

> *Mere anarchy is loosed upon the world.'*

– W. B. Yeats

As the monk became busy managing the cat, cow, wife and child—he lost his centre.

Was it in the institutional arrangements to take care of the centre or the centre burdened with institutional arrangements?

A STORY FOR A STORY

As children growing up in a provincial town in Karnataka, India, we had a story that was quite popular. Neither did we know its source or purpose. It just existed in our repetitions.

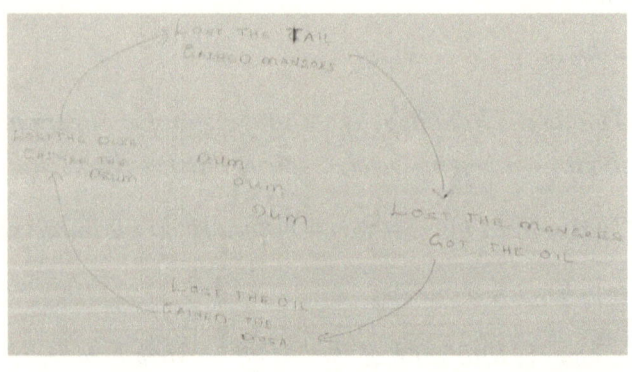

An emperor on a hunting spree comes across a monkey complaining about a thorn stuck in his tail. And the king in all benevolence tries to remove the thorn and in the process inadvertently cuts the tail. The monkey is terrified and protests; and in exchange, as compensation, demands the king's knife and gets it.

As the monkey travels further with the sword, he comes across a man selling mangoes sitting under a tree. Seeing the knife in the monkey's hand seeks it to cut the mangoes but breaks the knife's handle in the process. The angry monkey takes some mangoes in exchange and moves further.

Further, the monkey finds an oil-seller who exchanges oil for the mangoes; and then, as the story goes, an old lady exchanges dosas[31] *for the oil with the monkey.*

And finally, as the monkey travels with the packed dosas, a hungry drummer is tempted by the packed dosas in the monkey's hands and the monkey by the drum. They exchange.

And the monkey, not sure whether to be happy or sad, drums a song thus—

'Lost the tail, got the knife,

Dum Dum Dum

Lost the knife, got the mangoes,

Dum Dum Dum

Lost the mangoes, got the oil,

Dum Dum Dum

Lost the oil, got the drum,

Dum Dum Dum.'

And the typical questions were asked by the elders narrating the story—was the monkey an intelligent one?

And the story for us was not a simple question of right/wrong, intelligent/unintelligent but was dialogic—inconclusively dialogic. It didn't have a linear conclusion but was quite evocative and generated several reactions. And as children, we enjoyed debating the monkey's actions without an end.

To take an even more authentic example would be Herman Hesse's 'Siddhartha'. The novel depicts the trajectory of a virulent seeker, who drops his father's ways of forbearance and rituals to a more direct form of inquiry. A

---

31   a south Indian dish

delicately knit writing, simplicity itself being its essential stylistics, Herman Hesse examines Siddhartha spiralling into the vortex of life experiences including the pain of separation from his son born of a prostitute, the pain of loss, etc. only to be redeemed by the Boatman Vasudeva who teaches him to listen to the River. Once done, Vasudeva retreats![32]

Despite virulent commitment that we see in Siddhartha, the centre was lost and the constant striving for the invisible centre always continued incessantly! Never attained—hence never satisfying.

WHAT DID I WISH TO SAY?

Let me try establishing the links!

I will take two scenarios—one of how organizations other than 'commercial' ones function and within it a description about what makes a business thrive. Both are described from a general 'angle of view'.

Any social organization, 'spiritual organization' included, from the business perspective could be an error. Businesses thrive on the unique, in minimizing waste and quick iterations along with a search for the newer capital; from the business perspective, a 'spiritual' organization has no basis to thrive. Because a 'spiritual' organization is fulfilled and is complete in whatever is the current state and revolves around the tenaciously mundane - cooking, cleaning and washing - and celebration of 'waste' and the capital is what gets generated in its doing.

On the other hand, a 'business' outsources the repetitive, non-value-adding waste—cooking, cleaning, security and front office. 'Spirituality' is in being wholesome in our absolute attention to the work on hand—regeneration by focusing on the waste—sweeping, cleaning, etc. done as service.

---

32   I have read this from my friend's unpublished Kannada translation. This is a precise Occidental depiction of spiritual life and analytically appears like the reason for intriguing popularity of Buddha, an instant hit, in the West. Siddhartha appears like a tragic irony - being stuck into what he always wanted to escape from. The reader would easily see how important maintaining alertness was and the dread of missed alertness.

An Oriental would have written 'YOGA VASHISHTA' instead!

As case studies later in the book may suggest how a business may fail or remain inefficient and how a spiritual organization could collapse, an examination of what's 'essential' and what's not is by itself a fundamental self-inquiry!

Ideally, an idea should develop into the manifestation of the architecture, design and everything else that supports its existence. That's how a 'spiritual organization' can crystallize and consolidate all its efforts. Housekeeping, hospitality, maintenance, etc. should ideally emanate from the centre as an idea that's organically developing into a fully functional aesthetic organization. And when these are accrued from the outside, this 'gathering of instruments' brings with it a set of expectations and intentions, which cannot always be heard and completed. The manager wants a house, the worker wants better pay and the organization is completely engrossed in managing these 'upsets' and since it's impossible to manage these 'upsets', it becomes an 'upset organization'—angry, quarrelsome, gossipy, 'leg-pulling'[33] and spirit-less!

And more often it is these tiny little upsets that drive the organization!

That is—we are all the monks who went on to manage these tiny little upsets—the rat to the cat to the cow to the wife...

Are we really different? Look at these aspirational statements—

    a. 'the most admired company' status, or

    b. 'the most sought after by employees'

    c. 'the best place to work'

WHEN CHANDRASHEKHARA DIED...

Chandrashekhara died in circa 1967

And I was there...

Despite that, I was born only in 1974.

---

33 A colloquially used term to indicate the existence of infighting and internal sabotage

He died,

Drank poison in the dingy, dark Nagara house.

He died unexpressed!

His death got trivialized…

Remained unspoken,

And I had a bridge, but the destination was missing…

he remained unexpressed … and I remain unexpressed!

They said, 'he was an angry man!'

They further anecdoted, 'he threw hot coffee on Shankara Chikkappa's face.'

And Shankara Chikkappa[34], apparently calm, wiped and left.

Shankara Chikkappa should have just cursed him, banged him and thrown his tantrum

Why did he drop his anger?

Shankara Chikkappa's silence pulverized the inexpressibility!

Rotten and hidden, Chandrashekhara had to remain unexpressed

And they didn't say what he couldn't say—the unbearable distilled decoction of the entire universe that he was!

*They still say, 'he was a first-rate **Jyothishi**[35]; **veda parangata**[36]. Very sensitively intelligent.'*

How could that be expressed?

I am he …. the sensitive hyper-intellectual.

---

34   refers to uncle - father's younger brother
35   astrologer
36   mastery of the *vedas*

To stare at futility and decide to cease means courage but not freedom.

I chose

How odd I feel to refer to this dead man as 'Chikkappa'!

And yet, more unacknowledged, deeper you reside in me!

I will live a part of you

But consider exploration as not mere living…

I acknowledge you 'Chenshekhara' Chikkappa,

You died,

Demonstrating the futility of voluntary death,

We live on… Anna lives on,

52 years ago… yet I was there!

*   *   *   *   *

Where am I?

When did my life begin?

What's the source of my life?

How do I know it?

Who told me that?

*   *   *   *   *

Even at the risk of becoming autobiographical let me briefly explain the incidental relevance of the above almost autobiographical 'fictional' figment; that's just half the truth—any autobiography is fiction. It's not to demean great auto-biographies which have inspired all of us but that's the nature of the past—it doesn't exist except as if in dreams. Hence, the expression is in semi-poetic form—neither the complete truth nor is it the untruth! That explains why there are footnotes on some terms within the poem.

Let me try establishing simple parlance.

Anyone would recognize oneself in terms of these simple questions—

What are my coordinates? Are the coordinators real? When did this emerge and how did I know it?

What nobody would know is the subjectivity that I am. Personally, my now fondest, what was then densest, memories are of my childhood. Amongst five siblings, I remained largely unexpressed but intrigued about—a silent feeling of senselessness in the Math and language and handwriting I learnt in school, my parents' incomprehensible worry about my 60th rank in a class of sixty children, the fear of being attacked by other children, the boisterous joy of a small town, happy intermingling dirtiness of my affectionate family and many more portrayals. My childhood, like everyone's, wasn't a single romantic string but a complex web.

The organized institutions like family didn't make sense to me—school, family, relationship and categorization of individuals. Amongst all these was a strange feeling that I knew where I came from—I am not very different from Chandrashekhara, the one who lived amongst us, children, as a dead man. It was a family secret and we never talked much. Death is inauspicious even in our family of *vedantin*[37]*s* and suicide was certainly out-of-bounds!

My visits to my ancestral home in Chamarajanagara, then a small township within Mysore District, depicted this sultry unpleasantness of a death that hasn't been revoked and completed with; it lay hanging like Eliot's wasteland, 'breeding lilacs out of the dead land', 'mixing memory and desire'. Even the few photographs of Chandrashekhara had been cleverly hidden.

It was only later during the ceremonies that accompanied my grandfather's death that I could reconcile with this partially. My grandfather died when

---

37   one who has the knowledge of the *vedas*

I was thirteen and the chanting that accompanied these ceremonies was strangely rhythmic and aesthetic. It gave me a vague understanding that sound without sense can be quite meaningful. I never understood the chanting but the feeling was one of pride about my identity, which I still carry—a bit shamelessly in a world of secular values.

Somehow, Chandrashekhara was acknowledged! I had inherited a past. This acknowledgement drove my performance. I still feel proud to mention this (even if it's slightly out of context)—I went on to score very well after that—scoring the recorded highest in my family during my board exams in 10th, which was a fiercely contested competition then. It's ridiculous to speak about exam scores and my simple effort here is to relate performance with an acknowledgement of a past that we never thought existed!

Performance in a strange way was related to my acknowledgement of Chandrashekhara—actively revoking and acknowledging the past, without uttering it outside, but being absolutely sure of the same in my poetry and diary entries. It had a strange kind of interconnection to everything I did including a shift in my poor academics till then to a performance I am proud of and, more importantly, transformation from a constant rivalry with my eleven months younger brother in particular and the complaining 'wronged' feeling in general.

I had reasons to look into this aspect though logically it didn't fit into a valid conception. As probably is visible in this writing, my style is convoluted into an internal cascade that spirals down into my own personal space without a culmination, I draw your attention into yet another digression. Of course, I believe it to be important.

ANGER, URGENCY AND A SENSE OF IT'S STILL NOT THE POINT!

Anger is the only emotion possible when things are not the way you think they should be! Look at the contexts below—

1. I deposit money in a bank and the bankers are unable to pay me back at that instant due to a technical glitch or lack of staff.

2. A teacher expects homework from her students only to find incomplete work.

Both result in anger, which can be expressed as disappointment, irritation, upset, anger or to be utterly frozen with emotion. In both the above cases the situation can be easily augmented. The context can be varied and it can be moved by just creating another promise for the deliverables. 'When will you give me the money back? Or when will you complete the homework?' has an answer. Without a valid answer and a re-commitment to executing what is expected, it results in one of the feelings described—from disappointment to anger.

Think of another situation—what existed before God?

If the question is serious enough, it can never be answered in the way we answer factual questions (like 'when will you complete the homework') and neither is there a way to find out whether the answer given is the right one. It implies that if the questioner is dependent on an external agent for an answer, one could expect her to be perennially angry.

I had experienced this situation as a child—whatever my family members and relatives opinion of me was never true; it wasn't the answer. One of the easiest descriptions my family members had of me was as 'Durvasa', the familiar recluse in Indian mythology, who was perennially angry cursing all and sundry. One of the popular anecdotes that keeps getting circulated amongst my family members is about how I would ask for sugarcane to be cut into pieces only to demand the same in its original fullness; all this with hysterical tantrum!

Since a valid conception of myself was impossible, the easiest alternative was to consider what was being offered to me as an explanation of who I was and always have been. My behaviour continually endorsed this notion, and all my mind distortions and mental ailments could be traced to the primordial identity of who I was! I landed in a state of the family in an order of birth that was perfectly suited for the complete expression of who Chadrashekara was—the family could never reconcile Chandrashekara's aggression with his intellect; and Chandrashekara, I guess, could never be satisfied with the artificial fabrications of a family. There's an inheritance that I see!

This argument gels with a recent meditation I did with Shreans Daga on 'Soul Contracts' and 'lives between lives' though I found Shreans' style too objective and knowledge delivery too rudimentary. What I realised was that who I am is passed on to me, intact, from the past of who I had been. Chandrashekara appears to be one easy association in the family but I know now, intuitively, that it goes far beyond it.

Like the earlier piece we saw on 'necessity' it became convenient for me to handle these distractions as me rather than the really - and more fundamentally - question that I always had—what existed before God? The distractions were much easier rather than this primordially unanswerable question—to pass an entrance test, to pressurize my family members to do well, to feel anxious, anger, etc. were far better than handling the problematic primordial question.

Whether I am like Chandrashekhara or I have acquired his characteristics are immaterial; the point is that none of us truly have enough time and space to truly explore our fundamental question!

My surmise is that it's true of all human enterprises and it's not uncommon to see such digressions in all endeavours.

JUST ONE MORE ADDITION BEFORE WE PROCEED

In a light-hearted conversation with my friend Ravishankar, an eternal sceptic, we each discovered the fundamental acts of our lives; a fundamental question that's driving everything we do and the kind of cynicism or enthusiasm that characterizes our experience with things. I discovered mine to be the question about what existed before God while Ravishankar saw his in 'why we should know?'. This Ravishankar called this 'beejamantra'—the seed question. That is also the seed capital on which we have constructed our lives!

In our own ways of articulation as children and subsequent suppression of the same, we have evolved in our lives. These questions were oppressed as the interesting distractions provided immediate relief whereas this question had no end. We knew it. As we have grown into adults, a chance conversation showed both of us our 'seeds' from what we could excavate from our memories.

Children are such. As Meerama of Shivanetra tradition (she drives a surprisingly beautiful organization called 'Temple of Learning' in Bangalore) suggests, children have a far greater connection to the cosmic world than the way they relate to the parents. This connection to the cosmic and ethereal if understood (forget nurturing; we have no way of doing it) causes an enormous difference to the way we nurture and educate our children. Just that I am replacing 'children' with 'our enterprises' as leaders.

So, just ask yourselves without the urgency of finding the answers.

What is the 'fundamental act of life' that has driven you?

What 's the 'fundamental act' of your organization'?

As CEO and senior leaders, you have an extraordinary chance to discover and connect and thereby establish a lineage of 'discovery'!

CHAPTER 2

A Discourse on Upset

No suffering befalls the man not attached to name and form

And calls nothing his own.

He who holds back rising anger

Like a rolling chariot,

Him, I call a real driver.

Other people are but holding the reins.

– Dhammapada

As we keep shuttling between what, probably, was too 'esoteric' to the exigencies that organizations and businesses handle, we have to deal with certain questions circumstantially. There are these unexplored and continually suppressed 'fundamental acts of life' that come in the company's transactions. Any organization for that matter deals with these fundamental acts. How leadership drives these questions seriously is not just metaphysical but eminently connected to the ways we are creating our world.

This is essentially what a learning organization does—helping each player to identify and learn how they have constantly been trying to improve 'things' around them ranging from better nutrition for themselves to their children's better spelling. This penchant for the better—which extends into 'more, different and faster' in the language of an admirable book

'**The Three Laws of Performance**'—refuses to decline in our inability to see the point that 'the more things change, the more they stay the same'!

Having just transferred ourselves from a world of esoteric associations, I invite you to revisit a small description in the earlier piece on 'Chandrashekhara'. It is about anger and the source of anger as a question that remains unanswered. That's the point from which the next part of the 'discourse' begins.

WHAT WE DO WITH 'UPSETS'!

An 'upset'[38] has to be managed!

An 'upset' can be managed and dissolved because it's finite! An 'upset' that 'adds on' becomes a story, an epic—an infinite narrative; an epic is beyond a happening in the present!

An epic is very difficult to handle—one can refer back to it and recreate meanings of the narratives but one can't have a mastery over it—even to aspire for it is futile. Nevertheless, one can make connections of the 'here and now' with certain narratives in the epic. Likewise, an organization cannot handle the 'epics' of built-up stories but on the questions of 'here and now'.

This brings me to a point I would want you to consider. This is a point of intersection of the two—a spiritual organization and a business entity. Both are same. A 'spiritual organization' has to answer the big questions of individuals from the 'here and now' of repetitive work and create a business

---

38 I was enamoured by this term when my wife explained to me after a seminar that she attended with Landmark. Landmark Education provided me with unique conversations but this I got it from my wife's sharing with me about what she experienced. This is a personalised version of another personalised version that I heard from my wife. Landmark education provides an edge which is unmatched in my experience. The point here is to point out a happening in an organisation for an insight The Three Laws of Performance is also a wok that has originated from the principles Landmark adheres to. As I am reviewing it I see that parts of the section are completely influenced by the understanding that I drew from my conversation with my wife and my participation in Landmark programs.

so that more of humanity can participate in it; and a business entity has to answer the 'here and now' questions of humanity and turn them into the big questions of individuals. In other words, it boils to two questions—

1. *What's my role and how does it fit into the larger scheme of things?*

2. *What's the team/company/my life up to and what's my role within it?*

'Upset' is a discontinuity. Existentially, humans appear to dislike discontinuity. That explains the popularity of movies, theatre and novels. They exhibit a portable continuity—as one integrated whole—that can be consumed. Each of these—novel, cinema, story and theatre—present a matrix that can be transposed into our own lives and generate empathetic participation—without a complaint.

As a corollary what follows, therefore, is that 'upset' is 'mandatory prioritization'—excluding some for the sake of others. Like we go to work and give up our desire—in that sense exclude—to spend a day with our families. This is the kind of dilemma that Arjuna also experienced when confronted with an inevitable war with his own relatives—winning the war will exclude his happiness with them. In other words, the choices we make with work and personal lives causes discontinuity with other equally important preferences in our lives. Krishna on the other hand is fully expressed. Krishna probably would advocate inclusiveness—'be happy and also kill the relatives in the war'! So, it's understandable that Krishna had several wives and all of them fully satisfied by Krishna's simultaneous prioritization of everyone.

Like Aldous Huxley's portrayal of a dystopian reality, 'upset' is the epitome of 'stuckiness'. Every action in Aldous Huxley's 'Brave New World' has an 'ethical gain' and a corresponding 'ethical loss' and it's human tragedy to choose between the two. Organizations, like us mortals, fail to see the circularity of 'gain-loss' cyclical waves. And what we see is that we are stranded in a world that is absolutely not free from 'upsets'—it's impossible to see a point where there's no gain and no loss. It's absurd.

This 'discontinuity' is continuous with two previously touched conceptualizations—the triumvirate of relationships (as seen in the diagram representing three triangles arranged vertically with a thin line passing through them all) and organizational violence in Chapter 3 of the previous section. The crises we experience is not exclusive to us as individuals but is continuous with the crises of the entire humanity and the way to grow out of it is to participate in this 'continuous' crises. We are going to explore this theme once again in the next chapter and in another called 'Transformation is a Design'. In contrast to this theme, we insulate ourselves in neat differential equations with boundary conditions attached to it. That explains why Newton competed with Leibniz in his claims on the discovery of Calculus and in the conception of space: the mechanism of arriving at an understanding by breaking things apart into its tiny parts had an advantage. Newton pioneered the cause of breaking down the whole into fragmentary mechanical entities. To break down into fragments and to insulate was the primordial sin and the original act of corruption. A very popular household Indian chanting goes like this—

> '*Papoham papa sambhoham*
>
> *Papatma papa sambhavaha*'
>
> *Loosely translated as—*
>
> '*I am sin manifest, born and nurtured in it.*'

Unless one shows the courage to cut this 'discontinuity' mercilessly, one is eternally stuck in a cycle of mediocrity—changing and revolving all the time like a fly stuck in phlegm; a more friendly metaphor could be like a rat running on a spinning wheel, deluded by static movement. The sin is the momentum of cyclical motion.

Without a discerning organizational intelligence, everything appears meaningless and a manifestation of a set of discontinuities. Everything is 'except the one that I am proposing' kind of narcissism gets into play. In PVI, therefore, one trustee wanted only sessions on knowledge, another better ambience and accommodation, yet another a beautiful garden—all strands without a central knot; each a discontinuous intense personal desire. None of them referred to the core of what the organization had stood by. Instead of being 'absurd', organizations can become self-referential by referencing all actions to one central core mission. Absurdity can be meaningful self-referentially!

I have taken one instance for a full exploration of this 'upset' and discontinuity with reference to PVI but I am tempted to mention one right away. PVI advocates vegetarianism. Patriji, the spiritual Master of the place, doesn't compromise with vegetarianism. His adherence is so virulent that when two names cropped up during a discussion on inviting a celebrity for the upcoming Global Festival of Spiritual Scientists, Patriji rejected one on the grounds that of being non-vegetarian. One of the trustees attempted to explain how even a non-vegetarian guest may positively be transformed, only to be snubbed. It did appear naive and childish, but what's important for us is organizationally it was a 'discontinuity' with the larger realities of people's lifestyle choices and the discontinuous violence in striking out a possibility expressed by another stakeholder.

All of the above-mentioned - including the episode on the ludicrous non-vegetarian and vegetarian conundrum -cosmetics sorely focused on the body of the organization. For Buddha, the attention to the body without interest to know the causal reality was ignorance. A body, something that's just held within the bag of our skin, is discontinuous.

As said, it's not 'upsets' that we are out to handle. 'upsets' happen like the exhaust of an automobile. There's no meaning to it and there's no reason why one should deal with it, except that one could observe the pattern and change the technology so that less 'upset'—or toxic exhaust—is released; because 'upset' is a question that's waiting to be answered! In fact an 'upset' has the capacity to draw all attention to itself.

It's not 'upsets' that we are out to handle but a question on how to make sense of the more universal 'discontinuity'!

An Illustration—(Names Used Here are Illustrative But the Narrative is True)

Pyramid Valley International, the spiritual organization I have been referring to on the outskirts of Bangalore, made some changes to its operations. It decided to close its gates for visitors, unless informed, by 7 PM. Here comes the story!

In a meeting with the Joint Managing Trustee, two representative trustees and the newly hired consulting firm on improving visitor experience and hospitality, we came across the data-base from Google and our own records that most visits happen between 11 am and 4 pm except for the weekends. Instead of stretching our resources too thin and becoming frivolous in our offering, the decision taken was to limit visits to between 9 am and 5 pm to all except those who have hired rooms in the campus. And even the guests who stay would have a time limit of upto 7 pm. Secondly to maintain the exclusivity of the privileges that guests can enjoy without a violation to their privacy, entry of the general visitors to certain areas were to be restricted. These appeared commonsensical and in line with the intended transformation.

Pradeep, one of the elite visitors and well-wishers of PVI, has a meeting with the trustee who resides just outside the gate and comes late; the guard refuses entry with a refrain, 'rules have changed!' In fact, Pradeep brings numerous overseas guests that contribute to the organization's treasury and is a respected figure amongst the PVI circles. 'Rules have changed!' retort could have been shocking to him.

Pradeep experiences the same refrain, 'rules have changed' at Meditation Lab! (Meditation Lab is the institution where the benefits of meditation are institutionalized. The Heart Rate Variability instrument and Subtle Energy complex and such other devices not only measure the life parameters but also advocate practices. A discourse on Meditation Lab and the way it was created and struggle to sustain it is a story by itself)

To this, adds Pratap Sinha, 'Yes! I have also experienced the same. I wanted to just go for a walk into the surrounding hills and saw that there was a gate and it was locked; then tried moving over the wooden-bridge and that was also locked. It was surprising', with a sarcastic smile! Pratap Sinha brought about the creation of Meditation Lab in an interesting twist from his understanding of Quantum Mechanics through Prof Amit Goswami and also from his own spiritual practices. The whole enterprise of Meditation Lab by itself was another attempt at cosmetics. It appeared that the organisation was so enamoured by the cosmetics that nothing useful could ever happen - this time finding refuge in Quantum mechanics! (And I was 'upset' with that)

It doesn't stop there—Patri madam, as we all affectionately call her, and is the wife of the Master Patriji, encounters one such aberration— she is stopped by a new security guard (enthusiastically recruited by the security agency but never oriented!)

In the first chapter of the book, as I began developing an apology for the Organizational Buddhahood, I had used a rhetorical question on whether an organization can ever attain Buddhahood. I had responded with two alternatives corresponding to the 'YES' and 'NO' scenarios. You may refer back to the context. The Buddhahood, I had replied there, wouldn't be possible 'if it's terribly limited by its own stories; limited by its own understanding of its vision! A vision that's not discretionally accommodative but brackets itself into suffocatingly narrower domains as it progresses.'

THE PROBLEM OF FINITENESS AND DISCONTINUITIES

They blame him who sits silent,
They blame him who speaks much,
They also blame him who says little,
There's no one on earth who is not blamed.

– **Dhammapada**

I could see no reason why Pratap Sinha travelled all the way from Dehradun, bearing expensive flight tickets to and fro. His presence hardly filled a gap but concretized a discontinuity. He had started the 'Meditation Lab', which itself appeared absurd and the Lab was a target of several trustees including the moribund senior Managing Trustee's contempt (I am conscious of the implication of using a word like 'moribund' but diplomacy is no way to deal with a new reality). The senior Managing Trustee himself was a 'discontinuous' entity having become a trustee without an agenda—except that he had retired and nothing much existed in his career. The laboratory was another instance of discontinuity with quasi-scientific justification from 'Quantum Physics Quackery'. The lab looked more like an inventory of exotic instruments gathered from around the world.

Forget all these, my own appearance as a learning consultant (everyone called me a General Manager there) was 'discontinuous' with everyone's agenda of what needs to be done. I looked like a half-baked school principal hardly enough to steer an elite organization. The senior Managing Trustee hilariously went on advising me about how he would train me to be leading a spiritual organisation and to take sessions on spiritual matters! It was an irritant at best and a cosmic absurdity at its worst.

What we had was a perfect battlefield of 'fault-finding' experts. There were several such and I am taking this one for exploration with reference to the disruption of new timings I described above.

This takes us to an important concept in understanding human cognition: Fundamental Attribution Errors—(I became familiar with this term in Rolf Dobelli's 'The Art of Thinking Clearly')

Attribution 1—'new rules' is the reason for the 'upset'

Attribution 2—Jagdish is the reason behind the 'rules';

Attribution 3—Jagdish doesn't understand 'change management'

Actual analysis—

Actual analysis is my part of the story here! There cannot be anything 'actual' in the factual happening.

Jagdish has made those changes, which is reversible, in constant consultations with the trustees, staff and volunteers—a product of weekly and monthly review meetings for around twelve consecutive weeks and consistent attempts at change! The Treasurer and the Joint Managing trustee who were to look after the operations on behalf of the whole trust and to whom Jagdish had to report were involved in the whole enterprise.

The whole of these and other changes were part of an exercise - which is summarized below - as was created back then. The intent was to design a holistic model, which include the discussions and meetings cited above but designed out of constant interaction with one of the lean management experts from Israel who had offered her services free of cost to us during her visit to India.

As a Lead Learning Consultant (at least that is the way I looked at myself), with help from an expert, Jagdish had created the following model, which invokes participation amongst all, including visitors, volunteers, employees, trustees and also vendors. The following is the dashboard on which the transformation was envisioned. The tables that are mentioned here were to be a part of our communication to the world outside and to ourselves! They were designed to appear as aesthetic notices in the forefront - near the reception area of the campus - of our presentation to the world.

What can you expect from PVI!

Expectation is personal! It varies. Broadly, we expect ourselves to be—

1. Organizationally Efficient
2. Socially Responsible
3. Legally Right
4. Scientifically Authentic
5. Attentive to the needs of the world!

We aspire to the above...

Organizationally Efficient

We aren't wasteful!

Neither we waste our time nor do we want you to waste yours.

Our success is in the quickest way we can take you to what we do best—MEDITATION, SHARING EXPERIENCES, BOOK READING and HOW YOU CAN GROW WITH US and ALSO HELP US GROW!

How best can we enhance your meditative experience? Is our constant reflection.

Feed us back on when we aren't quick; quick without hurrying!

Socially Responsible

INTELLECTUAL GROWTH, EMOTIONAL SECURITY and MASTERY are our keywords.

'Meditation' and 'inner-scapes' are our ultimate Dharma!

We believe these lead to aesthetics and symmetry; symmetry in our ethical consumption and in the way we treat mother earth, fellow human beings and the way we manage our space.

We aspire to be plastic-free, lesser wasteful each day and cause least collateral damage; we seek your participation in this.

Satisfaction is in RESPONSIBILITY; emotional security is in SERVICE; intellectual growth is in EXCELLENCE.

We abide by them.

Legally Right

We enjoy following the rules of the game.

We exhibit extraordinariness in our adaptability and malleability! Because we intend to serve.

We go beyond just following the norms. We adhere to the ethical spirit behind what we follow.

Pollution Free, Water and Waste Management, Safe Human Environment and Statutorily complete are our mantras!

Scientifically Authentic

The campus is an invitation to experience your inner landscape authentically.

There's no ideal 'inner-scape' and whatever is, is good enough.

We only communicate our experience and nothing else. We, to the best possible way, substantiate what we say.

Our laboratory, our BookSpace are explorations of our actual collective experiences.

We will remain genuine.

Attentive to the needs of the world

Be it sustainability, stress, health, human aspirations, relationships… or whatever the present world needs are, we stand by it.

We will respond to it in completion. We will not be wasteful but be productive and volunteer to serve.

We are going to be 'unreasonable' in our quest to a better world.

We will remain malleable to suit ourselves to the needs of the world.

The steps towards these broadly defined outcomes and framework had their own benefits and travails. Certain outcomes are listed below.

Outcome—

1. Increase in General Donations and donations in kind by around 500%

2. Creation of an organic farm—in 2 months making us self-sufficient in vegetables; PVI practices 'Nitya Annadana' (free food served to all visitors) and we became self-sufficient; total market value of vegetables grown—80k

3. Spic and span campus (images available from a presentation made to the board)

4. Establishing legal structure and statutory compliances—immediately recall property insurance, visitor database, foreign

guests database, electrical line, FSSAI licensing and CCTV coverage

Jagdish had also tried softer handling and had found it difficult to influence certain departments—chiefly security, MeditationLab and BookSpace. Because all of them were discrete entities and attempts at unifying them as an integrated offering of one institution also had resulted in another refrain on Jagdish—'a control freak'. A security team is never completely available for a fulsome interaction. At the same time, attempts were being made to fix some standard formats and people at key interface points and train them extensively in softer visitor management. Similarly, tags for residents and cards for privileged visitors had been thought out and implementation planned. (the passive voice is intentional—it's a 'newspaper report' LOL)

This kind of Fundamental Attribution Error as in, "Hitler was responsible for World War 2" or "Edison invented the light bulb" minimizes and trivializes the whole complexity of the context. This is reflective of the 'strands' of the story that become alive fragmentarily as characterized by modern narratives described in the introduction. Hitler's hate towards Jews had at least a millennium worth of background, spanning across a continent and is embedded in the theology of certain religions. Anti-Semitism is not an offshoot thought of a Hitler. It has a background. When we care to know this in entirety, we would never trivialize or escape in easy condemnation or eulogy. The background to Hitler's peculiar hatred is also seen emanating in the rich texts of Shakespeare and Marlowe and modern intellectuals like George Bernard Shaw. Hitler wasn't alone. He was a context.

Similarly, to fundamentally attribute a security guard's tangential behaviour is to be under the clutches of a personal story, always sanctified and refined in its multiple narratives. (I do not intend to describe it as something wrong but the very way in which human beings operate and I am not an exception to it). A personal story is still a personal story, a small narrative and not an epic still!

Probably this simple narrative has a broader background—an unemployed Nepali youth had newly joined the organization as a security guard. And the decision about a new procedure (of closing the gate after 7 pm and restricting entry of general visitors to general areas) reaches this poor employee in a grossly exaggerated form, and he is all eager to do his job well in all his insecurity. The obliging nature of a hapless employee, absence of an appropriate support system, etc. would have led to entry restriction at the gate - without the flexibility of a seasoned employee. The ever-saluting, helpless security guard is a quintessential representative of our broader society—hierarchical, command-follow system.

Our responsibility lies in broadening these narratives. Even I was refused an entry by an unfamiliar guard, but that didn't perturb me as the entire story was available to me. When troubled, we have just ended up with discrete Quantum Mechanical particulate, thinking that to be universal, without even aspiring to see the wave-qualities of the whole continuous entity. The 'upsets' we all experienced were part of humanity's story of feudal entitlement and privileges; there's nothing substantial about it. These 'upsets' ultimately found its way to the Board Meetings and the whole pandemonium that resulted was reverse confabulation: disjointed series of upsets without a head or tail to it. It was the ultimate knee-jerk activism! There's was no one who could narrate the entire story and there was no sane voice that emerged from these meetings. All the interest was in assuaging 'upsets'.

Within your organization what attributions are fundamental and tacit but present? There's a story that remains incomplete and thousands of these incompletions are running the company; not really the space that was once created.

What's the solution?

I would suggest several out of which two are critically important as far this model goes!

A. **Criticality of creating a prototype.** PVI being a public trust remained amorphous; a crystallized central prototype was missing. Work was too random and not all questions were equally treated as is listed in the boxes described as our project. When prototype isn't created in the form of 'knowledge transfer' models or transition from one Managing Trustee to another, as in the case of PVI, work remains arbitrary and random and nobody takes responsibility. My journal notes during these times of transition are recorded thus—

Humans are ontological. The ontological essence of a human being lives on stories. Stories many times aren't limited to the present but a projection of a past; they invariably generate multiple versions even within a single enterprise and creates chaos if it has not yoked itself to the centre. It has happened with PVI and the examples from the world of corporate are many.

Many a time, our own upsets with a particular form of governance, organizational culture, etc. generate actions for us. There's a momentum to our being, which should be acknowledged....

.... and that takes us to the 2nd critical element here—

B. **Handling 'upsets'** and distinguishing between the models that handle them while treating all human 'upsets' as equally significant!

Many a time the real issue is when 'upsets' are seen as infinite. It follows from a refusal to acknowledge the finiteness of any upset. When upset becomes the *'sanatana'*, what it causes is the repetitiveness of a past momentum. So, it would be valuable to see that—

1. *'Upsets' are finite.*

2. *It's located within—what, when and how something happened.*

3. *A 'finite upset' can be resolved—it's just easy!*

4. *We don't dissolve it but add-on because there's an advantage in that—it becomes a source of our evening conversation or helps us avoid responsibility and truthful communication.*

'Upsets' possess an extraordinary appetite—it can dissolve anything into itself and appropriate the same. 'Upsets' do not allow anything to stand on its own—in its bare skeletal framework. It builds its muscles, strength and density from the numerous stories it continues to create. What it generates is the reasons for the existence of everything mediocre—including the absence of excellence.

Reasons cripple the whole enterprise called excellence!

A matter of being unreasonable—

Transformation stops with reasons.

Transformation demands unreasonableness

When organizations are built or when people get into it for specific reasons—better pay, pleasant environment, freedom, even influenced by declared organisational missions etc. (which are by themselves very important), and limit themselves to it because their previous 'upsets' have not been resolved in their earlier avatars, we can no longer take them to the intended point of the organization itself.

What is actually needed? Commitment!

Commitment demands 'unreasonableness'—doing something even when no agreement exists, striving for agreement, continuing even when criticized, ability to take blame and criticism, working hard, going beyond formulae, accepting failures and mistakes. How does it become impossible to achieve in some organizations? Read the box describing a *'Chakli Organization.'*

Well-crafted 'upsets' and leaders who are articulate and adept with their stories may not forge excellence! Many a time, their satisfaction with their articulation alone becomes sufficient for them and is the chief barrier.

CHAKLI Organisation

'Chakli' is a popular South Indian snack familiar to the Indian readers here. Made of flour and fried, it is characterised by a continuous spiralling convolution of strands tightly knit. Rather than depending on the description here one may check the internet images for it.

Just like a 'chakli' an organisation may be convoluted. When everybody has access to everyone else, and especially if the vision and mission are unclear, it's a perfect case of 'chakli' organisation. And politics is the only way out - not merit or excellence!

Without active learning apparatuses with in an organisation, the vision statements may become childish defences of inefficiency. Many Chakli organisations defend their mediocrity and lack of productivity by resorting to the vision statements and values. The organisational leadership may refuse to see that values are to be understood in newer versions. For instance, an organisation may refuse to fire an incongruous employee because that apparently contradicts their value of compassion.

And everyone has access to everyone else without the needed discipline of an established communication chain, these very access becomes cause of self-defence and furthering of politics: coteries and build-up of support structure to ward off one's own insecurity.

'CHAKLI ORGANISATION' is a term that I invented during one of my conversations with my brother

In the next chapter, there's an examination of the presence of 'ghosts'—the pasts that are determining who we are in the present!

"Turning and turning

in the widening gyre,

the Falcon cannot hear the Falconer."

As we come to the end of the chapter, it could be meaningful to look into the prominent questions here—

1. What 'upsets' remain in the organization—either expressed or unexpressed? Not to start solving it and become yet another knee-

jerk series or re-activism as was seen in the beginning of the story 'necessity' earlier in the section, but to start looking at the eternal quality of these 'upsets'—the substratum of sorrow playfully put!

2. How are these 'upsets'—either in trying to prevent its onset again or reacting to what's already there—preventing you from looking at what really needs to be done? In other words, is the '*Paramahamsa*' alive or the '*Purohita*' at work? If neither of them is, then there a substantial amount of attention we may have to put into this; just to ensure that we are either absolving the team from its past or trying to invent a new vision.

3. What is 'upset' for you in the organization? In the attempts to look at it, we may be looking at it very personally or vaguely. The exercise itself needs attention. There's a substratum of inner work that's generating quite a bit of these 'upsets', which are personal, tangentially orbiting around the central locus.

Examine the chapters 'WHERE ARE THE GHOSTS?' In this section and also 'REGENERATION OF THE CEO' in the next; try putting the 3rd question in context. When upsets are personal organizational leadership will have to take a skewed look at developing people but not handling 'upsets' there. (skewed look is to look at it bending our head to one side so that what appears starts appearing different.)

CHAPTER 3

Where Are the Ghosts?

All that we are is a result of what we have thought,

It is founded on our thoughts,

It is made up of our thoughts.

– Dhammapada

Life precedes sound,

Sound precedes language,

Language has nothing…

– ANONYMOUS

'Here, life is the end and Ghosts have no meaning'—page 57, Zen and the Art of Motorcycle Maintenance

When Ghosts have no meaning, transformation becomes impossible!

'Apa sarpantu ye bhoota

Ye bhoota Bhoomisamstita

Ye Bhoota Vignakartaraha

Tenashyantu Shivagnya.'

(Lose translation of the above verse as per my own understanding: **the all pervading existence - populated by ghosts - is the entire world and**

creation; they are the barrier and the rift and let them be annihilated by the orders of Shiva)

Bhagiratha, one of the greatest kings of the lineage of the Sun God, takes on the enterprise of bringing Ganga down to the earth from the abode of the Gods. The reason is to liberate all his ancestors who had been burnt to ashes due to sage Agastya's inadvertent gaze (a detailed story by itself). The sacred Ganges flowing over their ashes would liberate them!

Earlier his ancestors including Emperors Sagara and Dilipa had failed. The project of bringing the Ganga was by no means a mean task. Just being a part of such a project looked good, it's historical and has huge impact and dimensions. But without a past they were crippled - nobody before had tried doing it; also, human efforts are diluted by dropping out in-between - both had dropped out.

Bhagiratha takes it on. Equipped with the story of the past and resolved with his emotional skills he somehow convinces both Ganga and the gods for this noble enterprise - liberating his ancestors. Having been permitted by the gods the issues remain to be resolved: the flow of Ganga is indisputably a blessing, but the current can destroy the world itself? Who will handle this? Who is equipped to handle the violence of the cascade?

To search for someone who will handle the vibrations, waste and noise is an imminent necessity. The thrill of creation isn't a match to the drudgery of protection. Bhagiratha had to search for one such. He found lord Shiva who himself is a recluse. Continuous prayers and Shiva agrees to hold Ganga in his flowing hair. The cascade was harnessed.

Shiva removes the noise and necessary toxins of any endeavour. He is the destroyer who harmonises everything.

The enterprise is never as romantic as the summarization portrays it!

Since our life ends here, our search doesn't go beyond life. Our obsession for the search also, like the famous story where the lost pin is searched for where the light is instead of where it was lost, doesn't end! It attains a feverish pitch—an immeasurable cascade! A 'cascade' is a 'cascade'. It flows uncontrollably. As the famous story from the *Puranas* on the descent of River

Ganga goes, even a well-intended cascade should be held benevolently. To just summarize the story for the context, find it in the adjoining box!

It So Happened—[39]

> *The furious Ashwathama vengefully wanted to end the whole of Kuru Clan. And with the lone promise of Uttara's pregnancy carrying the Kuru offspring from the late Abhimanyu, Yudhisthira sighed relief.*
>
> *Ashwthama's notorious anger and Yudhisthira's single hope emanated from the same womb. The former had no qualms using the Brahmastra (the epitome of all astras—weapons) on the hapless, young widowed pregnant woman.*
>
> *Uttara, carrying the baby in the womb, fears not for her life but for her unborn one. She resorts to the refuge of all Pandavas—Krishna; she prays to save the baby. Krishna enters the womb and neutralizes the Brahmastra!*
>
> *And the story continues....*
>
> *The baby born as Vishnurata is keen to meet the one it had met, as a foetus, in the womb. So Vishnurata starts examining everyone he meets to check whether the person is an acquaintance from the womb. This examination is called 'pariksha' in Sanskrit and the young toddler comes to be called 'Parikshita'—the one who examines! Since Parikshita keeps searching himself for something he got acquainted before birth, he may have to reach the point he was in before birth!*
>
> *Instead, his empirical search reaches nowhere!*

---

39 The story is quite popular to be described from its source. As the story goes Ashwathama, Dronacharya's son, is lenient towards Duryodhana - the Kaurava king. Durodhana in his constant opposition to the Pandavas and what in popular legends is termed as injustice to the Pandavas, wages a war and loses it. The fallen Duryodhana generates uncontrollable grief in Ashwatama out of which he decides to end the whole Pandava clan and also kill the new born growing in the Uttara's womb - the child would be Parikhshita and is the third generation for the Pandavas. The version of the story here is one of the several!

The days go by and the 'fundamental act' of his creation is forgotten (the convenience of being forgetful)...

Once on a hunting spree, tired and exhausted, he reaches Rishi Shamika's Ashram (hermit). He seeks water and Rishi Shamika, unaware, doesn't respond. Angry and thirsty Parikshita garlands the Rishi with a dead snake. But the Rishi, still unaware, continues his meditation.

A little later, Rishi Shamika's son Shinagi notices this absurdity and curses king Parikshita with death by snakebite in 7 days.

The news of curse cascades into Parikshita's awareness...

Parikshita stares

at the visible end

blunt meaninglessness...

What's the meaning?

As death stares at him, and devoid of any meaning, he is shaken. Seeks Shuka's counsel in pain.

Futility... dry futility; what is it all?

And Shuka narrates the Mahabharata!

Pariskhita's intense interest in life (to know life itself) begins with 'death'.

Without the end in perspective, the current attains no meaning.

His interest grows about his ancestors—the Bhootas that brought him into the world—why did Vidura go for a pilgrimage? What happened in Khandava Dahana? He wants to inherit his whole past; acknowledge every inch of his existence!

* * * * *

Knowledge Is Entropic and the CEO Inherits the Past!

When Vyasa narrated Mahabharata for the first time, it was 8000 verses. Probably it was succinct, pithy and elliptical (details left-out as it was understood, known). By the time Janamejaya (son of Parikshita, grandson of Abhimanyu and great-grandson of Arjuna) hears 'Bharata' from Vaishampayana, it had expanded to a total of 26,000 verses—the total narrative of the core story—Kurukshetra, family feuds and tussles, etc., it still remained a mystery till about seven centuries later, when it expanded to 100000 verses[40].

No longer was the original sufficient. In fact, the hidden, related stories of Rishya-Shrunga, Vashishta's suicide attempt, Nala-Damayanthi, Nahusha, Bruhadashva and Yayati are far more beautiful than the clichéd Pandava-Kaurava conflict and the Kurukshetra. It expands and becomes relevant as it progresses.

As we are dwelling into it, we need even further elaborations of certain stories within the Mahabharata. And not just one version of it but several of them!

Similarly, these narratives which are added with time also expand and vary with region. So knowledge, that adapts itself to the situation and time, is never and can never remain the same!

The cosmology of a speck of sand

is the Universe

The cosmology of the Mahabharata lives on. It's ever alive and omnipresent!

It's all the Kshetra

that's the entirety,

---

40   I have heard several versions similar to this on the development of Mahabharata into an epic. The version mentioned here is the notes I took from listing to Shatavadhani R. Ganesh, an immaculate scholar. Numbers mentioned could be in variation with what was mentioned.

that hillock over there is where

Krishna lived, Rama rested and Bheema slayed Baka...

That's all to life!

The Fundamental act of Creation

Building on 'what we know'—a theme that I became acquainted with from the book 'Creative Intelligence'—there's really no scope for creating anything. Creation, including great businesses and products, is essentially 'knowledge mining'. The hugely successful Roomba Robots, described in the book, wasn't a 'flash of insight' but an investment of time and hardwork—floating in a space that doesn't exist. That is a difficult space to be in. For in that space, nothing really happens and the ghosts hovering around simply want to occupy anybody like the exigencies of an unemployed youth ready to take on any job or work. It's hard to be in that space, disembodied and identity-less. But that's the space, one can presume, the MIT Roboticists occupied when they were creating Roomba. Infosys and Narayana Murthy represent that ambiguity in a struggle that appeared to reach nowhere.

Herbalife, a global giant in nutrition we will discuss briefly later in Section 3, was a product of its Founder's, Mark Hughes', six-year hiatus in the vacuum of ghosts-land attending Chinese symposia on herbal medicine and several hitherto untested concoctions before the creation of an everlasting masterpiece of a company. Mark Hughes died in 2000, but his legacy has grown in stature and Herbalife is a highly respected global 'cult' today!

One may tentatively conclude that it's when the leaders exhibit phenomenal emotional strength to withstand the ghost-land do they create stories—the *Puranas*—that the 'cult' considers it worthy of pursuing. To acknowledge the ghosts that were once, and hence constantly operating through us now, is to expand the domain of what was always known. In the expanded domain of knowing is born **Buddha, The CEO; Buddha, The CEO** is born in the ghost-world. In other words, Buddha, The CEO is born in a spiritual realm what Master Patriji had once referred to as 'the science of the invisible'.

Without having had the privilege of spending enough time in the ghost-land Maulvik, our protagonist form Chapter 2 of Section 1, created an accidental renaissance! A renaissance that could never replicate itself. Without replicability and without an availability to attain avatars, leadership is stuck in a mould.

There are several kinds of ghosts. One that's prominent in organizations is described in Steve Saffron and Dave Logan's enviably simple but a profound masterpiece 'Three Laws of Performance', referred to in the previous chapter. It describes a general scenario thus—

> *'If you went into the company (described earlier), and got employees talking about their future, they will talk something like **it will never work out. We're mired in politics, so when we do bring a product to market, it's two years too late, and that's not going to change. Our leaders will never lead—it's not in them. We'll just waste away until we are bought or shut down.***

> *Although most people have never really articulated what they think will happen to them personally or organizationally, they live every moment as if it's destined to come about. Employees are reduced to going through the motions, never fully engaging, never taking on the politics that they believe is holding the company back.*

> *If you interviewed the leaders in this company, you'd hear a future that is correlated with what the employees describe, something like **people here don't care, and they never will. We invite their ideas, but they never come through with anything good. We don't have the money to replace them with star performers'***

The ghosts hang, unarticulated and never acknowledged. Without appropriate company rituals to propitiate them into embodiment, they remain and perpetuate their existence subliminally. Euphemistically referred to as company culture, it is dominated by these 'ghosts' and despite years of toil in the art of improvement—towards 'more, better, different and faster'—the wheel appears to be stuck as the above-described scenario that the company demonstrates. The book goes on to describe the three fundamental laws of performance and one that is pertinent to us here is the first one—'*how people perform correlates to how situations occur to them*'.

Buddha dealt with the reality of things. The 'nature of things' as is described by David Bohm reflecting Nagarjuna's theory that reverentially replicated Buddha's teachings into the scholarship of the then ancient university thesis. In the traditions of Indian logic, there is a similar one that is succinctly mentioned—a characteristic of Sanskrit language—as '*rajjusarpo nyaya*'—the logic of a rope appearing as a snake. As long as a rope appears to be a snake, our handling it lacks the simplicity of a rope. There's an inherent complexity in the handling of a 'snake'. It's 'Buddhahood' in leadership that would see that the nature of things is not what's painted by our mind. At the level of 'Buddhahood' it is not difficult to see what an expensive bargain it is to either miss the point or misunderstand it in terms of the possibility of performance in a company, but reaching Buddhahood may have a transitional point—ideal self-expression of the Rama Avatar which in turn follows the need for discipline in cutting away the fears that dominate leadership.

'Three Laws of Performance' goes on to describe inspiring stories of transformation. One stands apart among others. This is the story of the South African Mining Company Lonmin Corporation, the third-largest producer of platinum in the world. Endowed with suspicion between the local populace of blacks living in abject conditions and their disparity with their leadership form the richer Whites community, Lonmin suffered extensive damage and was at the brink of closure. Brad Mills, the new CEO, initiates new action that tackles the ghosts of suspicion and disparity head-on—not merely in sloganeering and rhetoric but in action; authentic action that included Mills having had to sleep in the workers' hostels despite the expressed dangers of doing so. What ensues is an emotionally reverberating transformation of not just a company but the community itself.

In a 'future rewritten,' it turned out into an extraordinary act of courage and community enterprise. Here's a brief that I have sculled out from the book—

1. Productivity reached historical heights of one-million-plus platinum ounces.

2. Decrease in lost-time injuries by approximately 43 percent. A reduction that continues to be sustained.

3. International Financial Corporation (IFC) of the World Bank invested $100 million towards a self-sufficient Greater Lonmin Community.

The above are the tangibles but a shift in the whole populace about the possibility of living a life of freedom and happiness is what actually the most gratifying thing about this transformation exercise is.

As described in the previous chapter, I failed in such a possibility of transformation in Pyramid Valley International. Without being able to build a community that trusts and despite my strong feelings for it, I could never help my leadership see the need for dropping a counter lawsuit on one of its own trustees and building reparation not only with the trustees who felt wronged but also with the local community who had carried a hope (based on a promise) that Pyramid Valley would bring about a huge transformation in their lives. And most importantly, to begin with, were the volunteers and employees who never saw a commitment from any leadership there. Senior and powerful trustees would order the hapless employees around to bring them cigars and liquor, food from the cafeteria and the *annadana*, which was never accounted for. Trust meetings, as some employees who had access could see, hardly focused on real work but terrible bickering. The safest thing was to remain indecisive and be a part of a coterie rather than being part of the whole story.

For me to have been able to do that, what I needed was not just intelligence and higher emotional quotients—which are both important—but an ability to propitiate the ghosts. My chief ghosts were insecurity and a fear that compelled me to diplomacy where I should not have been. And such!

The point is Pyramid Valley International could never translate into reality what is described in the boxes in the previous chapter—especially one that related to working so that the 'globe pays attention to it'. Without having propitiated the ghosts of performance, Lonmin would have never catapulted itself into an extraordinary community of camaraderie that created a world, which would renew itself in a thousand different ways. All along Lonmin was 'on a collision course with the *default* future'. A *default* future where, as the book says, 73 percent of change efforts fail and 70 percent of new strategies fall short of expectations.

Here's where our circle is getting into shape. We had seen the following passage, almost verbatim, in the introduction. We are arriving at it again, iterating it here with a new set of experiences—

The moment a CEO becomes part of an organization, she inherits the organization's entire past. A CEO inherits the complete spectrum of an organization's past. And it depends on the CEO how meaningfully she inherits the past, iteratively; 'iteration' is to reuse knowledge in much more functional and meaningful ways by integrating new experiences into the past of who we are or who we have become. The significance of this formulation can be amplified as we go ahead in the exercise of reading the book.

To explicate the above point a little further, it could be appropriate to explore some interesting theorizations on the way things exist. David Bohm in his now-famous interview with David Suzuki, suggests an 'implicate order' to things. There's an 'enfolded' order to the nature of things. We have access to only the 'explicate order'—the 'unfolded' nature of things. What is explicit is just microscopical vis-à-vis the continuum of causation.

Lest we become too esoteric, and also because unless used up in a context familiar to us, this will continue to be slippery, it makes sense to look at a corresponding allegory. Imagine there's a towel in front of you (or anything!). That towel exists because there's a form, shape and colour to it, which our retina captures. And our retina is able to cause this visibility due to the physiology, which supports it from the background, and the physiology in turn because of the support system in the form of life-energy within the body and so forth ad infinitum.

Nagarjuna, a proponent of Buddhist practices and widely acknowledged for the spread of Buddhism in a structured format, propounds a similar theory in his *'pratitya samutpada'* explicated in his *karikas*. He reasons out a continuum of cause-effect juxtapositions. As we saw in the towel illustration, what exists is actually an infinite series of cause-effect couples! There's no reality to address!

In that sense, the battles we are waging are not even ours.

In other words, it's simply as the adapted quote from Philip Roth's 'The Counterlife' in **'Insights and Distinctions, Landmark Essays Volume 1'**—'the worm in the dream is always the past, that impediment to all renewal'.

THE POINT WHERE EVERYTHING BEGINS[41]

So, the event is not at all ours. It all began somewhere in the infinite past. Without a grip on this past, one cannot substantially manoeuvre the present and also that in the present can one access the infinite past.

What's new in the leadership cupboard? What's getting cooked? What's occupying the leadership's consciousness? Could be the most important questions of the present.

This present point is where we begin!

The point where everything begins - the present - is a point of 'pure' potential. A

A DIMENSIONLESS POINT

---

point where 100% more is still possible. That's the moment available to all of us right now.

It is a point where no leadership is possible; or to put it slightly differently, a special kind of leadership alone can stay there. Leader is '*nayaka*' and '*vinyaka*' can mean special leadership or the absence of leadership itself—absolute anarchy! The prefix 'vi' here stands for '*vishesh*'—special. Or it can also mean, 'nothing is sure; anything could happen' as if it's pure anarchy!

Another name is '*dhumra varna*'—the smoke coloured; foggy. Still unclear as to what it will manifest as.

Because manifestation is a single point game—you either manifest something or not. But the point is a station of infinite possibilities. It's a junction. All categories co-exist there. That is the place of '*ganapathy*'—the lord of all (infinite) possibilities.

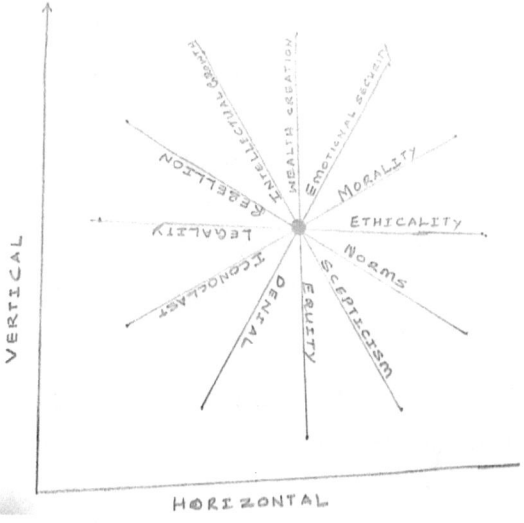

And the Indian knowledge systems speak of him as someone who resides in the '*mooladhara*'—the bottom-most chakra. '*mooladhare sthitosi nityam*'—you are the one established at the point, says one of the *vedamantra*.

The 'point' is maintained by some kind of equilibrium. Look at the corresponding diagram. The *ethics, morality, norms, legality, a desire to be different, rebellion, growth and cynicism* hold the point. A point of high tension and stress—a point of infinite possibilities.

There's no leadership here. No one can lead. All possibilities are fully alive. It's really foggy.

Constantly human lives and organizational patterns come to these points of standstill. And every point is a point of 100 percent more. And every point is foggy.

THE GROWTH MIND

Hold and Release...

The human biology is designed to 'sustain' and 'evolve'!

The combination of mitochondria and nucleus is what helps us! The sustaining force is the mitochondria with its ability to process the raw material and converting it into propulsion; the nucleus provides the blueprint, a directionality to the energy that's being consumed.

'Enough of poetry', one may probably say. But 'poetic prose' is the cutting edge of life itself. When one is sure that it can never be said but saying becomes important, one resorts to poetry. Poetry, with its figures and licentious use of language, obliterates our sense of reality and there's no way to distinguish it from what's unreal. Prose happens a long time after the poetry. In the history of literature, prose is relatively a recent phenomenon. Prose explicates what poetry captures. Hence, let me begin with some prosaic formulations also—

As societies and communities grow in complexity, knowledge gets reduced to its utmost simplicity—the basic tenets and commandments. For our ordinary circumstances, we may not want to ponder into the intricacies of Biblical verses. The commandments will do. But as we dwell deep into the Bible, knowledge starts emanating in different forms.

Knowledge is essentially complex and intricate; it's the 'truth'—a multiplicity web; dialogic like the *Rudra*[42]. In the *Vedic* traditions, *Rudra*

---

42 *Rudra* is the shorter expression of *Namakam* chantings one finds in the *vedas*. It invokes the names of Shiva and in the invocation one finds that Rudra is the celebration of existence in its varied forms. Rudra celebrates the low and the high, the thief and the righteous, the chariot and charioteer - all binaries are unified into one whole!

is the sum total of all potential manifestations and in our human capacity, we invoke the gentler one—Shankara; but Rudra is the celebration of everything.

But knowledge is (probably has to be) reduced to the basic tenets and as commandments, penal codes and constitutional law take over, knowledge tends to become subservient to the social needs, - the necessities of the subsistence of the collective! It almost becomes impossible to penetrate what is 'known' and shift into the realm of what we are collectively indifferent about.

This is a sentiment that's Buddha reflects in his advice to Maha Kassapa when the latter spurns to advice the monks contemptuous of the degradation he sees in the new monks. Buddha advises calmly and with compassion to compile His teachings into texts, which will obviously be not the same, but the *Dhamma* will not be affected. *Dhamma*, Buddha says, will be affected only if one lacks respect for the five things—the Buddha—the wise one; the *Sangha*—the congregation; the *Dhamma*—the path; for the training and meditative contemplation. The Buddha recognizes the inevitability of knowledge boiling down to 'engineering ego' (an expression I came across in a newspaper article that criticized the flood management methods)—to see that everything can be broken down to its mechanistic entities and each of these can be solved separately to get to the final solution. The belief, as we saw in Chapter 1 of Section 1, is that everything can be overhauled. Without the contemplative practices - and guidance - the great learning will remain mechanistic fragments—nicely packaged seminar presentations!

There's a static text and dynamic possibilities. How do we reconcile these dynamics in the terrains of the eternal dance of the 'static' and the 'dynamic'?

Let me begin by putting a popular chant for our reckoning right away—

Om bhuhu

Om bhuvaha

Ogum suvaha

Om mahaha

Om Janaha

Om tapaha

Ogum satyam

Tatsa viturvarenyam

Bhargo devasa dheemahi

Dheeyoyonaha prachodayaat

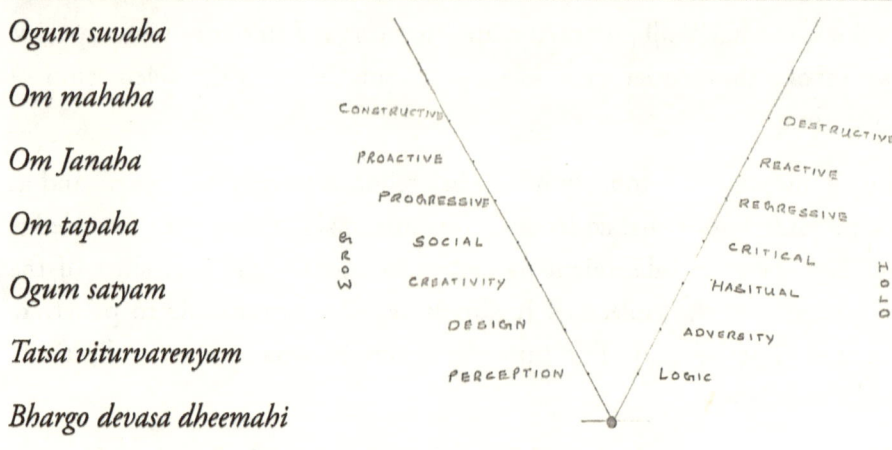

This is the popular chanting that most of us from India are familiar with. Familiarity doesn't mean mastery, but these chanting are ubiquitous in temples, rituals and many other occasions of public gathering. Probably friends from communities other than the Hindu should also be quite familiar with the sounds. It is the initial beginning mantras in the *Sandhyavandana*—the prayer for and of the transition.

Each of these sounds represents what are called '*lokas*'—the dimensions of our contributing mindset represented in the diagram by the left wing of the 'v'. The contributing mindset is balanced by the countering limiting factors termed as '*talas*'—here the right part of 'v'.

Unlike the depiction in the popular culture '*lokas*' and '*talas*' are not the domain of the gods and demons respectively but the confluence of apparent contradictions, beneficial when together.

Coming to the point—the diagram, which for representational purposes is shown as a 'V' is, in fact, a zig-zag ladder (an eternal dance of strands) when lines are drawn between one on the left wing to the right and from the one on the right to the next on the left. A zig-zag ladder is more comprehensive. One may recall the 'basis of life' and 'unit of life' illustrations that mimicked DNA strands in the earlier chapter of the previous section.

This is a scheme I adopted from a session I attended called 'Know Yourself' with the Temple of Learning in Bangalore. The logic is this—an entity, or a business, begins when one perceives a possibility of an idea. And once an idea is conceived, it has a romantic edge and excitement about it and remains too effervescent until it's held by logical questions like—where will the money come from? Is it unique? Is it worth it? etc. Once these dimensions put forth by 'logic' is accepted as necessary frames, we 'design' a system, which in turn will have to be nurtured by 'adverse' situations that crop up. Like this, the zig-zag ladder lines connecting 'perception' to 'logic' to 'design' to 'adversity' and so on, goes all the way to the level of being 'constructive'.

Equally evocative and pertinent to the point of our discussion is another I heard from Vilas, my friend who runs courses on Bagawadgeeta and Buddhist scriptures, in one of his sessions with us. I list them along with the notes I made as I heard him—

'Bhuhu' is the first existence while 'bhuvaha' is re-existence, which happens in forgetting the reasons for existence thereby creating incessant cycles of existential repetition; 'suvaha' is when, for the first time, the being realizes that there's a 'mistake'—something absurd about this repetition. This is a plane where one starts looking at what exactly this futile repetition is for. Since things, which appear, and end, it cannot have a definite meaning in these to be taken very seriously.

'Mahaha' involves a search for the body—an existence where this can be examined and experimented with again. To be happy in realization.

'Janaha' and 'tapaha' is to see the cycle of repetitions. Strategies, process and to see that, as mentioned in Three Laws of Performance, 70 percent don't yield results. It's available socially to see how the 'best practices' looks meaninglessly absurd to the employees while they hurry to end the day and reach home—a rodent also has an existence; and there is nothing despicable about it. This critical insight is also an opportunity to dismantle and see what 'is'

And the ultimate 'satyam'—the eternal truth without birth and death.

What this 'birth and death' cycle means is to see that it's all continuous re-cycling and regeneration (a theme we will be taking up in a while in Section 3)

Examining Its Relevance—

As the text is growing in its complexity (at least more esoteric), as probably one may see here, we must catch up with it in terms of our own lived realities. Similarly, when the going gets too concrete, it needs to be sublimated with something etheric. This is the nutshell of the above rumination—the 'holding' and 'growing' factors co-exist. What sublimates is held within the confines of what needs to be accomplished in the 'here and now' of our world.

In our ordinary circumstances, our cognitive domain is ill-equipped to grasp the entirety. If I ask you to imagine your house or street, you will probably get a small glimpse of just a negligible segment of the whole. Maybe you get your refrigerator door or the bathroom platform. What you get into your imagination is tangentially different but the whole isn't available to you. Similarly, if I ask a senior executive or a CEO to imagine her company, she may come out with a recent tiff with a colleague or the impending emergency, etc. Cognitively, in the state of survival, we are not equipped to look into the whole. It doesn't make any evolutionary sense— we have been taught since ages to be circumspective as we traverse the jungle observant of the immediate dangers.

In the *Katopansihad*, there's an examination of the sequentiality of the chain of causation—the equivalent of food cycle—in the world of thought and leadership. It goes like this—***the world of objects to be experienced lies lifeless without; its enlivened by our senses which by themselves have no life of their own unless the mind charges it up. And the mind, in turn, is nurtured by the intellect—an agent that distinguishes actions and thoughts as useful or wasteful; and the intellect is fed by the 'atma'—the self!***

These layers are the one that we see in of one of our earlier chapters—the web of excellence. As organizational leaders progress from objects being handled within the organization to the vision that's driving them, the journey is a gradual progression to higher entropy. And many a time, it's much easier handling the immediate ones available in the environment around—a meeting, a phone call or reprimanding someone. There's an element of excitement in handling the concrete but becomes embarrassingly difficult to defend abstract thoughts without the corresponding accomplishments. So grappling with the concrete 'realities' of performance and its apparent connecting factors appear far better than dealing with the abstract.

You may recall that 'the CEO inherits the entire past of the organization'. The sudden and immediate grasp of the entire chain or spectrum of an organization, if available to one, makes leadership extremely palatable. As the authors of 'The Three Laws of Performance', Steve Zafrron and Dave Logan mention in the book, 'there's a significant difference between the objective facts of the matter and the way those facts occur to each of us'. There's an 'occurring world' that we constantly grapple with. The contention is—the occurring world is hidden deeply in the past of who we are as much as the past of the organization.

HOW REAL ARE THESE?

Given the abstract nature of this discourse, a personal anecdote should do good here. I am reluctant narrating this here as it is too personal and small to be indicative of anything. But that's the best I have right now.

> In the year 2003, I dropped out of a government job out of absolute frustration. I was married and had a 9-month-old daughter then. The situation was extremely acute. Two instances should explain that well—once on a bike ride, crossing a railway-gate, my wife fell in a small accident and injured herself. I didn't have the 100 rupees needed for her basic first aid and more than the embarrassment, the frustration with what appeared like utter helplessness was demeaning. In the same line was when I had to shell out around 350 rupees

for my child's vaccination. Earning 5000 rupees in Bangalore was insufficient. It was during these trying times that I did my Sudarshan Kriya in an Art of Living Course and that appeared to be the finest thing that I had done till then. Of course, the breathing technique by itself was enlivening but more than that were the knowledge ingredients—one on acceptance was driven so fantastically by one of the senior AOL teachers Anand Rajendran that till now my grappling with real-life conundrums is guided by it.

The point I am arriving at is simple—acceptance of the present moment involved embracing the whole gamut of who you are and a simple equation with everything that surrounds you. It was profoundly simple.

What added on to my life from then on is tremendously beautiful. This may not be very unusual for many—there have been sudden paradigm changes in several lives. Mine just happened during the course 17 years ago, and that happened by a twist of acceptance.

GROWTH AND PROSPERITY

This is from the notes I took form during my reading of 'The Secret History of the World' by William Booth. And my journal entry mentioned this as from Chapter 23 of the book. These were not directly from the book but sudden and tangential thoughts that emanated from the realities I was grappling with—my daughter's university education and my reflections on what I should do for my life. I find those reflections apt here.

In the immediate section before this, we encountered two illustrations— one on growth that begins from a 'DIMENSIONLESS POINT' and another on the 'horizontal and vertical' growth. Before we dwell on what's growth and prosperity are for us, we may look into some suppositions here based on the notes from my reading of 'The Secret History of the World'.

Growth and prosperity both pre-suppose knowledge. To 'pre-suppose' is to know something even before there's evidence to show its existence. The scientists and explorers during the age of enlightenment were on

one such journey. They presupposed a world to be explored even before its full evidence was available to them; the science of alchemy was another—to create gold out of ordinary matter through occult science.

What may look like evidence is a strange conviction of the person who's stating it or a strange kind of connection to the occult the individual feels for. We all possess this kind of individualistic occult just like how the animals also come to know about the death of its near ones.

So, let's come back to our two initial words—growth and prosperity.

Growth is a vertical target while prosperity is a diffused horizontal spread. Individuals or entities grow because they accumulate more of what existed before—more money, more assets and more growth in other areas of life. As opposed to growth, individuals and entities become prosperous in a sudden realization of what never existed before. Growth entails stress and strain while prosperity let goes off it.

Like Emperor Nero, his mind occupied by the paramount necessity of the growth of his gold and territory that he couldn't even recognize how stressed he was; so stressed that he lost sight of the other equally important areas of life—say the welfare of his citizens. Recorded history is replete with such examples—Hermando Cortes[43] was murdered by his own men, impatient for the gold that lay before them; the same fate stuck Fransisco Pizzaro in Peru. Growth is terribly double-edged and it is risky carrying it all the time.

Prosperity beneficially blunts growth. Prosperity is instinctively known to the Marwari businessmen. The community is known for its philanthropy. Prosperity is to recognize what growth should be doing in the long run and making it happen in the current circumstances itself. In other words, philanthropy is holistic—establishing training

---

43   This incident is mentioned in the book 'The secret History of the World' along with the one that's mentioned about Francisco Pizzaro. Even without it movies like 'Mackennas Gold' make it evident for the modern consumer.

academy, health-care systems, holistic lifestyles, dealing with the highest knowledge.

Both growth and prosperity pre-suppose knowledge without evidence. The growth that we all aspire for is typically without a reason. Why we want to grow our sales by say 25% more or expand our market share by another ten percent can never be answered sufficiently. Growth and prosperity, primordially, presupposes knowledge. The former, if subservient to the latter, creates a phenomenal legacy. Engineering and other technical knowledge, marketing and sales skills which are all geared towards growth are not sufficiently balanced by liberal arts and what is recommended here at this stage is to begin dwelling into the need for internal organizational training academies that are holistic. Lest this appears too impractical and naive (it would be if it's not substantiated well. And even while doing so, one may turn that into objective knowledge of society and culture. I am looking at it not from a design perspective but from the ability to cognize and to be free from it), let me put forth an argument—

> A product that is to be designed is an 'idea'. Once designed and delivered it is done with and has a shape and form. Products have a shape and form while ideas don't have any. Ideas are much more free and one generally sees that despite all the care, the idea is still not the form it has taken. That explains the last minute preparations that we do in all our endeavours and keep on improvising it.

> An 'idea' without a shape is still alive while with a shape and form, it is dead. It does not grow in that form any more.

> The 'idea' has no existence if a human ceases to exist. Whatever 'idea' is already concretized on paper exists, and without it, it ceases. 'idea' happens because a human being 'is' and human being whose existence is ensured due to the 'life force' is more constant than the 'idea' itself.

The 'life force' is the point of 'ideas'—great and small. And 'life force' is given a character by an 'intelligence' as is explained by the Katopanishad.

So the question is—what should be nurtured? A product? Or an ability to think and generate ideas? Expand the 'life force' so that ideas have a source for emergence? Or should we build an organization that is learning and constantly expanding its intelligence?

How do we design our training programmes? What should we focus on?

Sufficient to say this much here—

1. History is still unsure of the great occult philosophy and esoteric knowledge that generated greatest discoveries, inventions and theories—Archimedes, Pythagoras, Newton, Copernicus, Galileo and several more.

2. Walter Raleigh, an anthropologist by modern standards, helped consolidate East India Company, which returned enormous dividends to its shareholders.

3. TESLA today is headed towards what no company has ever done before. A well-known maverick he is, a WhatsApp message that circulated once asked people to apply to TESLA and that their degrees don't matter! Not sure of the veracity but that kind of direct connections without intermediaries are a possibility.

And again, extending that a bit more—

1. A leader's struggle is only till 'success' is attained. To keep ambiguity alive even after 'success' is rather difficult. One more often sees successful businesspersons refusing to deal with ambiguity. This is not to say that one should not have a sophisticated mechanism to filter out what's clearly dung. All that the point tries to mention is that the culture of exploration is what keeps an organization or company free from complacency.

2. Entertain the most 'entropic' knowledge. Meditate, listen to occultists, talk to grandmothers and examine how they gravitate to a presupposed knowledge that lacks evidence.

3. Keep a check on the changing nature of our life orientation, philosophy, etc. which are never permanent.

4. Work on the field. Drop the book (not this one for some time, LOL), refuse to theorize without actual interest and appropriate application or without a background to the field.

IN CONCLUSION

I can urge the readers, who could be executing one or the other complex tasks of human endeavour to reflect on this. Just as *Bhagiratha* (mentioned in the box at the beginning of the chapter) had to consider the 'holder' before bringing down the Ganges from the heavens, any execution requires an examination of factors that would hold. An imagination that dwells on growth but doesn't reflect on the elements that hold fails to sustain and will consistently create false starts; and thought processes that persist on defensive 'holds' may never take—off! Balancing means to acknowledge who you are—and who you are is an acknowledgement of the past that you are!

The Intractability of Ghosts— Should an Organization Be Protected?

Good to begin with questions—

1. *What should be protected?*

2. *Is it worth protecting?*

3. *How does the 'protected' entity serve?*

4. *What's the essence and how will we clear the mess?*

The idea of protection as in the copyrights, patenting and property registration!

We will have to trudge back to the earlier chapter's concept—ghosts. The problem with ghosts is that they aren't traceable, and like the discerning intelligence of a scientist, one has to construct the real out of the faintest hints of indications. Rutherford, for instance, could investigate into a possibility of an atomic model different from his illustrious predecessor J. J. Thompson's just by a hint of the way his ray of alpha-particles bombarding an atom behaved. Though such discoveries are a fascinating reading on Wikipedia, we will have to come face-to-face with the ultimate civilizational questions—so what? What's in it for me?. As an illustration, one could examine how the intangible Quantum Physics, discerned from a pure perception of a scientist, is hacked by the 'serious' business of making bombs and in seminars on the 'Law of Attraction' and manifestation theories. Quantum Physics is used and abused left-right-and centre.

So, the question boils down to what should be protected—a product, the concept of the 'non-existent', or the ability to investigate? Right now, it appears that all are equally important; the tangibles—including systems and processes which are an intersection of need and the idea—and the intangible! As one can see it's a terrible limbo as explored in earlier chapters on 'Where are the Ghosts' and 'Exploring Stuckiness'. We also saw how feeding the 'pitrus'—those hanging out there—as essentially important to push the wait a little more lest they take any form and shape. The wait time has to be protected. The complete form needs a wait time and buildup of the critical mass—so to say.

In the *Mundakopanishad,* one comes across the following verses—

Satyena labhyastata hyesha atma

Smayag jnanena brhamcharyena nityam

Antahsharire jyotirmayo shubhro

Yam pashyanti yatayaha kshinadoshaha

By the practice of and the contemplation on the ultimate subliminal, permanent presence does reality dawn,

In seeing it, in the way of the great seers, as faultless and full of light,

And

Satyameva jayate naanrutam

Sateen panta vitato devayanaha

Yenakramanthrushayo hyaptakaama

Yatra tat satyasya paramam nidhanam

Truth triumphs, not the falsity,

The effortless path of the 'devas' includes this truth.

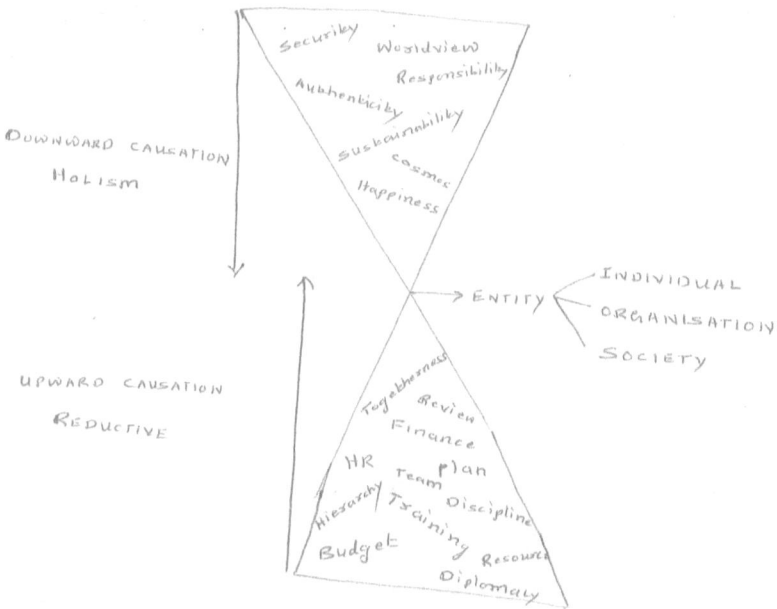

In the commentary, I came across in the book from Ramakrishna Ashrama from where I have quoted these, the Swamji's commentary refers to the path of the *pitrus* as temporary unlike that of the gods, which strike directly to the **ultimate**. The vision appears clear—to choose and protect the expressway of direct reach appears plainly practical. For us, however, since we are dealing with these principles as a transactional intersection between our business and organizational excellence on one side and the esoteric knowledge on the other, we may have to for some time protect both.

The diagram that I have inserted above looks at two triangles intersecting at a junction. I hope the diagram sufficiently represents the necessity of creating a predictable universe, a common shared world in which we all agree to operate, for extraordinary work to happen. It's not a fabian solution to the complex needs of an organization but something more tangible and mundane. It's something that 'regulates' and organizes. A division of the organization based on the functional criteria comes from a reductive approach.

Breakthroughs happen in dynamism. Dynamism is characterized by an exceptional environment of entropic knowledge that doesn't promise anything. When this happens it's holism at play.

Exceptional results are caused, if I am to believe my own train of thoughts, by unshackling ourselves from our conditioned responses. When the whole organization is uniquely structured around predictability but constantly shatters static patterns, exceptional results happen.

How will an 'intersection' point where holism meets 'reductionism' look like?

* * * * *

Traditionally, the protectors can be referred to as guards, and guards in the Indian tradition are called the '*dwarapalas*'![44]

(Right here, before you embark on the chapter, I would recommend you to just glimpse once the illustrations in Chapter 3 of SECTION 1. Especially the one that speaks about the PURUSHA and the ORGANIZATIONAL DNA!)

There's a design of this tradition. In their very formation, they are just the replica of what's being protected and nurtured. Hence, the '*dwarapalas*' are designed to look like the deity. *Vasihnavite* (those worshipping the God Vishnu) '*dwarapalas*' are ornamented, good looking and are docile while the *Shivite* (tradition of worshipping God Shiva) are ferocious '*veerabhadras*' with ferocious looks, canine teeth and body hair. Designed to filter out the evil forces, they are '*parivara-devathas*'—a part of the family; they are integrated and look-alikes of the deity! 'Parivara' refers to the family!

---

44 I found these interesting descriptions from my casual browsing when I came across these blogs called srinivasaroas.com. They not only appeared interesting but also extremely well researched and developed.

Just like all others, '*Dwarapala*' tradition also grew. The '*dwarapalas*' no longer managed the main gate but all the four—North, East, West and South—protecting *Jnana*, *Bhakti*, *karma* and *mantras*—the indigenous knowledge, quality commitment, wholesome action and repetitiveness respectively!

So, the questions turn out to be—

1. *What's your indigenous knowledge? What's the intellectual property and how do you protect it?*

2. *What are your rituals? How are they connected to your overall evolution and how will it serve the purpose?*

3. *How will we ensure the possibility of commitment? Who and how will the process be protected?*

4. *What's the repeating process? What do you really want to annihilate so that progress happens? What are you entrenched in that' not allowing you to progress?*

Unlike the '*dwarapalas*' who are designed to protect a particular element, there's another entity '*kshetrapala*' who protects the entire village or clan! '*kshetra*' is the field and '*palaka*' is the one who oversees or protects it. '*kshetrapala*' protects the field—the field of activity! It could be extrapolated this way—while '*dwarapalas*' protected the institutional mechanisms, the '*kshetrapalas*' took care of the community that held the institution. President, Operations and Head, CSR initiatives are the '*dwarapala*' and the '*kshetrapala*' respectively.

Though it may amount to yet another digression, it makes sense to glance cursorily at the Chapter 13 of the Bhagawadgeeta. Aptly termed as the *KshetraKshetrajna Yoga* the chapter is an examination of the field and the experience of the field. One of the inferences that draws out of this chapter is that field has its own dimensions and characteristics and has to be taken care of precisely the way it needs to be. When the field gets diluted with anything that doesn't belong to it, not only the identity but also the very efficiency for which it is made gets diluted.

And it isn't enough to just have the '*dwarapalaka*' who is at the entrance. A well-protected organization will also have guards all around—in all the directions. Direction is 'dik' and hence the term '*dikpalalkas*'!

So—

DWARAPALA—filters out evil; without having a protective shield, every attractive thing could become a potent activity within the organization. If an organization is a mere accumulation of ingredients without a central hub, it would remain ordinary. Probably the enlightened HR as viewed in one of the earlier chapters, the lean coach, etc. represent the DWARAPALA.

DIK-PALAKA—know-how, process, action, morality-ethics, treasure, resources and legality. Each head—R & D, sales, marketing and the training division constitute this.

KSHETRAPALA—the field of activity is to be protected. Unlike the entry point protected by the Dwarapala, Kshetrapala protects the field of action itself. Field of action is potentially toxic and is constantly struck by pangs of human inconsistency

Just as '*dwarapalas*' manage the purity by managing the entry and the '*kshetrapalas*' manage the space free from toxins by appropriate rituals and protect them, a spiritual organization or a business enterprise, highly ambiguous needs protection for its work to happen!

* * * * *

Having taken birth from the eyes of a spiritual Master or from the Paramahamsa leadership who sees the invisible, a spiritual organization or a business enterprise in its origins is ambiguous. So ambiguous that it would appear irrational. It's not surprising to see radical leadership of industry and business like Elon Musk and Steve Jobs of the business world have had to fight through a web of logic and 'common-sense', and Mahatma Gandhi's truth tactics appeared impractical in India's freedom struggle and bewildered many. In this vigorous logic-less irrationality, it remains utterly useless, cult-like and terribly vicious.

No worthy breakthrough business when initiated would have a logical frame. It makes no sense. Oyo, Ola, Uber, Flipkart, Paytm—none of them made any sense when it appeared on the horizon. It's just that these frames were made succulent by flesh by the leader who could, for some reason, manage ambiguity for a while!

That's how a spiritual organization also grows. It demands unreasonableness—in the form of tonsuring the head, silence for several months, fees that appear exorbitant and a demand that's put forth for service. One cannot function within the ambit of reason and leadership is in creating sufficient aesthetics, competence and integrity so that trust can be built. Otherwise, the whole enterprise is stupid and unworthy. Let's extend the consideration by adding these—

- *Spiritual Master is born out of disciples—unquestioning studentship. And the students of a Master just follow whatever the Master says.*

- *Master's statement, many a time, remains ambiguous; they can't be held within the container of logic; for instance, what can one make out of statements like—'all men are stupid people'; 'I don't like Telugu people'. Absolutely incorrect, politically at least. The only solace lies in the discretion of the disciples who should be good enough to look into their own lives of imbalance and make appropriate amendments. These statements, obviously illogical, need discerning intermediaries, which are caused by a strong learning organization. Imagine someone taking these statements seriously and believing them to be true! By the way, these statements were by Brahmarishi Patriji in one of the trust meetings of Pyramid Valley International where, as mentioned in several places before, I participated as a learning consultant.*

- *When one is capable of holding on to these statements; when one can hang between value—judgement and absolute acceptance, something transforms in the being and thereby in what one does in the life of the organization. There's no need for a sensible statement—any statement will do! The issue is when we don't hang. One clear instance is when some overseas delegates had to be hosted in the Pyramid Valley International campus. Some of them being Vegans, we had to cater to their vegan diet and also take enough care of certain allergies they had like peanut allergy. That was seen enough of a reason to construct a huge variety of offerings within our cafeteria. And the ground on which this was opposed by the then Managing Trustee was, 'Patriji is against vegan diet!'*

I am unsure what this meant but can just make a wild guess—Patriji probably, when questioned about the relevance of vegan diet (as the movement practices vegetarianism), in his characteristic flamboyance, would have brushed aside all these unnecessary extremes and advocated a simple and easy vegetarian diet. 'Patriji is against the vegan diet' is a gross and egregious interpretation. This was an interpretation by a leader within the organization and either it was made because of vested interest or gross misunderstanding.

- *Unless one has understood the power of ambiguity, leadership becomes a ritual of certainty—a way of reducing risk! Uncritical but aware participation with a Master brings about Transformation in the leadership!*

When 'ambiguity' is understood as a statement, or a principle or as an instruction it would start emanating a foul smell. 'smell' can be sensed but is not visible; not easy to trace. Unlike the real-life smell, this metaphoric organizational smell is even more difficult to locate.

The only hope is excavating the edifice itself; to look at the fullness of the construction as the only remedy. To locate this fullness is *'pooja'—'poojaat jayvee iti pooja'*—a ritual that gives birth to the fullness. To give a new birth with a fuller understanding!

And all poojas begin with the pooja of the *'Kshetrapala'*—the ultimate upkeep of everything that's valuable. The trustee.

And each of the '*palakas*' has to be assessed and alert—

1. '*Kshetrapala*' has to commit himself to a full understanding, the ultimate meaning.

2. The efficacy of the '*dik-palaks*' has to be assessed—are they capable?

3. The mandate of the '*ashta-dikpalakas*'—the eight guards—has to be crystal clear!

Coming back to the question of 'master'—

'Master' is alive only to the extent the disciple wants it! If the disciple ceases the 'master' ceases.

'Master' exists in the impossible, the inconceivable. And the only access a disciple has is in making an attempt to meet the Master's impossible demands.

Vignyana Bhairva—the ancient text on ascension form the India tradition says that life happens - and one is alive to the full possibility of life - only in the impossible!

Like pronouncing the sound 'ka' without the vowel attached to it. Pronouncing just the consonant. It's an impossibility.

Or freezing oneself in an overwhelming emotion!

Or in keeping the mind between 'desire' and its 'fulfilment'.

The 'impossibility' is the only possibility with the Master!

And conceiving the impossible is the only success. Remaining are all details!

It's not in achieving what's conceived. The mind stops when an impossibility is conceived! If the mind has stopped, something else is working for you

If the mind has stopped, logic has ceased and the universality of the vision, one has conceived a world-class work which is open to a possibility of a world-class organization. Master's statement, the company's vision and the subjective element that drives everything is what the chapter tried looking at.

CHAPTER 5

An Organization isn't Elephant—Dung!

He who says what is not, goes to hell

He also who having done a thing says, 'I have not done it'

After death both are equal

— **Dhammapada**

MASTER exists in the 'impossible', the inconceivable is the Master's abode. The true access to a Master is meeting his impossible demands.

So, we need to deal with the question of 'ambiguity'.

Fulfilment of a vision (which is very important) means to be hung in a limbo. The vision never gets fulfilled, and still, it's meaningless to be without a vision. So, to remain in between the vision and its fulfilment is a supreme act of leadership.

Let's understand with the help of a Master's voice!

When a Buddha expresses a wish, it's not a personal desire but a way for evolution.

But this wish can be conceived in two ways—

1. Total acceptance and jumping into action

2. Total dismissal and cynicism

And both are ELEPHANT DUNG!

No, not Bull-shit but ELEPHANT DUNG! While bull-shit connotes ugly trash worthy of being discarded, ELEPHANT DUNG is still a compound word whose meaning can be constructed by us now, in the present. Unlike 'bull-shit' which is a well-known expletive, ELEPHANT DUNG is ambiguous and we, as fresh users of the term, can turn it either way. To grasp the unique, one may have to fall back on the unique expressions!

Why elephants but? Elephants eat anywhere between 200 to 300 kilograms of food every day. Proportionally speaking, even to an elephant, this is a huge quantity of food. But the animal's alimentary canal is designed to eliminate the food almost as it is—on examining the excreta of an elephant, one can see the bark, leaves and foliage in almost the same form as was consumed.

To leave out just as was received, to give back the capital without interest implies an absence of an ethical dimension to it! As the famous parable in the Bible of a master going on a journey handing 5, 3 and 1 talent each to his three servants shows, the one servant who hides the money and returns it as it is, is punished and banished. The other two who turn their capital to gain are rewarded. This is the sentiment that's reflected in Milton's Sonnet 'On His Blindness'. Blinded, the poet laments, of what use his poetic talent is. To use one's talent and capital is to create a cycle of contribution.

Unused capital was an offence, a despicable act that lacks 'holy indifference' in the avoidance of risk. The popular Biblical parable reflects the sin of preserving the capital without turning it into profit.

ELEPHANT—DUNG is just that!

When 'vision' statements do not transmute itself into different 'transactable' dimensions in different departments like finance, sales, marketing, administration, housekeeping and security, it's just this—ELEPHANT—DUNG!

Let's examine this a bit further—

There are three interrelated aspects to understanding. This applies to everything that we do in the material world whether it's the school academics or company vision statements.

They are—

1. *SHRAVANA*

2. *MANANA*

3. *NIDHI-DHYASA*

SHRAVANA is the art of listening for absorption!

Once you listen, you've consumed and jumped into action or dismiss it, then there's ELEPHANT—DUNG in action.

SHRAVANA is the act of pristine reception. There's no value-judgement. It comes from being settled about what the Organization is meant for in the case of companies and contemplation on how something applies to one's personal life in the case of individuals. The pristine listening is multi-dimensional but myopic leadership, out of urgency or insecurity, many a time strives to make it uni-polar!

And the struggle begins. Maybe you can re-look at the piece on 'Necessity' at the beginning of this section. The struggle is the several conundrums that we come across in handling our 'talents'—spare capacity, surplus resources, attrition and fear of losing to the competition. It's in these circumstances that one has a chance to examine what's at stake and what's the truth. As we encountered in the case of 'vegan diet' episode of the previous chapter for overseas visitors, there are both—something at stake in the form of examining how well prepared we are to take care of our guests' needs and re-examining the complexity of yet another offering we may be unnecessarily building up to. Complexity is 'karma'—a momentum that cannot be controlled. When something cannot be controlled, the conundrum cannot be considered.

Unless the next step is fully conceived, the struggle continues!

The next step is MANANA!

MANANA is the practice. Practice exposes one to all kinds of contradictions. Quite a number of your experiences negate or contradict what you've consumed in SHRAVANA.

It involves voluntarily looking for the contradictions and negations. To look for actions, practices and exchanges that don't fall into the pattern of what you've experienced in SHRAVANA!

To examine the principles or vision from amongst all you have heard is the only way to concretize what you stand for.

To be sincere about these experiences and compiling all of it to be carried to the next level of examination is NIDHI-DHYASA!

An organization has to learn! The entire cycle of listening, contemplation and practice can be integrated into the learning cycle. Learning isn't linear, as basic principles of pedagogy suggest but spiral. A spiral has an identifiable beginning vortex and enlarging concentric circles that spiral out. Also, a spiral in its effusion keeps on gyrating out and also has a connection to the original question.

More relevant imagery could be one of spin. Any spinning entity—from sub-atomic particles to the cosmic—there's an inert spin, that is fatalistic and predetermined. None of the spinning objects has a choice in their orientation and speed. As basic laws of physics suggest, and as a famous legend about Archimedes suggests, to move anything would require a force and space to operate the force from. Given that, a spinning fatalism on its journey has hardly any chance of reorientation without access to the force and space where one can operate it from. Look at the diagram below. The axis is imaginary and the spin

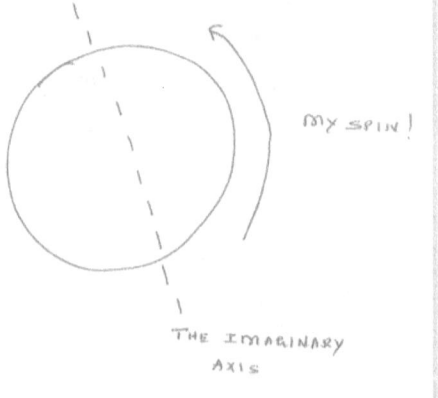

is real! By close observation of axes, we can shift for the creative output of multiple axes simultaneously. (Recall the illustration from the Chapter 2 of Section 1)

As I am writing this, my WhatsApp notifications ring a message from our local community support network. The neighbours are troubled by dry leaves, dumped waste in the community and such ones related to waste management. These messages have been circulating for the last several weeks around the same axis and the harassed in-charge responds defensively and, many a time switches off without a response. I was struck by the point I was trying to make. I immediately responded with a message which read like this—

To be fair to the already overburdened system, can we do something collectively about waste management? If we can come out with a solution ourselves as a community there are a few possibilities that open up—

1. *We will innovate more and more as no technology or system is foolproof. Innovation requires collaboration and brings the whole community closer in responsibility.*

2. *Our children will witness live how an empowered community functions so that we will never have to feel a need to lecture them about responsibility and civic sense.*

3. *Brings down the burden on administration.*

4. *Creates a workable model for other communities. In a sense, we will take on the responsibility of transferring valuable methods to other communities—both from our failures and successes.*

I am not sure how this can be brought about. Or how impractically romantic the idea is...

What I felt is that the axis of 'waste management' on which the whole discussion circulated hardly provided leeway for alternative action and thoughts. Can such immediate shifts in orbits be a possibility? Yes, in learning!

PUROHITA facilitates this learning!

PUROHITA comprises two words—'PURA' and 'HITA'; 'PURA' is the field, the *kshetra* and the centre of activity; 'HITA' means to nurture, manage the welfare and maintain. So 'PUROHITA is one who manages the welfare of the KSHETRA—the field of activity. By dropping all vested interests, the Purohita takes full care of the welfare of the organization. The field where action happens isn't a predetermined fatalistic field. A small technique—called *upaya* in Sanskrit—should be enough to mitigate the effects or completely change the orientations. Literally, Purohitas have been doing it for long in our traditions—through certain rituals to mitigate an inescapable momentum to life.

In that, *Pura*—the field—becomes even more elaborate than a mere field. Its welfare is in not being stuck in its own momentum but to be constantly in motion in a direction to the flow with a gentle nudge.

PUROHITA, like a Bodhisattva, makes it easy for you!

Without the PUROHITA the knowledge remains unconnected, irrelevant and scattered.

PANDAVAS had a PUROHITA.

PANDAVAS organized themselves Ito victory because they had the PARAMAHAMSA and the PUROHITA—

1. *Directionality of Krishna*

2. *Principles as guided by Dhaumya*

The story of Dhaumya—

Pandavas had Dhaumya for their priest—a teacher sans any vested interest!

They come across Dhaumya rather accidentally while one of the Pandavas Arjuna battles a Demi-God and subjugates him. In apology, the Gandharva requests Arjuna for his life, in return provides Arjuna with occult warfare techniques, and also advises the Pandavas on the importance of having a teacher; a teacher marks excellence. (It's rather difficult to differentiate between the purohita and the shikshaka—the priest and the teacher).

As the story goes, once a warrior named Saindhava abducts Draupadi when Pandavas are away during their exile in the forest. Dhaumya chases Saindhava. But the chariot is too fast for the hapless teacher that Dhaumya was.

Pandavas return to find the hermit empty and go in the direction of Saindhava in search of him. As they travel fast, they come across Dhaumya, exhausted by the arduous journey. Pandavas rest him for a while and then continue their chase.

The point is—who are you taking care of even when there is a crisis? Look back into the earlier chapter describing the sanatana—eternal knowledge!

WHO IS YOUR 'PUROHITA'?

CHAPTER 6

From the Sage Ashtavakra

'Kshamarjava daya tosha satyam pitushvadbhaja.'

Forgivness, sincerity, compassion, contentment and truth are to be worshipped like nectar!

Extraordinary organizations are made up of extraordinary human lives!

And what are extraordinary human lives made up of?

Unreasonable excitement defines extraordinary lives; not excitement as a destination but as the source. To be established in the 'current' and to be supremely satisfied is to hang in a state of possibilities. It's a very peculiar state—it negates complacency and also negates feverishness.

To be excited for no reason is the ultimate source of human excellence! For in it exists all possibilities.

How to create excitement? And how to sustain excitement? Should be the central questions organizations should counter. To be excited and to be conscious of it—there lies the central proposition!

Broadly, that also defines what it means to be human. Otherwise, the illusion of control and guarantee and attempts to reduce pain by themselves occupy human consciousness. In other words, the major part of the human consciousness in its ordinary state is—

1. *To avoid what cannot be controlled*—*hence, the focus is on small targets, achievable results and extreme feverishness to be 'practical'.*

Even to conceive a vision statement appears impractical and superfluous. Ordinary human consciousness is gripped by survival, practicality and the bottom line. It lacks excitement! And we get into superficial creativity—the packaging. It lacks excitement.

2. ***Avoids that which lacks assurance**—why to try something ambitious? Is the constant refrain. It entails avoidance of the game itself—avoids the very reason for which an organization in particular and human lives, in general, are created for. In the name of 'guarantee', there's nothing worth playing for and even in its success or accomplishment, it lacks excitement! In guaranteed outcomes, no real assets get created and the organizations and human beings suffer from perennial problem-solving!*

3. ***Avoids pain and searches for sources of excitement**—even the game of human development processes and welfare is reduced to compensatory outdoor events, trekking and games. The best way to avoid pain is to take on a 'bigger pain'. It's not uncommon for HR departments to look for the most exciting outdoor destination or the most entertaining trainer. And the moment you shift your life to outside factors, you want to control even what the trainer would do. (and so the HR departments should be made of real teachers—the purohitas—people who live beyond survival).*

It makes a lot of sense to look at Buddha at this juncture. Buddha uses 3 important terms—

Anichcha—whatever you have—pain or pleasure—diminishes. The excitement vanishes and the passion dwindles. What arises also subsides.

Dukha—the nature of the mind is to hold on; it wants to have a guaranteed effect for as long as possible, preferably eternally. And hold on to something, which is not. When the mind attempts this, it gets into pain and A CYCLE of actions to avoid the pain.

Anatta—you've no control over it. To control or attempting to control means illusion; fighting over something not even worth it. It lacks a central point called 'self'

To be 'excited' means to know the TRUTH that you're not in control.

Everything is changing and the flux of change is visible in our businesses and daily life today. It's so fast, it's impossible not to notice!

The shelf value of our products and services are dangerously depreciating. As one author claims that in the mid '90s, with the hardware technology changing so fast, the value of Apple's products depreciated at an astonishing pace of 2% every day. That had compelled to change its financial structure and re-calibrate their inventory. Shreans Daga, a businessman, Vice-Chairman of Pyramid Valley International and a meditation coach, refers to this as a phenomenon of the 'Quantum Age', wherein the earth has moved into the 'photon band' and we experience 'accelerated time'. In accelerated time, things move fast and time is contracted. The way events happen and manifestations show up is super-fast, and it is only when we are caught up in the events of life that time expands. Shreans Daga calls it 'missing in focus and vision' when we operate in expanded time! The following example will illustrate this better.

In the versions of the oversimplified Quantum Physics, shorn of its mathematical abstraction, the time between events 'A' and 'B' is a function of thoughts. There's no definiteness about time in their new dimensionality of time and space. This logic, though ubiquitous now, may not be palatable to serious students of physics nor is it the intention of study. But what we can take away is the simple aphorism that 'work occupies the time allotted to it'. Shreans Daga gives the example of travelling between Delhi and Bangalore is fast in flight and may take two hours without distractions. On the other hand, one may take two years if travelling by a bullock cart! It's not just the time of travel but the ways one may be caught up in the events of life—the bullocks may get tired, you would rest in a friend's house, fall in love with the ambience there and so on. So, there's no truth called time. It's all based on the thoughts that determine action.

When 'change' is visible and you contentedly witness these changes 'truth' is also visible. Because that's all 'truth' is. Like many 'pious illusions', as Sam Harris says, that religions suffer from, companies and organizations do suffer these illusions, which are constantly endorsed by the motivational seminar industry. Entertainment is great, but to make ourselves and our workspaces happier is not more of these 'pious illusions' but a clearer understanding of the way the flux is.

Coming back to the initial quote from Sage Ashtavakra, human excitement is a function of recognizing the truth of this flux. 'Excitement as a source' is possible where 'truth' is visible and we recognize that even the finest achievements have a shelf value and recognize the 'pious illusions' of a long-term target and a mission worthy of pursuit. There's none actually!

Ashtavakra has mentioned two more things—'kshama' and 'daya'—forgiveness and compassion!

So pervasive is the usage of 'forgiveness' and 'compassion' that we may have to distinguish them here for our purposes. We cannot afford to persist with ELEPHANT DUNG!

Forgiveness—there's a lot of didacticism associated with this word. We are not going by the sentimental feeling of it but into an inquiry into what forgiveness is.

Forgiveness is the art of being familiar with every layer of existence. Our existence transposes into and between survival, security, desire, ambition, purpose, confusion, ambiguity and dislike. A human being doesn't do anything to acquire these. They are just there. To be aware of the entire lineage of your existence, to know the entire story is 'to forgive'. Buddha could do it with Angulimala. If the Buddha were to be treated as a trainer, he would have been rated very highly—peak performance. When one knows the impermanence of any characteristic, when established in truth and when absolutely sure of the plasticity— you forgive—aware of the multiple layers of existence. It's personal, individualistic and subjective.

Compassion—while forgiveness is personal and subjective and sees multiple layers within a single entity or act, compassion is its opposite complement. Compassion is objective and projects itself into the society or community. In other words, compassion is the ability to see a single expression or entity within multiple manifestations! (Forgiveness was to see multiple layers within a single entity) In the Green School, Bali, as visitors, we were exposed to the model they called Compass Model. Look at the adjoining figure.

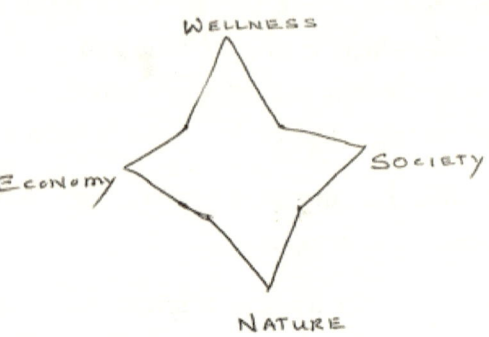

It is the constancy of the psychological essence. At a personal level whether old or young, rich or poor, we all know who we have been, have always remained the same and know what has changed are only the circumstances. Similarly, an organization is continuous with the leader. Actionable compassion will figure into teaching so that everyone functions optimally and punishiment is meted out so that discontinuities are flattened.

To extend the logic of compassion a bit more to be able to hold it relevant to what we are considering right now I will take recourse to my language, Kannada. Like many Indian languages which are sourced from Sanskrit, Kannada also is one and the word for *compassion* is '*anukampa*'. Without any expertise in etymology, I am tempted to make an analysis here based on dependable logic. '*Anu*' is a prefix for 'right' and '*kampana*' means to vibrate. Hence, *anukampa*' means to vibrate right. Without right vibrations, we would be acting as per the rule book and the rigidity of dogmas. Imagine a child seeking chocolate being lectured about the ephemeral nature of the body and the futility of having chocolate! That simply lacks '*anukampa*'— appropriate vibrations. This largely explains why leadership many a time stumbles with logical conclusions about what it conceived valuable!

The whole idea of the discourse is that we can construct an ability to respond. As the figure suggests, to be able to see holistically how any complex entity functions is compassion. The model divides that into four components—

Society—*happiness and predictability; strong welfare measures. Equity*

Nature—*sustenance; preservation*

Health—*wellbeing; fitness and sinewy; productivity*

Economy—*financial and operational leverage. Intellectual property! A sensitive measure of the tangible and intangible assets*

Coming back the two important points mentioned before—

1. Change is not a theory or hypothesis, a stock phrase, but visible and can be witnessed.

2. When things are changing, what can be called an asset is also under flux. (this flux has always been there but can be witnessed now. The assets during the slave trade, during empires, during colonization and territorial expansion have changed. Only that the change today is accelerated. Kodak has collapsed, Nokia sold off, and many more legends can be seen in our own contemporary business annals. What was an asset has collapsed in 'accelerated time').

Since these things are changing and no asset has any intrinsic value, it's worthwhile to examine what a real asset is!

Any company, worth its salt, would carefully examine assets, liabilities, debt, equity, financial leverage and operational leverage! The challenge is that, just like the absence of a 'stable self', these terms also don't have a stable meaning and watertight correspondence with value.

Each company or institution is uniquely situated. What's relevant for Harvard may not be for Indian universities; a software company is different from a commodity trader; and a school is not the same as a spiritual organization! Each has its own identity and has been incubated from the process of inception! High financial leverage could be good for real estate while high operational leverage is important for an automobile company; an NGO will be happy with low financial leverage and a school may still want to be low on operational leverage entity!

To excel is to be sincere with what you have identified yourself with! Krishna in advocating the path to Arjuna amidst a war calls it 'svadharma'—the duty that's righteously yours, and he proclaims further 'svadharme nidhanam shreyaha'—even failure and death in one's duty is better! If one can tear away the sentimentality of this off repeated line, one can see the value of 'time contraction' in locating one's duty in a specific role. This is easier said than done in an age of constant flux and tonnes of free-floating information. Real asset is in clear identification of one's role and the numerous possibilities in it.

Irrespective of where you come from and what your identity is an examination of what your assets are would make sense.

- *What skills do people have? Has the company been able to identify the right skills? Has the ''A to B' mapped well?*

- *What's the intellectual property that's driving the company? Do you identify the process? Or have you written the story of its creation?*

- *Who are your customers? Why should they not leave you? How are you connected?*

Building on these intangible assets breeds on how well one has identified the 'undercurrent drive' of the company!

'Kshamarjava daya tosha satsam piyushvadbhaja.'

To create a story,

To link the apparently unconnected,

To be in eternal ambiguity

Is leadership!

Do you want your company to be a leader? Then there should be learning as promoted by the 'PUROHITA' of the organization.

Let's depend on the famous cliche between Formula Vs Learning:

FORMULA—a method or a technique to be followed! And the end is in view.

LEARNING—discovery and is open ended; it's a process.

Humanity's penchant for formula-based knowledge isn't new. The age of '*mantra*', '*tantra*' and '*upaya*' have always existed since sage Bhrigu and 'sutras' enunciated these paths. Today, these extend to coaching institutes and guide books.

But learning is a different ball-game altogether. It's a commitment to the discovery of who you are and what the organization is about! It's a commitment to creating a self-aware organizations.

'Learning' is central to it and a 'learning organization' is a collective commitment to discovery!

SECTION 3

CHAPTER 1

Regeneration of a CEO—
A Hierarchy of Regeneration

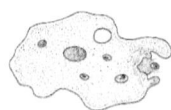

AMOEBA

- *Constant regeneration*

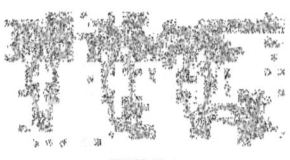

HYDRA

- *each tentacle capable of regenerating itself.*

LIZARD

- *Can re-grow the tail?*

- Can regenerate emotions; from that can regenerate actions! When it jumps to grab a fruit and misses it, the monkey doesn't sit and think and brood about it and blame his parents! The monkey will simply jump onto another fruit.

MONKEY

- *HUMAN—can re-grow only the vestigial ones—nail/hair, etc.*

- *When regeneration isn't easy or natural, one gets frozen—stopped everywhere.*

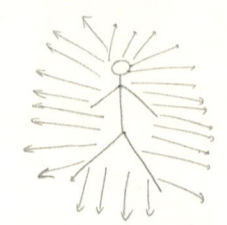

INFINITE POSSIBILITIES

Since the CEO is responsible for everything, as the illustration suggests, she cannot afford to be frozen. There's a need for constant regeneration! In an over-the-coffee conversation with my friend, deliberating on time, we discovered how a CEO's time is much faster, more packed than say an assembly-line worker. The same unit of time is more productive and, sometimes, infinitely more indiscernible as to where exactly her being, the nature of her existence, is impacting and being impacted. And without constant regeneration, CEOs will either be avoiding or somehow managing the issues!

EXPLANATION—Each of these numerous directions is potentially alive but not dynamically. It exists as a possibility. And when it is a dead-end, what may happen is a case for another illustration.

Each arrow turns back and what one experiences is one of organizational implosion, which could be visible in subtle breaks in the team, gossip and inefficiency; at a grosser level, worry and litigations are visible. This is a major cause for mediocrity as the only reason something continues to exist is that its absence causes a loss of self-worth. And value creation and preservation of self-worth are exclusive to each other!

Please refer to our repeated reference to Pyramid Valley International. The reason why the same actions continue in Pyramid Valley is because it is completely stranded and ceasing it means to have lost a cause and hence the self-worth of the leadership. The tyranny of a stable 'self-worth' is too powerful to be subverted!

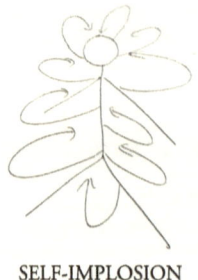

SELF-IMPLOSION

The changing nature of the business and the world is never visible, even though that's a constant refrain in educational and business discourses! What is starkly visible, on the contrary, is the mundane—preparing children for school, the early morning rush, the nagging spouse, morning walk, TV shows and news, phone calls, etc. in the domestic domain; and training, structuring appraisals, a meeting, review, etc. in the professional domain. The change (especially the speed of change) isn't an existential reality. Besides, change or stagnation, human beings are involved in action! It's just these actions, which are real. And the reality becomes available to us only in the attention to our actions!

WHAT GENERATES QUALITY ACTION?

Resolution of the roles we play—

We all play roles and the society and institutional mechanisms have a way of assigning relative value to these roles.

Just as the mundane is the most obvious, our immediate and urgent execution of organizational exigencies are also the most conspicuous. The overall target of the sum total of all actions isn't something that becomes starkly available to us. Instead, one may feel petrified by the fragments—at the thought of a deadline; frustration at the intransigence of a subordinate; a nagging worry about the project; anger at a follow-up call or some such things that are immediately available to us about the distant project. This is something that I am experiencing as I write this book. I am periodically doubtful about its relevance and how unnecessarily ambitious this work is, feeling the frustration of creation, fear tinged with a hope that it doesn't become controversial or the fear that it may look like an oversimplified version of some personal spiritual meanderings; the ultimate fear is that there's no way to say if the conception would match with what will manifest!

It's a fact that the mundane rules. As organizational heads, we distinguish and relegate the 'unimportant mundane' to an outsourced agency—the housekeeping, security, the pantry or a receptionist who can ward off the mundane 'evils'. These are all necessary. A project surely needs an adiabatic system which cannot be overexposed. No CEO or corporate leader needs to be told how dangerous casting a wide net is. Casting a wide net is invariably an office headache with unsurmountable questions being answered all the time. I am aware of such mistakes when, in my own small experience as a school principal, I had wrongly cast the rightly understood responsibility as I was 'blameable' for everything that happened in the school—including some lost pencil box or a small fight amongst children in the pre-primary classes. Management had some roles to play. I felt shy in relegating the role to the management of ensuring a high degree of standardization training to all staff and appropriate expenditure and budget towards it. Standardization certifications weren't necessary for my actual work there but would have served by not not-diluting into the broader questions at work.

So, it's clear that one has to ignore, marginalize, relegate or outsource a potentially mundane question of operation. The question is not that. It more relates to our civilizational ability to ignore primordial questions of survival and sustenance as we progressed. We no longer have to wait and fill water in tanks or trek miles to fetch a bucket-full; what we earn doesn't depend on the rainfall patterns and monsoon; our food doesn't come from long hours of wait in the silence of jungle for a prey, and certainly not bothered about an attack by the opponents. The food is largely available to us, water gushes out even from our toilet commodes, and many of us don't even notice that money has been credited to our bank accounts. All these dimensional growths of civilization have helped us ignore these questions so that collectively (based on what we think the collective is) either think of our national identity or pride, or space exploration or military superiority or the tally of our medals in Olympics; or individually plan to fulfil our bucket-list wishes—trekking to the Mount Everest or planning for the next exotic holiday.

Unrehearsed in the art of managing the mundane, we are untrained in focusing on the basics in the modern age. If our mundane activities are not to manage the subsistence, what do we manage then?

Our mundane is not bound by the questions of subsistence but by a sense of identity. Our questions of identity are, in fact, our mundane question. Identity, a pure illusion when looked at closely, has occupied our desire for subsistence. We handle the psychological—stock market and its impact on our company's performance and a search for a new identity in the wake of the contraction of global GDP; psychology of who we believe we are is our new identity. Within this deep desire for 'status' of identity, leadership misses the point that everything is part of a global phenomenon beyond 'time and space'. You may recall the illustration of the 'golden connecting thread' of the *Sanatana* (the Triumvirate of relationships triangle)in Chapter 3, Section 1.

It reflects on Krishna's hint at the inter-connectedness of things in Chapter 3 of the Bagawadgeeta[45], albeit succinctly. Krishna's virtuous cycle connects food to rain to the evaporation process. In this cyclicality, there's no gradation and privileging of roles and identities. What exists is inter-dependence and the next logical question, therefore, is—*how do organizations grade their roles and what's its function?*

Just as any machinery requires oiling, the organizational machinery's gradation provides for it. In an analogy I heard from Swami Suryapada from the Art of Living, in his discourse on Chapter 3 of the Bhagwadgeeta, he likened this inter-dependence to an oiled sugarcane crusher machine one usually finds on Indian roads. When you observe the whole machine working, it's hard to ascribe ownership of the product to any one thing. This, of course, is an analogy that most of us are familiar with but as far as organizational structure goes, gradation provides for a perfectly oiled organizational machinery. Therefore, a great organization, let's surmise, for now, is one which is perfectly oiled and which 'does nothing'.

The point is simple—organizations can show up this state of 'non-doing' by establishing rituals where 'ownership' and identity are dropped. Ownership and responsibility are perceived by a discerning intellect in the spirit of work. What we are looking at is the possibility of dropping fastidious attachment to identity. Each organization will have to indigenously arrive at these rituals that are appropriate for the organization. One of the ways we did this (both in PVI as its learning consultant and especially in Satpuda Valley Public School as its principal) was to take up cleaning up of the

---

45 I am specifically referring to verses 12-14 of the Chapter 3

entire premises, de-cluttering it once a month; sitting together, holding our hands clasped into each other in prayer before we have our meals and head to a set of games every Saturday afternoon; and most looked-forward-to of all was our monthly togetherness days where we celebrated focusing on learning, socializing, fun and recognition! This was a method and dropping requires creative rituals established and revamped now and then. The best way, of course, is to have a *Purohita*.

These are not very unfamiliar to many companies and some have forged even more sophisticated and effective ones into their schedule. Just that when we establish rituals of dropping ownership, a frozen identity is given up for flexibility that's simply reflecting what needs to be done. Maybe one could conclude logically that when identities are not frozen but flexible and that every role that we play is critical, the chances are more that people play out their functional roles extraordinarily well. The freedom one experiences when one sees that it's all role that we play is a critical factor for efficient functioning. Because whatever we do is just another role and to crave for another is like a prisoner looking for a better prison cell—maybe the one with an attached toilet!

Quality action, therefore, is an absence of identity. This is a corollary to one of the earlier ideas we explored—the absence of a stable self! The absence of a fixed self like 'boss' or CEO we all recognize naturally is also what determines our actions.

The absence of 'bossism' and hierarchy isn't just a romantic idea or politically safe rhetoric in an age that demands politically righteous egalitarianism. When exercised as a romantic idea, it would be counter-productive as it happened in the case of schools where corporal punishment was criminalized. Even more critical was when it was imposed as a statutory necessity in some countries without appropriate social preparation towards it. Only those schools which have recognized the significance of democratic values for a new global order have established a lasting legacy. In others, punishment was replaced by subtler ways of coercion, and the spirit behind the act was severely undermined.

That could be a problem with institutionalized processes which don't allow for spontaneous regeneration. Even these processes could be the 'exotic' new-age fashion—casual clothing and game-like environment. When resources to fulfil our mundane necessities are in surplus, we shift them to the next set of mundanes—the 'exotic' and 'what's worthy of a well-lived life'. Likewise, we also freeze and hoard our survival feelings that degenerates a high potential action to the mundane questions of survival and sustenance in an office space. So, '*Kamsa Consciousness*' is at play. And this is a perfect antidote to quality action! We will examine 'Kamsa Consciousness' in a short while form now.

We could begin analyzing the hierarchy of frozen things we handle—(since these are too popular imagery in the esoteric circles, we can as well go through it quickly in points)

1. *The most frozen is the body. As Deepak Chopra says in one of his audiobooks, the body is a frozen essence in time and space. Like the picture of an ocean, as Dr. Chopra says, is not the ocean but a frozen piece in time and space!*

2. *Slightly fluid is the 'life force' which keeps the frozen body active. A body can jump and shout and be thrilled all because there's this life force operating within it.*

3. *Absolutely unfrozen is our mind—just freely roaming around in its own created stories, imagination and superstition.*

4. *What's the source of this mind? Where did this 'source' originate from?*

And the corollaries are—

1. *Much like the body, one can only do as much with an institutionalized organizational framework (you may recall the Chapter 1 assertion about the irrelevance of an organization). It's frozen. Maybe one can colour the hair, get a facial done in the local saloon and be done with it. We could improvise it, make it look neater, but regeneration isn't possible. Like a product that we design and the service that is offered*

has something frozen and limiting about it, there's nothing much that can be done. Regeneration isn't possible but re-packaging is!

2. *Where did these products come from? The idea about a great business plan, a project, a cost-cutting measure, innovation, etc., ideas are aplenty. Ideas are more alive than the completed presentation. It has a potential before it's frozen into a body. These ideas again are limited by a pattern of thought—like a toymaker gets ideas about the toy, and also as the designer ideates on design—once someone leaves a company or dies the idea is dead. Though more flexible in regeneration, it again has a limit.*

3. *Where did these ideas come from? May be from an alive and enterprising coffee-club—a space of innovation and serendipity! This is more complex than the realm of 'ideas'. This is challenging as this requires a design where whatever comes in works the way it is supposed to—in tune with the bigger questions of the enterprise. Can one regenerate this culture merely by some case studies, observations and hiring a consultant?*

These questions trouble us every day—in our search of regenerating ourselves. That speaks about the popularity of courses on 'Law of Attraction', 'Manifestation', 'Creative Visualization', etc. which abound the 'enthusiastic trainer syndrome' market. The search for a quick-fix to defrost is too common to most of us.

Leaders in an organization have to grapple with deeply frozen entities. The organization, as a body of frameworks and vision, is a frozen entity. It only has life, as argued earlier, because it's out to cause something substantially important for humanity. Its importance is a function of what humanity deems valuable and to the extent, the organization listens to answer these demands.

It needs a little more elaboration and, certainly, some kind of a 'way-out-of-the-maze'! We don't have access to anything but action. So we must recognize an ability to regenerate through action.

There are two ways of action—

1. Acting towards a point you're going

2. Acting towards a point you're not sure you're going

As human beings, we are not bothered about the first category of actions—reaching the office on time, fixing the telephone, lunch-hour hunger bites, the coffee breaks, etc. What really bothers us is the second category of actions, which are uncertain—meeting with a client to strike a deal, selecting a CFO for the company, deciding on a high-stake payment or innovation, removal of employees and making sense of the existing financial/operational structures!

So, the first set of actions, which never bothers anyone including organization leadership, isn't where our current life is located while the 2nd set is our entire life. One can easily observe that there's a high degree of bias towards your 2nd set of actions!

Further—

The 1st set of actions are in the tacit domain—in the 'silent zone' and are 'taken for granted' while the 2nd set of actions are ludicrously boisterous! As the second set becomes increasingly boisterous, the first set gets into increasing oblivion! (Please refer to the small description called 'necessity' at the beginning of Section 2; here, businesses are built out of a focus on the 'extraordinary' and the avoidance of the 'mundane')

That becomes visible, either starkly or subtly, in our daily actions—unshaved dishevelled looks, scattered paper on the office table, unkept cupboards. (Of course, these may be characteristic of another way of expressing the joy of life!). More starkly in the paranoia and panic that organizations in general and the leadership, in particular, experience. We will come back to this later. It's sufficient to examine the psychosis of excellence at this juncture before we get back to this!

THE POPULAR STORY OF KAMSA IN THE BHAGAVATHA!

Amongst all the details, there is this event—

Kamsa, one of the greatest warriors and imperial powers of the time, is escorting his newly wedded sister Devaki along with her husband Vasudeva.

He hears the ethereal voice declaring a son born to Devaki to be Kamsa's death. In the simplified version of the story, Kamsa is furious and is about to execute the hapless woman. Only on a request by Vasudeva is she spared but incarcerated with an instruction—every child born will be surrendered to the imperial power.

Agreed!

Escaping the present Dracula is more pertinent than the later danger! And as the story goes, Kamsa is ultimately killed by Krishna born to Devaki.

This story doesn't catch the psychological depth in its simplified version.

Examining its relevance in the context of excellence in leadership—

There are a few questions!

What's this ethereal voice and how true is it? How do we really examine the truth of anything? What's substantial and what's 'phony'? What's the metaphoric 'pink elephant' that the CEO is fighting against?

'Kamsa' also means a bracket. A bracketed existence, unconnected to humanity, doesn't see itself as a function of cosmic 'inter-dependence'. The paranoia is part of *Kamsa* constantly listening to our ethereal voices and the organizations, without examining these, construct the 'panic pyramids' we examined earlier. Even linguistically speaking how much can one regenerate an explanation in a bracket. A bracket itself is an additional explanation, connected to the whole and it's syntactically absurd if separated from the whole. I have used this metaphor in my other upcoming book 'Bagawadgeeta for Your Worktable' contrasting it with another expansive

'*Vyasa* Consciousness'. *Vyasa* means the diameter—something that connects both ends of the periphery passing through the centre.

BACK ON THE COMPANY WORKTABLES.....

What dominates modern businesses is the psychological essence—the share value, implicit rivalry of businesses, potential attrition of high-value employees, etc. These are the ethereal voices that constantly hover around the CEO—how to make the 'out-of-control' zone work in predictable ways? Every event in these domains - a news report about differences within the board, litigation by a supplier, a politically distasteful commercial on TV and anything for that matter - is a cause for serious psychosis! The CEO's are compelled to act in 'Kamsa Consciousness'

A CEO, therefore, will have to examine the fundamentals and trace the entire growth trajectory. There's no 'psychosis' when the entire trajectory is visible! Death no longer terrified Parikshita when he heard the entire story. A self-generative CEO will know the entire trajectory.

In my workshops with executives, I sometimes deliberately make the room untidy before they enter for a particular session to be cleaned and set right by them. And the process is only a precursor to finding out how one feels redeemed when we know how to focus on the basics as well as our ideals simultaneously.

And that's a possibility we are talking about!

What Does a Buddha CEO Do?

To be 'spiritual' means to look at the non-obvious; to be able to look at things that have been ignored for too long and to be able to see, small or big, the stupid or intelligent, profitable or regular, with an equanimity. In other words to be able to see things with utmost love and compassion. (look at the description of 'compassion' in Section 2, Chapter on 'From the Sage Ashtavakra').

To be 'spiritual' means to be 'stupid'. Spirituality is the 'science' of stupidity. hence, one can afford to make a statement—'THE BOISTEROUS IS RESOLVED IN THE OBLIVION'

Let's examine some mundane instances—

What constitutes an active day is located chiefly within the restfulness of the night.

A good night's rest and sleep ensures freshness during the day.

Similarly, the extent an arrow can fly ahead depends on the extent to which the strings have been pulled backwards.

That means the complementary opposites are the function of any occurrence. To the extent I can do something is a function of its opposite—day/night, active/restful, shot/pull, etc.

Extending the same logic, extraordinary businesses which are grounded on the breakthrough innovations are in fact located within an immense capacity to engage with the mundane and the ordinary; to deal with total love and involvement what really matters to the whole humanity. Getting back what we saw in Section 1, Chapter 3 on the idea of triangles is a reflection of what is being said here. The chapter under reference looked at triangles of crises and moral dilemma individuals, organizations, communities and humanity at large face! In simpler expressions it happens when the Buddha, The CEO knows how to respond to an Angulimala.

When we talk of the 'mundane' as a way of redeeming the breakthrough business performances, we are looking starkly at engagement with humanity—GREAT ORGANIZATIONS AND BUSINESSES ARE BUILT OUT OF COMPASSION FOR WHAT IT MEANS TO BE HUMAN!

So, breakthrough performance, change management, complex change, transformation or whatever you call it is not easily visible but what would be visible are the actions towards these. So, it makes great sense for businesses to focus on the indirect switches that switch on the lights of humanity.

How to cause it?

Everyone and, more so, people with responsibility get stuck in actions due to an incapacity to regenerate—bad mood, anger, frustration, helplessness, etc. which do not appear easy to come out of. The only possibility is to come out of it through appropriate rituals that we looked into in the chapter on 'Should an Organization be Protected?'

For a CEO, without these humane rituals, the act of regeneration is a task next to impossible. It remains a difficult task when appropriate rituals are absent. It is indeed the most important thing to follow the right pathway— SAMMA KAMMA—The Wholesome Action!

An illustrative hierarchy for regeneration across the organization—

The security staff, housekeeping, cooks and the assistants—every moment regeneration; scold and abuse them, they generally don't collapse. (not a recommendation but an illustration for the capacity to regenerate). The tasks performed at this stage of an organization can be easily regenerated—'stand on the left rather than right', 'bring the black tray to serve coffee' kind of instructions are enough to bring a new set of actions.

The clerical staff—a memo or a notice would be enough. A drill on new accounting software or information system would do.

Sales/marketing/finance executive—regeneration is complex. Needs elaborate training. Many a time hand-holding and slightly longer mentoring process could be necessary. Not just the mundane skills but a focus on communication and training on the enhancement of emotional skills is a necessity.

Senior Manager—Mentoring and a lot of subjective understanding of the task. The number of objective indicators are far and few. What matters is the subjectivity of the tasks. Though targets are clear and performance bottom line is concrete, the ways of moving towards it isn't very objective. The number of parameters under consideration is far too many than the previous level.

CEO—The number of data points is so huge that anything can be a matter of concern—a report in the newspaper about a squabble is enough to finish the good work over the years. A small innuendo on sexual misconduct should be enough to shake up the CEO! This demands constant regeneration. It's only regeneration, the fantastic ability to see every moment freshly, that helps performance. There's no formula to help the CEO in this but an extraordinary commitment to understanding humanity (which means one's own self) completely!

The above hierarchy is also the hierarchy of ethicality (see the next chapter)!

In the programme on 'Know Yourself' which I have referred to earlier conducted by Meerama of Shivanetra tradition, the idea of rebirth is described quite surrealistically. Based on the *Garuda-Purana*, the potential for rebirth, it explains, is a function of the point from where you left your earlier body. And it's an inverse function—higher the point (called CHAKRA here—the node of energy junctions; you may want to explore this with a teacher who is well-versed with the knowledge of Ayurveda and Yoga) lower the capacity to regenerate; lower the chakra, higher the potential for regeneration.

Meerama gives a practical illustration for the same. She explains how infertility has never been a problem in the economically challenged lower strata of society. Here the society is not based on aesthetics but only on survival. Regeneration is a constant phenomenon. Infertility is in fact a major issue reflected in the numerous IVF clinics taking root in the thriving cities of our modern metropolis.

SURVIVAL—any platform is okay. Amoeba can thrive anywhere. They never die. An organism called amoeba never dies just keeps on being transformed.

Coming back to the point, transformation is a commitment to humanity. We may examine it in a bit more detail in the next chapter 'Transformation is a Design'.

CHAPTER 2

Transformation is a Design

Thou hast no provision for thy journey,

Make thyself an island, work hard, be wise.

– Dhammapada

Prashnopinshath *is one of the ten canonized* **Upanishads** *in the Rishi traditions.*

This Upanishad is a conversation between Pippalada, the mentor seer with other six sages which includes Bharadwaja. The conversation is through a series of questions that Pippalada answers. That's also the meaning of Upanishad—an intimate conversation. An intimate conversation considers all questions important and answers nothing beyond what is needed.

Bharadwaja asks the mentor Pippalada—I would like to know the sixteen talents attributed to human life and its culminating point—Purusha. Pippalada makes it look simple by explaining away the sixteen things that cause human life—5 senses, 5 elements, 5 vital forces and 1 mind. Examining what would establish for oneself the entire spectrum of these 16 divisions—is the exploration that happens throughout this part of the text.

In answering it, in the Socratic style of inquiry, it is further extended to another question—which one if separated from the body, the body ceases to function? The question culminates into the examination of Prana—the vital process that drives the body. Similar to the underlying processes that drive a business—like the interconnection between operations and production, production and quality assurance, Quality and marketing and the whole subsisting on a felt market needs—Pippalda says the body is driven by Prana which is the primary element of subsistence.

Just as market and social needs can be surveyed, tabulated, examined and analyzed—it's just the prana that can be subjected to study. All other philosophical inquiry that delves into the pre-critical phenomenon of 'want' and 'need' isn't appropriate in dealing with an enterprise. Similarly, the master Pippalada recognizes the imperfection in the pedagogy of beginning the inquiry from anything more abstract than 'Prana'. Probably it would be intellectually more stimulating to examine multi-verses, the cosmic energy to the intelligence that drives all design etc. But they would just remain that—intellectual stimulation.

From the discipline of the master stems the knowledge that's relevant to the disciples here. As the text unfurls Pippalada explains, how Prana itself is divided into sub-operative Pancha-Pranas, divisions of vitally important functions— circulation, digestion, respiration, (inhalation-exhalation) and excretion. Observing it—the imbalance, temperature, volume, texture, length and fluctuations—non-judgementally, one has access to something more profound and intrinsic—not by mere explanation or, even worse, by poetic description!

Pippalada describes the design of the human system in the subtlest amongst the tangibly observable—

Pana - Inhalation

Apana—Exhalation

Samana—Circulation

Vyana—Digestion

Udana—Excretion

Buddha's famous practice of 'anapanasati' comes to mind. Millions have benefitted since the Buddha revived it from an ancient tradition of breath observation. And the most popular reference to it can be found in the Bagawadgeeta in its Chapter 6.

These departmental divisions of prana carry multiple portfolios. As explained in commentaries on the Upanishad, Udana, for instance, helps in excretion. To excrete and discard what is not relevant. Not just the faeces, urine, sweat and phlegm but also in discarding the body when not needed—in fanciful imagination, in sleep and in death itself. Just that in the two former states, there's a return to the same body and memory is intact while the latter is a transfer to the next stage of life—the body is permanently discarded or excreted.

That's the design in the system. The body may be discarded but the universal principles of subsistence are carried forward as per Pippalada in the Prashnopanishad!

Business lies in Transformation! In transforming each subtle entity into a newer fresher gross product.

* * * * *

A good teacher or a Head of Learning and Development (you may recall the **Purohita**) knows the design of inquiry and the suitable nature of response that's appropriate. It's not mere FAQs that the *Purohita* handles but the entire design that involves sub-topical questions:

who's asking? Where would that be needed?

Should it be answered right away or stage wise?

How can the answer not only address the pertinent challenge but also create a need that was never felt before?

While a pre-eminent teacher's answer itself is a design, the Upanishads are also a part of the design for appropriately guided self-inquiry. Design rules.

The possibility of excellence is in design.

And transformation is a design! Bruce Nussbaum, in his 'Creative Intelligence' explains how International Design Excellence Awards—with metrics on R & D spending, patent listings and revenue generated by new products—could no longer assess the innovation and creativity of new companies on the block, which included Facebook and Apple without recalibrating the measurements. Apple and Facebook simply didn't fit.

'That made it clear', Bruce Nussbaum says, 'that something else was happening, something else was responsible for these big, disruptive innovations, something that we hadn't discovered how to quantify'. That largely explains the phenomenal success of Art of Living and its tremendous social impact. Because the design is such. Product innovation happened in Art of Living because the organization had a design that could sustain a habit. R and D for new services—which include *Natia-Yoga, Medha-Yoga, Ayurveda cooking, Vastu-Shastra,* etc. and more profound ones like *Sanyam, Vijnana Bhairav, Shakti Kriya* among others—was an organic outgrowth from the felt need of expanding participation. And all of the programmes are thriving. Like the Art of Living, Herbalife's phenomenal success and social impact—which we are about to see in detail—is largely due to a design to help people sustain a habit.

HOW DO DESIGNS COME ABOUT?

Design is an idea,

it's ergonomic!

Unless ergonomic, business is not.

It gently fits into the environment,

It listens for the shape of the body,

Occupies the form.

When businesses struggle, it lacks an ethical dimension. Real business don't struggle. An ethical dimension feeds and nurtures the quality of a society and the society, in turn, feeds the organization. And ethics is not trivialized 'right' and 'wrong' or simplified morality; it's an extension of who you ought to be!

There are several rounds of iteration that one can perform to make sense of fatalism in the discourse like in the statement, 'when businesses struggle it lacks an ethical dimension'. In each of these iterations meanings open up only to be discarded so that, in the flexibility of who we are, much more can be discovered by dropping it. A beginning question could be—what is struggle? And an extension of it—when do we say it's suffering? These questions will not be answered but we will be getting into a more concrete consideration.

When businesses don't care for the people who house it, and when they don't help them locate the template on which they are functioning the whole purpose and meaning of the business could be lost; it becomes fanciful, technically unsound and a struggle!

Buddha's *'sheela'*—the essence of mannerism for wholesome action—isn't directly related to the business and its processes but intimately connected to its organic success and the impact caused.

I should mention a personal observation here. The street I live in Bangalore is a school quite well known and offers dependable education to the neighbourhood. The popularity of the school is such that even children far from the school are enrolled in it. Since the school doesn't have transport, all the children are dropped by their parents and what we experience about the school stems from this—mayhem and morning pandemonium. That has largely defined how we see the school and we all have complaints about the school even without knowing about its pedagogy or actual output. With parents dropping their children parking their vehicles haphazardly many a time blocking the road for people in the neighbourhood hurrying to their offices, the school is seen as a nuisance to be tolerated.

We had looked at 'compassion' in one of the earlier chapters as a quality of leadership. Though the school in question need not respond in any way to the quagmire created by parents, there's an inherent issue in not being able to address it.

Let's look at it this way—

I am running a Nutrition Club.

All that I care for is people coming there and consuming my product; that's my business and my business matters to me.

People like the product and they come in hordes. Cash flow grows.

But without ever knowing it, something else is happening all around the club.

The customers who come to the club park their vehicles haphazardly, sometimes affecting the neighbours; such is the hurry sometimes that they look hurried and stressed; all that matters is the product that's served in the club and not the appearance—so the customers come unclean, unshaven and do not appear hygienic.

It also happens that they use the club very personally, with boisterous noise, loud music and direct display of excitement.

As a business owner, the club proprietor doesn't mind this; in fact, the owner's happy and excited about what's being offered. The illusion of an energetic and a happening place is too difficult to be ignored.

But without anyone realizing, there's an undercurrent that has been sucking the enterprise.

The neighbours are getting more and more disconnected. They gossip around about the noise, intrusion and filth that's getting generated; and look for ways that could bring down the disturbance and noise. But the club owner all along felt that the noise indicated and kept the excitement alive and excitement is an automatic invitation. (One can recall Osho's Commune at Oregon, USA)

To have imagined that is a false understanding. In fact, it's listening to one's own conditioning—noise being equated to excitement (the way teenagers equated smoking to machoism. Most of the time, this conditioning is inadequate and many a time counter-productive to the business.)

As the spiral of public gossip expands, it spirals into a new story; the original story—the reason for the formation of the club—is submerged in these noises. Ministry interferes, bureaucracy sends a notice and without you ever knowing, the actual game has shifted.

The above experience is something that has never happened in the nutrition club that I used to be a member of.

This isn't a hypothetical narration but what I have experienced first hand in the nutrition club that I frequent. It's run by my nutritional coach Arun and he is from Herbalife. I also have become a member of it but my inclination, priority and available time don't allow for my regular attendance there. What I have described above is precisely what, as personally witnessed by me, Arun never did. In fact, he is so scrupulous about the ethical standards he has learnt from the company that he doesn't even allow the guests visiting there to come there without a helmet—a rule that's not so stringently followed even by the traffic wardens within the neighbourhood; but that's certainly not something under Arun's purview and even distantly linked to Arun's business.

Lean and small built, ethically courageous Arun prides how unsuccessful and unhappy he was as a physics post-graduate. Though it had a demonstration value, that certificate hardly contributed anything beyond it. Instead, he recounts with a lot of gratitude how HerbaLife as an organization helped him grow. I have witnessed his struggle during my association with him for close to a decade now but have never seen him flinch from his ethical base.

That is the degree of ethicality and meticulous integrity practised all across the Multi-Level-Marketing company HerbaLife. They never have marketed their products to countries which haven't permitted their products and dissuade their distributors by warning to stripe off their licence to sell if they violate the rules of the game. Not just that, the distributors don't frisk away or hog other's customers. To hog and disengage from the ethical spirit hardly speaks well of a company and would hardly benefit the customers.

Why should have Arun bothered about whether the guests wear the helmet or not? And why does that become important? To grasp the impact of Arun's scrupulousness, one may have to understand Indian standards of public life. A predominantly oral society, India has nothing sacrosanct about a written word. It is quite a ubiquitous sight to witness boards that mention 'garbage not to be thrown here' with a heap of garbage just beneath it; there are ironically notices that read 'DO NOT URINATE HERE' where people are urinating peacefully. Train timings mentioned aren't adhered to (though this trend has largely changed). The mismatch between a written word and its application is too wide a gap for healthy and dependable public systems.

Herbalife, committed to standards of service and creating healthier and happier populations, needs to demonstrate integrity that's not limited to norms of the place. To be able to act with assurance and without cutting the corners by itself is a cornerstone of excellence. Just as the 'no conditions return policy' and its stringent label law of its products, not just the extraordinary products but an exemplary service that distinguishes Herbalife from several others. The robust systems are democratic and serve well to produce consistently dependable results irrespective of the input. And its innovation base is visible in the way their services base change and the way they perform.

To serve means to grow, and to serve means to follow the rules of the game. That practice is so well integrated that my initial compromise with its training and other integration practices while trying to make what appeared like easy additional income through selling its products hardly worked. And today Herbalife is a global nutritional leader and is the fastest-growing meal replacement brand. And it's true to its vision, mission, values and that's what everyone in the company does. The enthusiastic distributors in Herbalife dare sceptics to show an exception to this design.

Extraordinary companies and organizations somehow integrate by imbibing everything great admired by humanity all along. That's precisely the simple point. Let's look at Herbalife Vision and Mission statements which I have just copied from their website—

OUR WHY

Making the World Healthier and Happier.

The Purpose and unique value of our Company, our distributors and our Employees is to help people be Healthier and Happier through personalized nutrition and a proven business opportunity so that around the globe, every tomorrow is continually better.

OUR HOW

Through Purpose-Driven Distributors Who Are Our Difference

Beyond products that deliver on their promises, our customers receive irreplaceable knowledge, encouragement, respect, supportive coach, care, community. And an amazing opportunity. That is what our distributors truly distribute. We are driven by their needs and energized by their passion

OUR WHAT

To create inspiring Results for a Better Life

With effective products that taste great, distributors who provide guidance along the journey, the support of an entire company full of enthusiastic employees, and an encouraging community, we can give people around the world a simpler path to a healthier, happier life.

OUR VALUES

We Always Do What's Right

When we look in the mirror, we see integrity, honesty, humility and trust. We reflect the belief that ethical is never optional. And we honour and respect each other, our Distributors, our customers, and most importantly, ourselves.

We Work Together

We learn, we teach. We follow, we lead. We help one moment and accept help the next. We never stop collaborating, which makes us unstoppable. We have fun. We keep things simple. We celebrate the individual, and the team, in each of us.

We Build It Better

We're always looking up. Because that's where the opportunity is. To learn. To grow. To innovate. To excel and exceed. To be an agent of change in our communities. To turn an entrepreneurial spirit into daily inspiration as we make our customers' lives—and ours— Healthier and Happier.

It could be very personal that I am enamoured by the company. My family says it's too expensive; my brother says one need not go for 'unnatural food' to keep oneself healthy. Such disagreements exist and I respect it, but no one needs to be a linguistic expert well-versed in the art of stylistics to see the lyrical quality of this refreshingly straight forward statement. This is precisely what I have experienced in the company and the Nutrition Club led by Arun. It's just not my endorsement but also clarity that's visible in everyone who is a part of what they call Herbalife Family.

* * * * *

There's an ethical dimension to business.

In an article by India's former Chief Election Commissioner, who also is Mother Theresa's biographer, recounts an interesting episode in one of his trysts with the Mother in an article in The Hindu[46]. The puritan Catholic Mother ran an extraordinary organization in the communist heartland

---

46   The Hindu, Editorial 'Dignity Regained in a Calcutta Oasis' on 5th September, 2020

of India. Communism or no communism, Mother commanded respect, authority and admiration hardly equalled by any.

The incident the article recalls is this—Jyoti Basu, the late chief minister, requests the Mother to take care of some unfortunate women under confinement in an institution attached to the Kolkata Jail. Mother takes on and what she recounts from here is interesting!

The Mother recalls the visit by a group of Japanese monks to whom she had narrated the nuns' austerity of foregoing the day meal on Fridays to save money to feed the poor. The word spread amongst other monks in Japan and they, in turn, pool the money and send it to the Mother. And it is that money, she tells her biographer, that helped build a dormitory to these hapless women on land donated by the government. The Mother declares proudly to the author how twenty more are visiting in the subsequent week. "God has such wonderful ways of providing". The Mother just recognizes the design in which things happen. And what she lived with was an unadulterated tranquillity, that so many visitors frequently visited her to partake of; a tranquillity that will allow for more creations to happen.

Listen for what's ultimately needed. What we fancy may not be what's actually needed. There's a classical quality to understanding what's actually needed.

CHAPTER 3

'Buddha, The CEO' Leads a Design

How do we listen for what's important?

In spontaneity.

Today 'design' is the buzz word. So much so that my daughter who is about to enter a university wanted to get into 'design' and she spoke about how 'design' is natural to playing children. The way children 'gamify' is a natural design, and they are so particular about design that they are hardly attached to their creations. They are ready to dismantle their products and recreate something wholly new. Children's play is spontaneous and there's nothing that can be predicted about the way they go about designing their games. 'Design', she said, 'is intrinsically playful'.

So, what stops a game?

One of the barriers for 'play' and hence regeneration, which we examined earlier, is 'attachment'. The word is so much in space that I am hard-pressed to explain it in my terms, but I am sure that this would not require a separate footnote. Terms like 'commitment', 'humility', 'discipline' and 'dedication' are so used up that they hardly present anything of value when used. This is an aspect that would be examined in the next chapter—'Who Wants to Sell a Maruti?' Here we are going to just examine how lack of design is lack of insight and an inability to see beyond the obvious.

Let's begin with a story—

* * * * *

The Story of the Intelligent Monkey—

In the Mahabharata, there comes a story as a parable describing the importance of strategy in vanquishing what's dangerous to a kingdom or a community!

Once upon a time in a prosperous kingdom, there lived a band of happy-go-lucky monkeys in the royal garden. The princes in the court fed the monkeys well and the monkeys had nothing more to ask.

In the same premises lived a rogue ram who would simply barge into the royal kitchen and gorge on anything in the kitchen. And the general habit was to chase the ram away from the pantry.

Having observed this day in and day—out, one of the elderly monkeys in the band called for a meeting to discuss this apparently unconnected issue of the ram barging into the royal kitchen. It was rather unusual as it had no connection to the monkeys!

Nevertheless, the elderly monkey rationalized— 'The ram is being too roguish. Every time it goes to the kitchen, it runs out from the stable with some of the world's finest and most exquisite royal horses. One day, it may happen that the cook or an assistant in the kitchen may simply take burning firewood and throw it at the ram.

The ram with its thick fur may still run through the stable, lighting up the whole stable and burning several horses and injuring many in the mayhem!

As the ancient texts on horse health mentions, the fat under the monkey's skin happens to be the best medicine for the burn on the horses.

Beware! We will be the first ones to be caught mercilessly and killed for the fat, which would save the horses—our fat will be of immense value then. All said and done, the value of the horses for a kingdom is far more than the mere monkeys being fed in the garden!

It's ultimately foolish to succumb to the temporary easy pleasures of the royal garden. We will be doomed and our whole progeny may end.

Let's take no chance and exit from here!'

Saying thus, the elderly monkey opened the situation for a debate in the emergency meeting.

The younger monkeys scoffed at the suggestion. They laughed at the hyperbolic hallucination. They simply laughed it away and continued to relish their favourite garden with all its perks.

And as the story goes, it really did happen that horses were burnt and all of the monkeys were caught and killed for their fat—body fat that could treat the royal horses.

And the story continues further to say how the elderly monkey, the only one to escape the massacre, avenges the massacre of his kin.[47]

* * * * *

Being able to interact with, and believe in, what-is-not-there isn't an easy proposition. Even more difficult, as the monkey found, is to communicate to the team in realistic terms.

It's rather a difficult proposition to see something that is not visible and there's no evidence to its existence. As the *Paramahamsa* sees what is not, an extraordinarily perceptive Buddha CEO also locates what is not! And a Buddha CEO sets up the game—even if it means doing so is risky.

Setting up such a comprehensive game isn't easy as it obliterates the boundary question. The limits of a problem are essential in the differentiation of Newtonian Mechanics. Most of the games that science has ever played has been in the field of post Big-Bang and after. To deal with what existed

---

47   I heard the story from a discourse by Shatavadhani R Ganesh

before Big-Bang is absurd indeed (recall our discussion on 'Fundamental Act of Creation' in our earlier section in the small piece that explained 'When Chandrashekhara Died'). The incrementalism that many apologists of innovation defend, though necessary, lacks the fuller view that is a composite of 'Big-Bang' and the vacuum before the Big-Bang. This is the state of absolute resolution that Buddha calls '*shuddhastaka*'—the eight elemental constituents that make up everything. One cannot go further down.

There's an ethical dimension to excellence!

SAMMA KAMMA—the all-encompassing intention in Buddha's terms!

For the absence of an easy term 'samma kammo' is termed as 'right action'. I found another, more evocative, usage on the internet – 'wholesome action'. 'Wholesome action' pertains to the effects an action may cause, the way the action is designed, the brainstorming and inclusive strategies that get into the action. In other words, as briefly described in the previous chapter, 'wholesome action' answers five important questions—*planning, doing it as planned, doing it as it's required to be done, doing as is expected and completing the task.* While each of the terms has special significance, where one may inadvertently stumble is in getting 'completion' right. The spiritual programmes that we attend and the rituals that we perform have these important 'completion' processes as well. To take an example, if one goes to 'Vipassana' programmes, I am told, they undergo huge transformations when they attend a ten-day silence retreat and at the end of it, everyone participates in creating an intention of sharing the benefits and fruits of the retreat with the whole world. It intrinsically recognizes a 'cosmic design' in dropping what was created—in other words, to drop ownership and action.

Just to indicate how simple actions without awareness may degenerate the possibility of design, I will go back to an organization that I have exploited too much by now—Pyramid Valley International.

When I consulted with Pyramid Valley, a septuagenarian senior was its Managing Trustee. Having retired from a senior executive position in a bank and highly read and knowledgeable, his natural search was for an engagement. Seeking constant engagement, he would allow himself to be a part of the weekend sessions which were termed 'wisdom sessions' and was constantly on the lookout for some questions that he could elaborate and engage. So much so, that he would organize every visiting group for interaction with him.

This was an engagement that stemmed from an attachment to his identity— 'well read and knowledgeable'. Any question from a visitor would be quickly taken up by the elderly man—hardly providing scope for a design to emerge. Besides, any existing structure would also be undermined and remains un-nurtured in this kind of 'reverse spontaneity'. Not even a game has been set up. Without framing rules beyond personal identity and attachment to personal tastes, new and more meaningful frames can never be created.

Leaders create a design by going beyond their attachments to action and taste. In the example I have quoted somewhere else of a sugarcane crusher that one finds on Indian roadside, there's no choice for the smaller wheels but to rotate when the bigger wheel rotates. The axle, the gear, shaft and the entire design propels wheels into rotation when the big wheel does. The smaller wheels are part of the design and leadership exhibits that design— not for success and failure—but the way things are to be done, the way life can be lived.

'Samma Sankappo'—wholesome intention!

It's not very difficult to make sense of the above description and see its relevance for modern organizations.

Let us attempt explicating the exigencies of the modern organization by using two intimate terms of an organization—'growth' and 'prosperity'. Recall these passages from the earlier chapter on 'Where are the Ghosts?'

'Growth' and 'Prosperity' pre-suppose knowledge.

To pre-suppose is to know something even before evidence of its existence shows up. Even when we consider there's evidence, it's nothing but a strange conviction of the person who is stating it or our instinctive connection to the occult feeling that we should all grow. Growth is necessary in that sense.

So, let's examine these two terms—'growth' and 'prosperity' yet again! Since these two terms have been exhaustively dealt with in the Chapter 'Where are the Ghosts?' In the previous section a reference to its main points should be sufficient here.

- 'Growth' being vertical and 'prosperity' a diffused horizontal spread they complement each other . Growth alone is unstable; and egalitarian spread without growth would be shallow

- If one doesn't escape the stress and strain involved in any 'growth', 'prosperity' cannot happen.

- Emperor Nero was stressed as his desire to grow ignored the other equally important areas—say the welfare of its citizens. Recorded history is replete with such lopsided 'growth': Spanish explorers Hermando Cortes and Fransico Pizzaro's stories reflect this imbalance. Nero couldn't create a legacy but became a metaphor for a historical negation

- 'Prosperity' beneficially blunts the double-edged razor of 'growth'. 'prosperity' is already in action in several organizations—known or unknown to themselves.

- 'Growth' and 'prosperity', as said before, presupposes knowledge itself.

Nevertheless, when 'growth' is subservient to 'prosperity' phenomenal legacies are created.

In the present world, engineering and technical knowledge, which are geared towards 'growth, are not sufficiently balanced even by education in liberal arts and inter-disciplinary learning geared towards 'prosperity', let alone dabbling seriously with esoteric and invisible knowledge that this book is trying to emphasize on. We have grown; are we prosperous? Economic survey reports of the world would say 'no'! And the companies that we run or organizations that we nurture are just a fractal of this world.

CHAPTER 4

Who Wants to Sell a Maruthi?

It does happen that what we aspire for appears immensely more beautiful than what we have on hand!

Let's examine this through an imaginative anecdote:

A salesman in a Maruti showroom asks his boss to look at acquiring a Mercedes Benz showroom. His reason goes thus—'why don't you give me a Mercedes Benz to sell? It's not easy selling a Maruti nowadays. I would easily sell a Mercedes!'

Though gross, the example is indicative!

Like the metaphoric 'car salesman' used as a mocking derogation of the sales force, today many in India refer to 'Maruti 800' as a reference to the affluence of the neo - rich. I am not sure how ubiquitous it is and Maruti car owners and people working in the company should pardon me. I own a Maruti car and in the real sense, that statement doesn't make any difference to me. What is more pertinent here is a pointer to an age that's invariably prone to appearances. In a tribal community, ownership and territory matters but not as a show of affluence. Any community that thrives on 'what belongs to you belongs to everyone' kind of philosophy will not attach value to appearances. What is emphasized instead is the roles people will have to play.

A society that feeds on appearances will have to grapple with the danger of having to handle multiple diversions and carrots that are hanging everywhere else. We had begun with this term in Chapter 1 of Section

1 '*Ekatattvabhyasa*'—Sage Patanjali's dictum for a mind that is stuck in barriers. The roles we play and the practice we are involved in is shattered by innumerable appearances in the outside world. This is where, as some traditions practice, the ultimate is attained by practice of asceticism, which is symbolized by costumes that the practitioners wear. The costume by itself isn't important but it signals to the general public that the subject is 'under probation' and is a tacit request for staying away.

'*SANYASA*' as it is called in Hindu traditions is a way of excellence. Without this excellence which is demonstrative and living through the player, rookies keep falling on the players inviting them into an alternative system of practice. Even when betting controversy in Indian cricket was at its height, no rookie ever approached a star performer like Sachin Tendulkar. Sachin is the God of Cricket and no one approaches excellence with petty diversions. Desires stem and when one dwells on the desire the efforts thin out—that's the science of Buddha's monks.

Our inability to handle what's on hand is the desire that we experience. It's a piece that would complete the jigsaw puzzle. Instead of seeing what's incomplete within 'me' or within an organization, it's much easier for a human mind to look out for easy options outside; this looking out is much easier than the action and getting committed to the required action—to do what is on hand. This 'looking out' is sometimes, unfortunately, fulfilled or fulfilling. Somebody satisfies the desires by approving the expenditure and it creates an opportunity for engagement till the next round of actions; once this set of actions are concluded and have yielded no results, it begets another set of actions in a perennial search.

This 'finding' that there are actions that can be taken outside, into a domain beyond one's role to produce results, is an opportunity for a meeting, investment, repair, correction and many immense varieties of action. This will obviously remain unfulfilling, and this 'un-fulfilment' is the desire for more action. And then the cycle continues.

Our actions taken constantly on the outside is no way to produce results! That too ones that are not directly handling what is on hand. Patanjali calls it *vikalpa*—*a* fancy for what is not!

GETTING IT RIGHT

When we delve into this truth (in this case, desire) in the ordinary language of our conversations—in complaints, gossip, formal exchanges etc.—it comes out in the form of what we recognize as sterile exasperations like 'desire is the cause of misery', 'man's greed has no limit' or as 'we should control our desires', etc. When such unverified statements come forth, which are so universally clichéd, they invariably appear like anti-life gossip; and we inherently ignore it. Secondly, social norms and moral boundaries are such that thoughtfulness about them appear like inaction and being passive. A generation intoxicated by constant action, looking into the outside as a way of solving numerous issues around us, has been nothing more than knee-jerk 'reactionism'! And as Fritjoff Capra shows, it has consistently produced ad-hoc solutions that have generated later day problems.

And this is a predicament modern man and organizations are stuck in; and unless indigenously discovered and personified, this 'knowing' will remain terribly useless, even appearing in the form of allergy for more education and training—especially the one that relates to the asceticism required for the adiabatic processes of excellence. This was the kind of training we came across in the chapter on 'Transformation is a Design' that fails to produce results three times out of four. The problem is that any knowledge that remains undiscovered remains information!

This is not peculiar to organizations but a predicament of the whole humanity, as we saw, in the 'Eternal Triumvirate Triangles' in Chapter 1 of Section 1!

What should individual leadership and organizations do?

Take on; head on

Deal. Be straight. Challenge yourself!

Because—

When one tries to handle an organization or ventures into leadership, you are alone and left lonely and unsupported. There's no support mechanism or formula to rely on because there's no template available. In the absence of any perceivable support and a scaffold to hang on to, leadership finds it perplexing and the inevitable 'looking for help' happens with a leadership periscope searching for help in the ocean. Secondly, a proposition from the position of leadership, unless within the boisterous zone of action and target, will remain fanciful to the team. Say a suggestion to meditate together as a way of resolving a cumbersome knot in the company is inherently initiated, and it could be certainly mockable if it has come from 'looking outside for a Mercedes Benz' syndrome without appropriate discipline for the search and articulating it. Hence, the only option for leadership is not a formula to rely on but only a commitment to discovering oneself. In the absence of a stable self, a Buddha CEO constantly regenerates into more action with ease and resolve.

Since what we discover about ourselves is not always palatable, we find it convenient to bounce back to the age-old habit—doing, correcting, changing, suggesting, collecting, advising and several other innumerable ways of avoiding our 'being'—a term quite familiar today from seminars on excellence through spiritual courses.

A few more pitfalls—

1. Our attachments appearing as commitment.

2. Our preferences and priorities appearing as dedication.

3. Our fears may appear like discipline and respect.

4. Our under confidence may appear like humility.

What does it mean to learn or discover?

To discover means to encounter all of these without sympathy, self-pity, remorse, regret and guilt. Because it's easy to escape into all these subversive tactics, a transformative coach will not let you escape into these. Refer to the chapter 'Elephant Dung' where the *Purohita* mediates experiences, vision, actions and issues into learning!

The coach becomes the space within which these qualities in the list above are extinguished. That *space* of a coach is not supposed to be reasonable, compromising and the coach doesn't work out a conspiracy with you to be ordinary! To somehow survive and allow 'hook or crook'!

That's why it's recommended to do Guru seva—the service to the Master. The space of the coach and the Master is supposed to appear cruel, unsympathetic, un-understanding, lacking in kindness etc. The Guru stories are meant to be the pantheon of modern organizations—a precursor to the legends that are yet to be born in the organization!

So Transformation begins with your commitment—being settled about what it takes to transform!

None of these 'conditionings' like meditation, team-building etc. and other fair practices that organisations build, either born out of experiences or through a logical extrapolation of what's thought valuable, is ever enough to build and sustain a top-class business! It takes something more than that. We could examine it in the nature of our desires and demands that we put on the people around us!

CHAPTER 5

Yoga-Kshema

When thy impurities are blown away,

And thou are free from guilt, thou will enter

The heavenly world of the elect, Arya.

– Dhammapada

Sanskrit is derivative.

There are thousands of inflexions that Sanskrit opens up itself to. There are several sets of meanings a particular word or syntax can produce!

It emanates and propels itself into more derivatives and since a major part of the transactional knowledge is unavailable to us, we may have to depend on certain standard expressions to arrive at it. Let's look at the word *'namaste'*! I am using what I came across this in one of my brother's presentation.

'Namaste' in ordinary contexts means 'salutations. But *'namaste'* need not stay as and limit itself to 'salutations' as its etymological bases and its inherent complex, creative derivations may mean any of the following:

'Na Maha, The'—*not me but you!*

Na the, Maha'—*not you but me!*

Or as, 'Maha Na, the' or 'the, na maha', etc. arriving at the same meaning!

It's a complex semiotic exuberance. The contexts and complexity are hugely evocative and 'celebrational'! Only a comprehensive society could have produced this kind of unhinged flowery language; a society that was incapable of producing any tragedies in literature at all! Probably tragedies are a product of finiteness—to see events within time and space. Its popular version is—'we have but one life; let's make the most of it'. It's tragic when we don't make the most of it. In contrast the cosmic inter-connectedness of words to events, and events to ideas and ideas to impressions, words no longer have tiny meanings.

The very cosmology present in the air probably made a language!

The expression 'Yoga-kshema' also comes from Sanskrit!

'Yoga' means the 'sum total of' or 'good' or 'additive' or 'integrative' and keeps on expanding as the contexts of life expands!

'Kshema' means 'to secure' or 'to protect' or 'to preserve'

Any act of 'security' or 'preservation' involves stress; a part of you or what the enterprise is rubs away in stress!

So, the chief questions at this juncture are—

Can we keep on growing into goodness, add more, grow and preserve without rubbing ourselves away?

Can organizations be Yogic? Is a question that we could venture into now!

Ever saw a business that grew out of individual fancy?

Let's consider a scenario—

Edison was enamoured by the 'Jugaad'[48] (unlike the description of Edison as a scientist, he was a champion 'Jugaadist'). His actual hands-on work was designed around his contemplation or vice-versa—all his contemplation constantly circumambulated the productive work (who knows whether

---

48 an Indian colloquial term that refers to some kind of indigenous contrivance in making something operate

it was so. Neither have I checked with his official biographer. It doesn't matter much here because the legends around Edison suffice.)

I surmise that he was simply enamoured by the 'Jugaad' and just went on testing different combinations—of course, based on certain hypothesis or assumptions; all these permutations and combinations remained unimportant till the light bulb saw its light! No denying that he was deeply interested in and was patient enough to test 1000 or 10000 times (whatever!) as the legend goes. If he had been interested in showing off his every interest and had gone on to make it public, he would have remained an unsuccessful idiot. It was his success (however serendipitously) that brought the world's attention on the details, never vice versa. This broad description of Edison found its reflection when I inadvertently came across Matt Ridley's 'How Innovation works—And Why it Flourishes in Freedom'.

Matt Ridley writes, 'having hubristically claimed to have made a light bulb that would last a long time before failing, he (Edison) began a frantic search to prove his boast true.' A typical 'fake till you make it story'. And Edison tried more than 6000 different plant material in trying to find an ideal match for his filament. In the history of the evolution of science and technology, Edison's tinkering labs played a huge role in showing the world the importance of innovation in improvising a new invention. Innovation requires discipline for a clear focus of the product (the way Edison had declared about a bulb that would last) and a respect for what market and economy have been looking up to.

In an age hungry for innovation and coming on the toes of yet another scientific revolution, the strategy proved right for Edison. Besides, he was set to prove his claim with reference to a single product right. Edison exhibited a significant brilliance in strategic communication with a publicly recognized success already behind him—the way modern corporates launch products in advance that would stymie other competitive products within its market share!

While Edison claimed an objective possibility hubristically, Pyramid Valley suffers from its opposite: because of the open and confident claims on something more subjective and mostly subliminal—the effects of meditation inside the Pyramid. Meditation under a pyramid has a valuable output and many would stand by it including me. Hence, the enthusiasm is understandable but the problem is something else—enthusiasm disoriented in the art of purposeful communication. When an experience, like meditation under a pyramid, is so true and authentic it becomes even more complex. Without building the necessary intellectual paraphernalia and discipline for coherence, in communicating this subjective experience, Pyramid Valley has evolved more and more complex talks on spirituality with a belief that by becoming 'more scientific' and by going into digital ways, they will somehow crack it. A few visitors ending up in the air-conditioned room for a session on a weekend afternoon will listen to the speaker on varied topics of 'spirituality'—neither the listener nor the speaker has any declared intention. Yet, one advantage is clearly evident—teachers (in PVI they are called 'speakers') taking these weekend sessions who otherwise would hardly get any audience for their talks happen to get a few!

Without a coherent powerful design that includes, as explained in Chapter 2 of Section 2, responsible social behaviour, scientific authenticity and organizational efficiency Pyramid Valley came out with strands of immature information, that lacked even entertainment value, competing for its primacy. Look at the list below—

1. Law of Karma

2. Life After Death

3. Past Life Regression

4. Healing Yourself

5. You are the Placebo

6. The Power of Now

And many more. All interesting topics and that's the chief reason for its redundancy. When organizations innovate because it 'appears interesting', the competition shifts to 'making it look good' rather than 'making it valuable'. Having conveniently ignored the more important questions of excellence like sustenance and measurable progress, the enthusiastic members of PVI never balanced themselves with an inquiry on how this 'spiritual knowledge' has helped them and the organization they are 'contributing to'. The perceived value of Pyramid Meditation got stymied at the level of design itself. Without a core offering the organization constantly remained unsettled!

Imagine two scenarios—

Scenario 1—I ask you on a day to take the nutrition of Herbal Life, to take an Art of Living programme on the next day, asking you to try Pyramid Meditation on another day. I will be left stranded and you would probably desist my presence because I am unsettled about what I offer. You may recall the father of *Yoga Shastra*, Sage Patanjal's dictum from Chapter 1—'*ekatattvabhayasa*'.

Scenario 2—Edison, out of nowhere, comes out with the idea of an electric bulb; suddenly and from nowhere; and he explains the science of the vacuum tube, incandescence in elements and properties of certain filaments he is considering!.

Unlike the above scenario, Edison was 'intelligently' happy in his own tinkering lab and it was circumstantial that he created natural insulation and necessary adiabatic system. Despite Edison's nastiness in snubbing his former employee and a scientific genius Nikola Tesla (which we are able to see in retrospect). Edison remained a master innovator with over 400 patents. Edison had hired a huge number of artisans and craftsmen in his massive laboratory—massive for the age. He knew the value of innovation and turning an invention into a more economical product. The 'learning organization' that the unschooled Edison famously built went on progressing in reducing the cost of its products and also the product basket and thereby widening the participation net. Efficiency, wider participation and growing relevance are the hallmarks of a world-class organization.

Pyramid Valley instead stumbled from one product to another, hopped from one offering to another and had unnecessarily bifurcated into a thousand pathways—a self-implosion. Small flickering flames that hardly looked at the organization as an interaction between and a complex interplay of market, society, spiritual principles, organizational excellence and personal discipline. It had none!

Many organizations and enthusiastic teachers do not appreciate the importance of such adiabatic systems.

For a business to succeed, the driver of the business should learn the art of ignoring details however interesting or sentimental the driver feels about it. Business is driven by market needs; everything, including the volume of the products, pricing, demography for distribution, etc. are all determined by the market forces. There's no point in getting into narcissistic self-love about the way the business is built as what matters is how well integrated it was with the market—'yogic' organizations add well, and they are ergonomic!

The degree to which the market considers a particular product a breakthrough innovation, to that extent, the product or business will support other auxiliary businesses. Like the breakthrough in aviation industry brought in air-hostess and other training industry, hospitality, catering, on-air merchandising, tourism, pest control, etc. There's a rhythm to this additive property! There's a 'yoga' to it.

A good business, worth its salt, will focus on this fundamental creativity and the breakthrough. A business person has to keep on the 'activism' of excellence! (refer to Chapter 1 on the 'Organizational Buddhahood'); and an extraordinary ability to discard what's not getting organically added! A businessperson will keep on undoing what the market hardly recognizes as useful!

Look at Chapter 3 in Section 1 on the triumvirate of 'organizational—social—humanity' crisis and we will observe that just as a business is driven by the market, an organization is driven by society—schools, spiritual organizations, trusts, NGOs, activist/pressure groups are all driven by the social norms, its exigencies, needs and the well-articulated social problems.

But is there a way out?

YES—if the organization can understand the art of 'retreat'.

NO—if the organizations start 'solving problems'; in fact, the beginning point of excellence is to stop 'solving problems'.

But then, what is a 'retreat' for the organization? Let's make an attempt at it.

When we do '*aasanas*'—the yogic stretches, focus on breath and pay attention to our feelings—it's exhilarating. In fact, we become obsessed with it. And the benign construct around 'Yoga' and 'meditation' gives us, sometimes at least, a feeling of gratification—'I got into something benign; I didn't lose myself in a discotheque' kind of gratification. This could be a good beginning but very limiting in its dimension and self-congratulation.

This feeling is natural.

Joe Dispenza, the world-renowned new-age consciousness teacher uses the practices of Indian Yogis a lot. Unlike the popularity of 'aasanas' as the real yoga, Joe Dispenza touches upon several higher strands of yoga including the *Dharana* and *Dhyana*. He largely exploits electromagnetism and other significant developments of Modern Physics to explain this. With breathing and the control of the intrinsic muscles, Dr. Dispenza explains, how a 'person will have an inner vision and that is more real than the world you are sitting in right now'. In other words, the artificial divisions between the real and unreal vanish.

Yoga in its original definition means unison. Stretching ourselves such that the 'limitless' itself is the 'limit'. That is to say, for our purposes here, in the triumvirate of relationships, the moral dilemma between 'the organizational and the human crisis' simply ceases to exist—when you serve the organization, you serve humanity; you serve humanity by happily playing out your role in the organization.

You may refer to Chapter 1—'The Organizational Buddhahood' where the four symptoms of a dysfunctional enterprise are explained! When you stretch appropriately under guidance, it expands your ability to hold pain and bitterness (*dukha and dhuarmansya*) and also in coordinated efforts (*angamejayatva and shwas-nishwasa vikshepa*).

The problem is that this feeling of gratification doesn't remain consistent. It is extremely slippery. No formula holds true for too long. We don't want to let go of that good feeling, but it remains slippery—it happens and appears to work on particular days but remains slippery. So, we look into other variables—darker room, nature, Himalaya, Pyramid, etc. Or it may result in shopping syndrome—searching for solutions in the training and seminar industry, technology markets, better Human Resource and recruitment, etc., and the journey goes on and on without us ever feeling the futility of it!

That's where the fundamentals come into play. In Yogic parlance, they are called '*yama and niyama*'—personal discipline and social ethics!

You may refer to Chapter 4, Section 2 on 'From the Sage Ashtavakra', where the importance of the *Purohita*—the teacher for the organization is explained. At the level of fundamentals, ethics and discipline have to be distinguished with extreme care.

Let me cite a few examples—

When we examine closely terms like 'need', 'want' 'desire', etc.—they don't have a definite meaning; they're pre-critical phenomena and are basically psychological essence. Similarly, how do we examine '*shoucha*'—cleanliness? When do we say that we are clean? Should I bathe every time I eat or have sex or come from outside. Likewise, what are '*satya*' (truth), '*ahimsa*' (non-violence)?

One can never investigate from the gallery but from on the ground and in the court[49]! A coach—the *purohita*—creates the contexts where these fundamentals can be examined!

Organizations retreat so that these fundamental questions are examined. Fundamental questions don't have a meaning. One will have to impose a temporary meaning in a retreat and deconstruct it in the next.

The pure absence of 'self' and 'meaning'. I stop here.

CONCLUSION

A fault of others is easily perceived

But that of oneself is difficult to perceive

– Dhammapada

How do we develop the whole organization into Buddhahood? Rather, how does a commitment towards an Organizational Buddhahood look?

To develop into one, we may have some recommendations but the process of discovery is certainly beyond formulaic prescriptions. Nevertheless, a beginning without a structure and intention would remain volatile and easily sublimates.

The first point is to build an uncompromising ritual of togetherness; a togetherness that goes beyond any agenda is the one. This is a critical element before one goes ahead.

Phase 1—Discovering the Meaning of It All

Discovering the meaning behind it all—working in groups and causing a difference. Since this is an ongoing project and is the chief point around which stakeholders are mentored, this is of primary importance beginning

---

49   I owe the usage of these terms to the excellent conversation at the Landmark Education Centre in the numerous courses I attended with them!

with the first day of the programme when everyone declares what they would like to cause.

Reading and Reflection exercises—covering the nature of tangible and the intangible; the relative and the absolute knowledge. Training the team into focusing on the tangible, the intangible makes an important part of the conversation here.

The first phase is critically important where enthusiastic practitioners, like the way it happened in Pyramid Valley, may whitewash all problems of our world life into easy compartments of 'karma', 'soul', 'ignorance' and such. The market is abound with videos and literature on these terms. What is critical, however, is not the knowledge of these terms but 'swadhyaya'—the self-study and inquiry.

It may begin like this—imagine the team is working on a project. Invariably, teamwork involves necessary angst, differences, a sense of alienation, etc. A commonsensical approach would be to see 'meditation' practice as a key to handling them; and to make it appear more scientific, one may colour it with a bit of Quantum Mechanics and stuff. Unlike Edison's futuristic declaration, these declarations about how meditation or Quantum Mechanics would help lacks strategy and inquiry. The one-to-one correspondence is wrong. That's why Buddha was silent on a lot of questions.

A more classical approach would be to see all these as valuable, but one is facilitated into inquiring into these in aesthetic pedagogies. I will not be able to explain that in a book because that is the work of a '*purohita*' and *Purohita*'s work also will be a '*jugaad*' of a different kind.

An elaborate discipline of constructing the intellectual paraphernalia around the practice is as important as the practice itself. The importance of 'yama' and 'niyama' cannot be emphasized more.

Practising Mindfulness—exercises in awareness!

Phase 2—Examining the Nature of Barriers

Examining what really stops in making a difference in the project taken up—the ongoing project that's the undercurrent to this course. Since practice is best done not exactly on the task at hand, inventing a genuine area of service is ideal. It's important here to note that the most knotty aspects get resolved in mere commitment to something that apparently has no stake in who I am.

Combined with the above, a volunteer project that drops the false sense of dignity and orientation to pleasure is the key. Modern neuroscience can explain this better—how our ability to remain excited unreasonably stems from developing a capacity to contribute to what is not of practical value to me.

Practising and deepening of Feather in Space Meditation—to see oneself as the feather that floats; an identity exists only to be shared and there's nothing to defend.

Phase 3—Volatility and Entropic Knowledge

Entropic knowledge involves looking at what is most volatile—this is an inquiry into who you are on the one hand and what is the nature of responsible relationship with what surrounds you; there's a zeitgeist to this kind of knowledge!

Some meditational practices that could make sense here—

Awareness Meditation—Becoming the pervasive impermanence joyfully is the focus here. Reduced to a simple practice of observing the breath, this recognizes the total lack of control of breath—the fundamental process of life. This practice is too well known. However, organizations will have to build meanings by making closer observations of it.

The Silver-Thread Meditation—an attempt to recognize what's holding it all. When we shift from gross holdings to subtler ones, it becomes easier and more flexible. And when we recognize that, there's nothing to even hold on to its freedom. Freedom based on causal elements, one sees, is hardly enough to build extraordinary institutions.

The Expanding Sheet Meditation—practising the immensity of who you are! In one of the revered ancient Indian texts 'Yoga Vashishta', Sage Vashishta tutors young Rama. And most of this conversation derails Rama's ignorance and turns his very conceptualization fragile. To be able to see the futility of it and yet be excited about it is the 'pre-critical' happiness.

Phase 4—Looking into the context of the project on hand

Though an organization should never ignore the task at hand, this phase is a rather later aspect of actual performance.

Performance follows absolute clarity on what constitutes an entity and how they are assembled? There's a hierarchy of complexity when it comes to the ways things are assembled!

Silver-Thread Meditation, as described, is an enquiry into what surrounds 'you' and what has been collected; how much of it do you identify with? Is there an escape? Determines how precise and playful we are in dealing with a project, seeing freshly. Escape from oneself is to be 'limitless'—to be in peak performance!

A CONCLUSION TO THE CONCLUSION

Yoga is too familiar a term to be explained. In fact, the world needs a purgative to cleanse itself of all the unnecessary meaning associated with yoga rather than yet another explanation about it.

But the meaning of 'yoga' is still essential for thorough exploitation of the concepts we have dealt with till now. Yoga means to add up—to sum up everything. So, a sum total of all the knowledge and experiences is yoga. It could be summed up into a simple chant or recitation. In another sense, it could be meeting the highest potential of a being. Referred to as *purushartha*, this interpretation gels well with the theme we opened the whole book with—an analogy of the 'ink bottle'.

When is full self-expression really possible? Let me put a small note to make sense of that here. This refers to a conversation I had an opportunity to be a part of with a master. Look at the absurdity of it while I attempt to show the very beauty and symmetry of it. The conversation went like this—(all the names and terms are familiar to the world today. But one may look up for the details on the internet).

(A group of dedicated people sit across with a master facing them. And the master talks spontaneously opening up into what he calls 'new concept'. This particular conversation opened up due to a question on the relevance of asanas—the yogic postures. The organization doesn't emphasis on asanas and hence the important question emanated from the all-pervading presence of yoga).

Master—Can someone tell me what is 'Ashtanga Yoga'?

Silence

Master—(one by one) Can you say what it is?

Silence

Master—It has eight limbs (and lists them as yama-niyama, asana, pranyama, pratyahara, dharana, dhyana and Samadhi). And in the 20th century, each of these limbs was mastered and propounded by different people. Can you tell who they were?

Silence

Master—Who mastered yama-niyama in the 20th century?

Participant 1—(after deep thought) Gandhiji

Master—Yes, (he shakes hand with Participant 1 and looking at him) you appear to know my mind. Gandhiji practised yama-niyama. Who mastered asana and pranayama?

Participant 1—B. K. S. Iyengar.

Master—Arre... how do you know? Do you already know my mind? (Everybody laughs). Who was the chief proponent of pratyahara and Dharana?

(Different names crop up including the master's name.)

Master—It was Mahesh Yogi. He spread Dharana to the world.

Participant 2—But he taught TM. By taking the mantra one goes to Samadhi.

Master—No. Mantra is just Dharana. You focus the mind on to something and that is what he taught. Who taught Dhyana?

(The group crops out different names including the Master's. The Master rejects them all.)

Master—It was Osho. Osho focused only on meditation. Then who brought Samadhi?

(Everyone took the Master's name in chorus.)

Master—Yes. So, when you are learning Samadhi, one need not go into any of the stages of the ashtanga.

(The conversation continued on these lines...)

It was, of course, a very private conversation and obviously, nobody sensible took the conversation seriously. It was clear trash or had an element of sectarian viewpoint in that. Any serious student of Indian spirituality of the 20th century will vouch for it. But that had important points I would like to note here—

1. All spiritual traditions may practice what are different ways of offering obeisance to the earlier masters. Here in the conversation, the Master referred to a tradition that is already established that he also belongs to. In that sense, a master offers an integrated experience and knowledge. It does not lie outside the cosmos of

knowledge. Here, the Master located himself within a previously defined domain.

2. Master simply believes that he is the peak. Many may get this as fanaticism or narcissism. But it is not. Even this conversation happened amongst a select group of the inner circle. In fact, many of us do believe that we are the best and may be due to our own lack of boldness or afraid that such a statement smacks of arrogance, we keep quiet! A Master, by this example at least, shows no timidity in declarations.

It is, many a time, important conversations like these that put the followers off-balance. The Master did a wonderful job in making a conversation interesting and not talking about anything outside of his own network of the inner circle. Probably, my presence there was the only anomaly.

When such conversations are taken seriously without the necessary discerning intelligence and self-study (which is called as *swadhyaya)*, what results is a degeneration of the highest order.

Buddha, the CEO prevents that degeneration!